Praise for *The NORTA*

"The NORTAV Method for Writers is a great book for crafting stories. Writer's block just became a thing of the past!"

–GEMMA HALLIDAY, New York Times bestselling author

"An innovative project crossing the border from narrative theory to the hands-on practice of story writing. The author's close reading of narrative passages sheds considerable light on narrative styles. I can foresee the NORTAV Method generating illuminating discussions at conferences on narrative theory as well as being used in courses on creative writing."

–MANFRED JAHN, Professor of English (ret.), University of Cologne, and author of *Narratology: A Guide to Narrative Theory*

"The NORTAV Method taught me more about writing in five weeks than I've learned in the past five years. I owe Mr. Abbiati a tremendous debt of gratitude."

–MICHAEL SYNAKOWSKI, writing student, Quaker Hill, Connecticut

"Jim's expertise shines through as he examines the fundamentals of prose construction. There's something in this book for every writer, young or old, beginner or expert!"

–STEPHANIE VERNI, author of *Beneath the Mimosa Tree*

"Simply the best book on writing I've come across since Strunk & White!"

–RAKESH PATEL, writing student, Reston, Virginia

THE

[N][O][R][T][A][V]

METHOD
for WRITERS

*The Secret to Constructing
Prose Like the Pros*

A. J. ABBIATI

ISBN 10: 0615655130
ISBN 13: 978-0615655130

Published by LAK Publishing.
Cover design and interior layout by LAK Publishing.

LAK Publishing
http:\\lakpublishing.info

This book is for all who are as passionate about the craft as I am.

My heartfelt thanks to Todd Potter, best friend and life-long sounding board. Without his enthusiastic participation, this book would not exist. Thanks also to my family, friends, professors, students, work-shoppers, and to all those who encouraged me to continue.

My eternal gratitude to the pros who lent their prose to this project. Your generosity is surpassed only by your talent.

I could never have developed the NORTAV Method without standing on the shoulders of Manfred Jahn, Franz Stanzel, Mieke Bal, Gerard Genette, David Herman, and a host of other brilliant narratologists. I admire you all.

Finally, my thanks to Evan Marshall, Karen Wiesner, Jason Scott Bell, Elizabeth George, Jack Bickham, and Stephen King. I may have stood on the shoulders of the narratologists, but without all of you, I would not have known what to look for.

Contents

CHAPTER 6: The Narrative Schema

CHAPTER 7: Incorporating the NORTAV Method into Your Writing Process

CHAPTER 8: Adding the Final Polish to Your Prose

APPENDIX: Fifteen Additional NORTAV Analyses

Introduction

WHAT ON EARTH IS A NORTAV?

NORTAV is an acronym. It's shorthand for Narration, Observation, Reaction, Thought, Action, and Vocalization. By the end of this book you'll know exactly what that means!

WHO IS THIS BOOK FOR?

The NORTAV Method for Writers: The Secret to Constructing Prose Like the Pros is for any writer who is serious about the craft of writing and wants to learn, or learn more, about the fundamentals of prose construction. I imagine you right-brained folks out there, those who live solely in the creative world, must be rolling your eyes and fidgeting in your chairs. I've already used such left-brained terms as *method*, *fundamentals*, and *construction*, and we're not even half way through the first page! Many (dare I say most) writers cringe at the thought of having to learn more theory. We're artists not scientists, right? So before we go any further, let's chase off the herd of elephants that just stampeded into the room.

IS THIS A COMPLICATED BOOK ON WRITING THEORY?

The answer is yes ... and no. This book does represent a body of knowledge or writing "theory;" however, I've designed the presentation of that knowledge to be as *theory-lite* as possible. I keep the tone of the book conversational and introduce the NORTAV Method through the use of a few simple analogies, lots of examples, and a smattering of useful diagrams.

So yes, this *is* a book on writing theory, but no, this *is not* an overly complicated book on writing theory. In fact, I could have titled this book *NORTAVs for Newbies*, but I didn't want to give the impression that this book is only for beginning writers. Writers of all experience levels can learn a lot from the NORTAV Method.

WHO AM I AND WHY SHOULD YOU LISTEN TO ME?

Ah, the second elephant. Why should you listen to what I have to say about prose construction? After all, you've probably never heard of me. Well, I've published several short stories and the episodic fantasy novel *Fell's Hollow* (Summer 2012). I'm currently at work on my second novel. And I used the NORTAV Method to write each and every word. If you'd like to read some my work, you can find samples on my website: http://ajabbiati.com/.

Should you listen to me because of my experience?

Maybe.

In addition to my experience, I have an MFA in Creative Writing and a BA in English. I'm qualified to teach writing at the college level. For what it's worth, I also have a BS in Computer Science.

Should you listen to me because of my education?

Perhaps.

Not too long ago I was in the same boat you're probably in now. I desperately wanted to learn how to construct professional quality prose. I understood the elements of fiction. I had the stories and I had the language skills. But I still couldn't construct prose that resembled the work of those professional authors I most admired. My prose was unpolished, clunky, and difficult to read. No matter how hard I searched, I could find nothing, no how-to book, no workshop, no university program, that was teaching what I wanted to learn: the nuts and bolts of prose construction.

Sound familiar?

During my search, however, I did come across some savvy how-to instructors and narrative theorists, giants if you will, who touched on parts of the prose construction process, and I stood on their shoulders to develop the NORTAV Method. But no one covered everything, and what was covered was often somewhat inaccurate. So I went on a journey of discovery and returned eight years later with a stunning secret. A secret every professional writer is using, yet few if any know they possess. And I used that secret (in a relatively short period of time) to teach myself how to construct professional quality prose. Now I'm offering that secret to you.

Should you listen to me because you also want to discover the secret to constructing professional quality prose?

I would hope so!

And that shoos off the second elephant.

WILL THE NORTAV METHOD KILL THE MAGIC OF MY WRITING PROCESS?

Here is the third and perhaps largest elephant we need to deal with. Is the NORTAV Method a left-brained formula for constructing prose? Is it designed for logical, process-driven writers only? Is it some kind of outline strategy on steroids? The answers are *no*, *no*, and *no*! The NORTAV Method is simply a powerful body of knowledge that no one, as far as I know, is teaching anywhere else. This knowledge, once learned, can be used *in any way that comes natural to you*. It can be used explicitly (i.e. consciously) during the writing process by left-brained, logic-driven writers (I call these writers *planners*, for they delight in planning out every aspect of their work before they write a single word). It can be used organically (i.e. subconsciously) during the writing process by right-brained, muse-driven writers (I call these writers *wingers*, for they simply wing it when they write and wouldn't pre-plan their work if their lives depended on it). It can be used explicitly and/or organically by writers who fall somewhere between a planner and a winger. And it can be used by every writer during the editing and revision process. Or, instead of using the NORTAV Method to learn how to construct your own prose, the NORTAV Method can be used as a tool for analysis and criticism. That is, it can be used to illustrate how other authors are correctly and incorrectly constructing their prose.

> A **Planner** is a writer who plans her work before she writes.

> A **Winger** is a writer who lets her work develop organically.

Let me emphasize my point with our first analogy.

Sometime back when you were in school, perhaps in Mrs. Rice's Language Arts class, you learned how to use sentence structures. You remember the concept of simple, compound, complex, and compound-complex sentences, right? You spent lots of time examining sentences, determining their structure, and notating that structure on your homework sheet. Then you practiced using the different sentence structures over and over until their use became second nature. Now you work with all four sentence structures every time you write, and you probably never give them a second thought. Or maybe you do. It all depends on what kind of writer you are.

Learning the NORTAV Method works the same way. You learn the knowledge and then apply it in whatever way works best for you. Let me say that again: You learn the knowledge and then apply it *in whatever way works best for you*. Thus, the NORTAV Method will not kill the magic of your writing process! It won't scare off your muse any more than Mrs. Rice did when she told you that simple sentences express a complete thought through a single subject and verb. This is such an important concept to keep in mind, especially for you extreme wingers out there, I will repeat it at the end of every chapter.

And there goes the third and, I hope, last of the elephants.

With that done, let's go over how to use this book so we can prevent any more elephants from charging into the room.

HOW TO USE THIS BOOK

The concepts presented in this book build on each other. Working through this book in the order in which the information is presented ensures you are only getting one new, simple (or relatively simple) concept at a time. This keeps things simple. If you skip around the book, you may have to deal with multiple new concepts at once, some without explanation, which will make things unnecessarily compli-cated.

> This is a *Definition Box* used to define important terms.

> This is **NORTAV Tip Box** used to display helpful tips.

I strongly suggest you go through the chapters *in order* while you are first learning the NORTAV Method. After that, come back and skip around to your heart's delight. And as you may have noticed, when I want to impress upon you the importance of understanding a term, I will repeat its definition in a *definition box*. When I want to offer a useful tip, I will provide the tip within a *NORTAV tip box*.

There is no silver bullet to learning how to construct professional quality prose. Most amateur writers fail to move beyond the amateur level, for when it comes time to learn this vital part of the craft they have no choice but to do it through *years* of trial-and-error practice and endless subconscious emulation of their favorite authors.

The NORTAV Method cuts this learning curve dramatically by removing certain portions of the trial-and-error and subconscious aspects of the process. The NORTAV Method will teach you, step by step, how professional quality prose is constructed. Nevertheless, you will still have to work hard. Take your time with this book. Think of this book as a writing course or workshop, not as a book you simply read quickly from cover to cover. Make an effort to do *all* the assignments and exercises. They are an integral part of the learning process.

Phew! Now that we have all that introduction stuff out of the way, we can move on to Chapter 1: An Overview of the NORTAV Method.

Let's get started.

Chapter 1

An Overview of the NORTAV Method

Setting the Stage

THE BASIC FOUR-STEP PROSE CONSTRUCTION PROCESS

Here in Chapter 1, I want to set the stage for the rest of the book. I want to show you the basic four-step process for constructing prose. I want to show you, at a high level, how a unit of rough prose is actually formed. And I want to show you where the NORTAV Method fits into the big picture, and how I will cover it throughout the rest of the book.

Constructing prose is an extremely complex task. If it were easy, anyone could do it, and you certainly wouldn't need this or any other book on writing. Defining the entire prose construction process in detail would fall well outside the scope of a theory-lite book such as this, so for our purposes we will simplify things a bit.

Take a look at this diagram:

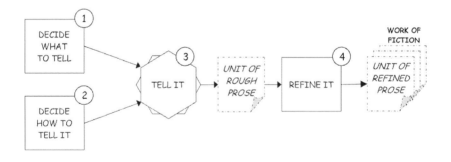

The Basic Four-Step Prose Construction Process

Constructing prose can be boiled down to these four basic steps. The writer decides what to tell and how to tell it. Then she tells it. Then she refines it. It's as simple as that. Some of you might be scratching your heads thinking this process is nothing like how you construct your prose.

Let me stress two important points:

First, each writer will feel she has her own unique way of combining and/or iterating through these four basic steps. For instance, a highly experienced writer might feel she goes through Steps 1-4 simultaneously, spitting out a work of fiction in refined prose in a single shot. An extreme winger might feel she starts with Step 3 and lets Steps 1 and 2 work themselves out organically. An extreme planner might rigidly follow this process one step at a time, in order. Regardless of how a writer feels she works with the process, Steps 1 and 2 can occur in any order and will *always* occur prior to Step 3, even if they occur a mere millisecond beforehand, deep within a writer's subconscious mind. And Step 4 will *always* occur after Step 3, even if it occurs a mere millisecond afterward, deep within a writer's subconscious mind.

Thus, though a particular writer may feel she is working with Steps 1-4 in her own unique way, all writers follow this basic four-step process when constructing prose.

Second, a work of fiction is composed of individual units of refined prose. How a writer breaks up her work of fiction into units of prose is up to the writer. I don't want to give you the impression that a writer has to determine everything she wants to tell in a work of fiction all at once, and then construct the prose all at once, and then refine it all at once, etc. When a writer decides what unit (i.e. what portion) of the work of fiction she wants to deal with, be it a beat, a scene segment, a scene, a chapter, or an entire novel, she will go through the basic four-step prose construction process in her own unique way to produce the prose for that beat, scene segment, scene, chapter, or novel.

So far, so good?

HOW A UNIT OF ROUGH PROSE IS FORMED

I broke the prose construction process into these four basic steps for a reason. I wanted to set the stage for the following diagram, which is where the magic happens.

Take a look:

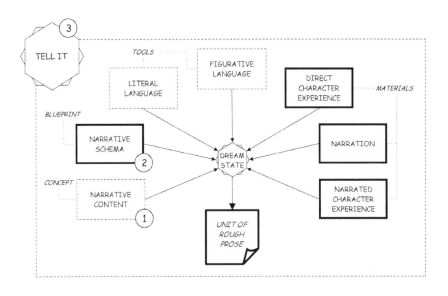

Step 3 of the Basic Prose Construction Process

Don't panic!

This diagram may seem difficult or confusing at first, but it really isn't. I'm going to explain each piece of this diagram separately, one piece at a time. When I'm done, you will understand how a unit of rough prose is formed (at a very basic level), where our current creative writing pedagogy (how creative writing is taught today) succeeds and where it fails, and what the NORTAV Method represents and how it fits into the big picture.

Are you ready?

Notice the big symbol in the upper left corner of the diagram. This symbol simply indicates that the entire diagram represents an exploded view of the details within Step 3 of the basic prose construction process. (Go back to the basic four-step prose construction process diagram and orient yourself if you need to.)

Now notice this same symbol in the center of the diagram. This smaller symbol represents the white-hot dreamstate (a Robert Olen Butler term) a writer enters when she accesses her creative center to conjure up prose from the depths of her subconscious. During this creative trance (a Stephen King term), the writer's subconscious mind has to deal with several sources of information simultaneously, referencing it, merging it, transforming it, until a unit of rough prose is formed. These sources of information are represented by the seven rectangular boxes feeding into the dreamstate symbol.

The single square box feeding out of the dreamstate symbol represents the unit of rough prose that's created.

Now let's define each of the seven sources of information one at a time, starting with the lower left rectangular box and working our way clockwise through the diagram.

Narrative content is the output from Step 1 of the prose construction process. (Go back to the basic four-step prose construction process diagram and orient yourself if you need to.) It represents what the writer wants to tell the reader. It includes the specific characters, events, settings, themes, etc. and the order in which it will be presented in the story. It draws upon the writer's knowledge of the elements of fiction (i.e. plot, character, setting, theme, etc.), elements of genre (i.e. specific traits of mystery, sci-fi, fantasy, mainstream, literary, etc.), and the elements of story structure (i.e. dramatic arcs, scenes and sequels, climax, denouement, etc.).

> **Narrative Content** represents what the writer wants to tell the reader and the structure and order in which it will be presented in the story.

Narrative content also draws upon the story universe the writer has researched or invented (i.e. the world background, politics, history, people, etc. where the story takes place). In respect to understanding and developing narrative content, there is an abundance of excellent how-to books, workshops, and university programs that will explain each aspect in detail. This is one aspect of the craft of writing where our pedagogy shines.

The next rectangular box represents the narrative schema. The narrative schema is the output from Step 2 of the prose construction process. (Go back to the basic four-step prose construction process diagram and orient yourself if you need to.) Put simply, a narrative schema is one or more unique styles of writing based upon a specific use of narrators, narrative intrusion, points of view, narrative tense, prose types, and other storytelling factors, and the pattern for using those unique styles of writing throughout a work of fiction. Here is where our pedagogy stumbles. It covers only portions of this information, and what it does cover, it often covers inaccurately. Writers are therefore forced to learn this part of the process, *one of the most critical parts of the prose construction process*, through trial and error and by subconsciously emulating the narrative schemas of professional authors.

The next rectangular box represents literal language. Literal language covers the writer's knowledge of the technical aspects of language: spelling, grammar, punctuation, syntax, sentence structures, vocabulary, etc. Our pedagogy does a wonderful job covering this aspect of the craft of writing.

The next rectangular box represents figurative language. Figurative language covers the writer's knowledge of the artistic aspects of language: similes, metaphors, alliteration, hyperbole, onomatopoeia, etc. Our pedagogy also handles this aspect extremely well.

The last three rectangular boxes represent Direct Character

Experience, Narration, and Narrated Character Experience. These are the three types of prose a writer can construct.

Three types of prose?

Yes, that's right.

There are three types of prose every writer can construct, whether she realizes it or not. The type of prose that can be constructed at any given point in a work of fiction is determined by the narrative schema. Our pedagogy is nearly silent on prose types. Writers are forced to learn this part of the process, *another critical part of the prose construction process*, through trial and error and by subconsciously emulating the prose types used by professional authors.

Now that you understand the basics of how a unit of prose is formed, I want to reinforce what I've just said with an analogy.

Imagine you want to build a shed. To build a shed, you first need to decide on the concept, that is, you need to decide what type of shed you want to build. Then you'll need a set of blueprints, tools, and materials. In this analogy, the shed is our unit of rough prose. The narrative content defines the concept, or the kind of shed we want to build. A potting shed, for instance. The narrative schema gives us the plan or blueprint that will tell us how to build the potting shed. Literal language and figurative language are the tools we'll use to construct the potting shed. And the three types of prose, Direct Character Experience, Narration, and Narrated Character Experience, are the materials we'll use to build our potting shed, based on what the plan calls for.

Thus, when a writer enters her dreamstate, she considers what it is she wants to build (narrative content), references her blueprint (narrative schema), and uses the appropriate tools (literal and figurative language) and the appropriate materials (Direct Character Experience, Narration, and Narrated Character Experience) to construct her prose.

This should explain the labels *concept, blueprint, tools,* and *materials* used in the diagram. Once the shed is built (Steps 1-3 of the basic prose construction process), it is cleaned and polished (Step 4 of the basic prose construction process) and ready for use.

A SIMPLE EXAMPLE

What follows is a simple example of the basic four-step prose construction process in action.

Let's say a writer wants to present to the reader an example of prose that represents the following information: A character, we'll call him Larry, feels sad and angry when he catches sight of a photo of his mother and his abusive stepfather. This bit of story can include many aspects within the elements of fiction, genre, story structure, and the story universe simultaneously. This is the narrative content.

In current pedagogical terms, the entire example will be written in the third-person, past tense. It will use a narrator whose presence should be hidden from the reader. Larry will be the point-of-view character. The style of writing should allow the reader to intimately experience what Larry is seeing and feeling, and it is the only style of writing to be used throughout the example. This is the narrative schema.

The writer then falls into her dreamstate, references the above narrative content and narrative schema, taps into what literal and figurative language skills she has, and forms a unit of rough prose. The resulting unit of rough prose might look something like this:

> Larry stared at the photo. His stepfather stood there, smiling, his arm wrapped around Larry's mother. The photo was taken in the fall. They were at the county fair in Bristol. It must have been several years ago. Before his stepfather lost his job. Before he lost his self-respect. Before he had starting beating Larry's mother. Larry's blood began to simmer, and a lump of emotion settled into his throat.

Do you see how this example reflects the narrative content?

Do you see how this example conforms to the narrative schema?

Do you see how it contains elements of literal language (i.e. punctuation, spelling, vocabulary, sentence structures, sentence fragments, etc.)?

And figurative language (i.e. metaphor and anaphora)?

This is how a unit of rough prose is formed. The fourth and final step would be to review and refine this prose, cleaning and polishing away any blemishes. Make sense? If not, go over this section again until it does. I'll wait until you're ready.

WHERE THE NORTAV METHOD FITS IN

Ready? Great! So now that you understand the big picture of the prose construction process and the basics of how a unit of rough prose is formed, where exactly does the NORTAV Method fit in?

Go back to the Step 3 diagram. Notice the bold boxes? This is the body of knowledge covered by the NORTAV Method. The NORTAV Method defines the narrative schema, which will replace such inadequate terms from our pedagogy such as *first-person point of view, third-person omniscient point of view, third-person limited point of view, frame narrative*, etc. The NORTAV Method defines how a unit of prose functions. The NORTAV Method defines the three types of prose (the three basic styles of writing), and how each is constructed, all of which is currently ignored by our pedagogy.

I will break the NORTAV Method into parts and present them to you one part at a time.

In Chapter 2 of this book I will define prose and explain in detail how a unit of prose functions.

In Chapter 3, I will explain in detail how to construct the first type of prose: Direct Character Experience.

In Chapter 4, I will explain in detail how to construct the second type of prose: Narration.

In Chapter 5, I will explain in detail how to construct the third type of prose: Narrated Character Experience.

In Chapter 6, I will explain in detail how to create a narrative schema. To facilitate the learning process, I will provide some preliminary explanation of narrative schemas throughout Chapters 3-5.

In Chapter 7, I will offer some advice on how the NORTAV Method can be incorporated into your own writing process.

Chapter 8 of this book falls outside the NORTAV Method itself. It is the final step in constructing professional quality prose. The NORTAV Method will teach you how to construct units of professional-yet-rough quality prose. You will still need to clean and polish it if you want it to shine like the prose of your favorite authors. In this chapter I will provide several recommendations on how to give your prose a sparkling sheen.

Throughout this book you will be analyzing quite a few samples of prose written by professional authors. The type of analysis you'll be performing (a NORTAV analysis) is designed to break apart and examine a sample of prose based on how it conforms to the NORTAV Method. You will learn how to perform a full NORTAV analysis as you work through this book.

Finally I will provide an appendix of fifteen extra NORTAV analyses so that when you finish this book so you can continue on with your learning process.

LET'S RECAP

Here in Chapter 1 my goal was to show you how the basic four-step prose construction process works, how a unit of rough prose is formed at a high level, what the NORTAV Method covers and how it fits into our current pedagogy, and how I will teach the NORTAV Method throughout the rest of the book. We will build on the concepts I've just covered here. Make sure you understand everything in Chapter 1 before moving on to Chapter 2.

Remember: the NORTAV Method is not a silver bullet or a magic formula for constructing prose. It is a critical body of knowledge that every professional writer should understand. Your goal in this book is to learn this body of knowledge and apply it to your own unique writing process *in whatever way comes natural to you.*

Now let's move on to Chapter 2, where you will learn the definition of prose and how a unit of prose functions.

Chapter 2

WHAT IS PROSE?

Discovering the Basics of Prose

WHERE ARE WE IN THE BIG PICTURE?

When appropriate, I will provide you with another look at a previous diagram to remind you where you are in the big picture of the learning process. Here in Chapter 2, I will define prose and explain how a unit of prose functions.

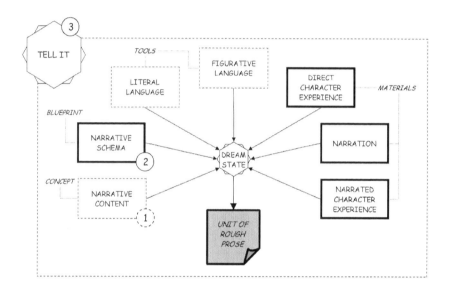

The Unit of Prose

WHAT IS PROSE?

Take a look at these three examples:

> Sue gazed up at me. Tears tracked down her pale cheeks, and her eyes were red-rimmed and swollen. My hate evaporated in an instant. She could never have written that letter. It would have been impossible.

Sit down and get comfortable. I'm going to tell you a story about a man, a woman, and a letter forged by a lonely, jealous sister.

I ran into the room where Sue was waiting, hating her and loving her all at once. At the time I had no idea she had nothing to do with the letter.

In current pedagogical terms, all three of these prose examples would be labeled as first-person, past tense. And that's about all you'd get from how-to books, workshops, or university programs in respect to understanding how to construct prose like this. The fact is, person and tense have little to do with the rules of constructing prose.

Each of these examples is constructed differently. Each adheres to a different set of construction rules, or guidelines, if you prefer. They are as different as apples and oranges and bananas.

According to Merriam-Webster.com, prose is...

a literary medium distinguished from poetry especially by its greater irregularity and variety of rhythm and its closer correspondence to the patterns of everyday speech.

While you might think this definition is adequate, I want to use a more restrictive and accurate definition. In this book, when I use the term "prose" I am referring specifically to *narrative prose*, a distilled set of writing that portrays a story or story segment through a narrator

> **Narrative Prose** is a distilled set of writing that portrays a story or story segment through a narrator and/or through a character's senses.

and/or through a character's senses. Notice two things about this definition. First, narrative prose is not like everyday speech. It is far more concise and more precise than normal discourse. It is, in a word, *distilled*. We will cover the distilling process in Chapter 8. Second, narrative prose portrays a story *through a narrator and/or through a character's senses*. This is an extremely important concept to understand, so let's take a look at this in more detail.

NARRATORS, CHARACTERS, AND THE THREE TYPES OF PROSE

When a reader reads prose she may get the sensation, in her mind's eye, that someone is telling her a story, like a voice-over narrator in a movie. Or she may experience the illusion that she is inside or beside a character, experiencing the events of the story as the character experiences the events. Or the reader may feel somewhere in between these two sensations, as if a narrator is telling her about the events experienced by a character.

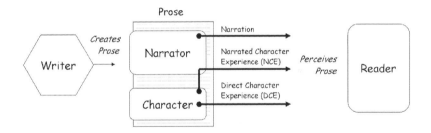

The Three Types of Prose

If you look back at those three prose examples, you can start to get an idea of what I mean. Reread them, and try to notice how you perceive each example in your mind's eye. Does the example make you feel as if someone is telling you a story? Does the example make you feel as if you are inside or beside a character, experiencing the story as he does, moment to moment? Does the example make you feel somewhere in between those two sensations?

Now take a look at the previous diagram.

Here we see how the reader can perceive prose in one of three ways. That is, the writer's choice of portraying a story through a narrator and/or a character results in the possibility of *three types of prose.*

> The **Three Types of Prose** are Direct Character Experience, Narration, and Narrated Character Experience.

When the writer uses only the moment-to-moment perceptions and activities of a character to portray the story to the reader, with little-to-no sense of a narrator's presence at all, we call this first type of prose Direct Character Experience, or DCE. When the writer uses a narrator to portray parts of the story that do not involve a character's perceptions and activities at all, we call this second type of prose Narration. When a writer blends these two approaches by using a narrator to tell the reader about the perceptions or activities of a character, whether those perceptions or activities are moment-to-moment or not, we call this third type of prose Narrated Character Experience, or NCE. Take a few moments to re-examine the previous diagram and reread this paragraph. This concept is the foundation of the NORTAV Method, and it's crucial that you understand what each of the three types of prose represent.

Now look at those three prose examples again:

> Sue gazed up at me. Tears tracked down her pale cheeks, and her eyes were red-rimmed and swollen. My hate evaporated in an instant. She could never have written that letter. It would have been impossible.

Sit down and get comfortable. I'm going to tell you a story about a man, a woman, and a letter forged by a lonely, jealous sister.

I ran into the room where Sue was waiting, hating her and loving her all at once. At the time I had no idea she had nothing to do with the letter.

Can you guess which example represents which type of prose? See if you can figure it out.

Done? Great!

The first example is Direct Character Experience, or DCE. It contains little-to-no sense of a narrator. The reader experiences the perceptions and activities of the character (in this case, the character is "I") directly, as they happen, moment to moment.

The second example is Narration. There are no character perceptions or activities being revealed to the reader in this example at all. This is simply the narrator telling the reader information about the story itself.

The third example is Narrated Character Experience, or NCE. Here we get the perceptions and activities of the character "I", but we are also given thoughts and information from the narrator "I" as he performs his role as a storyteller. That is, the narrator "I" is telling us about events that happened to him as a character at some point in the past. Thus, because we perceive both the character's perceptions and activities and the narrator, this is an example of NCE.

This will become clearer as we go. At this point, all you need to remember is that prose comes in three types: Direct Character Experience, which are the moment-to-moment perceptions and activities of a character with little-to-no evidence of a narrator; Narration, which is story information that comes directly from a narrator and has nothing to do with a character's perceptions or activities; and Narrated Character Experience, which is a narrator telling the reader about a character's perceptions and activities.

BEATS AND LINKS

Before we can get into the details of how to construct each of these three types of prose, we need to talk about two more concepts: beats and links.

Many amateur writers don't envision prose as having any structure below the scene level. They assume that a scene (or even an entire story) is created by simply writing one big long blob of prose that runs on for as long it needs to in order for the writer to say what she wants to say.

This is *not* how a unit of prose is constructed!

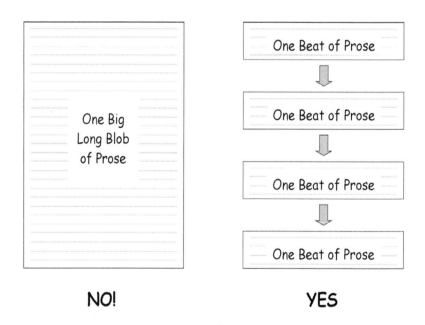

The Blob vs. Beats and Links

Take a look at the previous diagram.

Prose is constructed by linking together small bits and pieces of information called beats. A *beat* is small segment of prose that describes a single piece of story information, or one character perception or activity.

Beats can be of any length. They can consist of a single word or can run on for as long as a paragraph or two. For instance, a character's reaction to stubbing his toe (i.e. one character perception) might be represented as a beat that contains no more than a single word, as in: "Darn!" That same character's observation of a beach at sunset (i.e. another single character perception) may contain only a few words or it may run on for as long as a paragraph or more, depending on the situation and the character.

> A **Beat** is a small segment of prose
> that represents a single piece of
> story information or one character
> perception or activity.

Beats are tied together, one after another, through some kind of logical relationship. In other words, a writer doesn't randomly throw beats at the reader. The writer lays out the beats in a manner such that the reader can follow the prose logically from one beat to the next.

For instance:

The boy did this.

Then the boy did that.

Then the boy went home and climbed into bed.

If we consider each of these sentences to be a beat, we can see how one leads to the next, which leads to the next, in a way that the reader can follow and understand. In this example, the writer has established a pattern (a series of events) that logically connects each beat. The reader is not confused at all as she moves from beat to beat. She follows the unstated logic.

Here's another example:

> The old timer used to play baseball.
>
> Sally came home from school.
>
> My parents will never forgive me.

Confused?

Here there is no relationship or logic that connects these beats together. You probably thought as you read the example that there must be more to it than what you're reading. That's because you, the reader, are always looking for the relationship between beats such that they will make sense as they flow from one to the next. There aren't any in this example, and thus you the reader become confused. The point is, the reader must follow your prose from beat to beat, and therefore your beats must be connected by some kind of pattern or relationship or similarity or logic.

> A **Link** is any relationship that logically ties together two beats of prose.

Each beat must be connected to another beat by a *link* so that they form a chain the reader can follow from the beginning of the scene segment, scene, chapter, or novel, until the end. (Elizabeth George, one of my favorite aforementioned giants, does a great job explaining the concept of links in her book *Write Away*.)

So instead of thinking of prose as one big long blob that portrays an entire scene or story, think of prose as a series of small beats of story information or character perceptions or activities that are logically linked together to form a chain. I will cover the different types of beats and links and how they work throughout Chapters 3-5.

THE BEAT/LINK ANALYSIS

Let's reinforce your basic understanding of beats and links by performing a beat/link analysis. I'll be using this technique throughout the book, so you might as well get your first taste of it now. Here are two short paragraphs of prose:

> The house was huge, built in the late 1800s. It had three stories, a wrap-around deck, and a thick, russet chimney that stuck out of the roof like a fist. No one, not even David, knew that Jonah Keller had commissioned its construction.
>
> David opened the front door and stepped inside. A thick layer of dust covered a cavernous room. A smell of decay crept into David's nostrils, and he sneezed.

To perform a beat/link analysis, I will break apart this prose into what I think are the words, phrases, clauses, or sentences that make up the individual beats, and then I'll try to identify the relationships that link the beats into a chain. I will notate the start of each separate beat with a set of brackets [ ] and a reference number. Now let's get started.

> [1] The house was huge, built in the late 1800s. It had three stories, a wrap-around deck, and thick, russet chimney that stuck out of the roof like a fist.

Our first beat is a single piece of story information, presented in two sentences, which describes a house. As it is the first beat of the chain, it has no link to a previous beat.

[2] No one, not even David, knew that Jonah Keller had commissioned its construction.

Here is another piece of story information. This informs the reader that the house was commissioned by Jonah Keller and that David (an as-of-yet unknown character) is not aware of this.

One might argue this beat could be broken into two beats, as there are really two pieces of story information here (the commission and David's ignorance). Breaking out beats and identifying links is as much an art as it is a science. When you perform beat/link analyses, (which we'll soon be calling NORTAV analyses), simply break out the beats and define the links the best you can as you perceive them as a reader.

So, how does this beat link back to a previous beat? This information furthers the reader's knowledge of the house, so that "furthering" or "deepening" or "continuation" of the information (i.e. describing the house) is a pattern that establishes a link. One way to determine the link to a beat is to ask yourself this question: Why am I not confused by the appearance of this beat? The answer is most often the relationship or link back to a previous beat.

A NORTAV Tip:
Use the test question "Why am I not confused by the appearance of this beat?" in order to determine a beat's relationship or link back to a previous beat.

[3] David opened the front door and stepped inside.

Here is a single character activity. David is opening a door and step-ping into the house. There are two things here that provide a link back to a previous beat: David and the house. Both are mentioned in the previous beat. This beat brings the two thoughts or concepts together. So, why am I not confused by the appearance of this beat? Because I already knew that there was a house and a character named David, and that the two were somehow connected. The fact that David goes inside the house makes perfect sense given the situation at hand.

[4] A thick layer of dust covered a cavernous room. A smell of decay crept into David's nostrils,

Here is single character perception. David is observing the interior of the house. In the last beat, David performed the activity of entering the house. This beat is linked back to the previous beat because it is a logical activity that David would perform within the sequence of these story events, and thus the reader can follow the prose chain. That is, it's natural to assume that when a character enters a new setting, the first thing he or she will do is observe the setting. So, why am I not confused by the appearance of this beat? Because in the previous beat David entered the house and I would expect him to perform an imme-diate observation of the interior.

[5] and he sneezed.

Here is the final beat in our example. David performs another activity: he sneezes. This is a logical activity given the previous beat, where he got a nosefull of dust and a whiff of decay. Hence, this stimu-lus/response logic establishes the link. So, why am I not confused by the appearance of this beat? Because in the last beat he was hit with the dust and the smell, and these two things most likely caused him to sneeze.

And that's all there is to a beat/link analysis.

We use these analyses to examine how published authors have constructed their prose in order to *consciously* learn from their example. By the end of this book you will understand just how powerful a tool this is!

LINEAR AND NON-LINEAR PROSE CHAINS

There's one last concept I want to go over before I give you your first assignment. I explained that a writer links beats together, one after another, into a chain of prose that portrays a scene segment, scene, chapter, or novel. However, the term "chain" implies that beats are linked together, one after the other, in a linear or serial fashion.

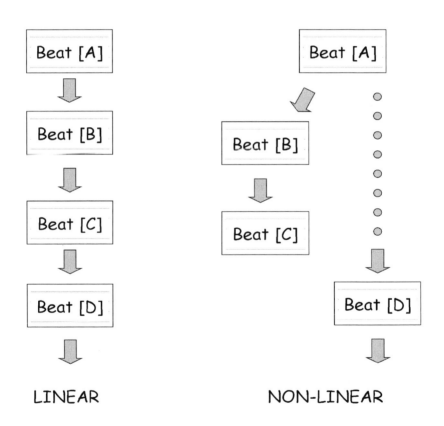

Linear and Non-Linear Prose Chains

For instance, Beat [A] links to Beat [B], which links to Beat [C], which links to Beat [D], and so forth. In actuality, this is often not the case. Every beat will have some kind of relationship or link back to a previous beat, but that previous beat may or may not be the *immediately* previous beat.

For example, Beat [A] might link to Beat [B], which might link to Beat [C], but Beat [C] might be a dead end. Beat [D] might link all the way back to Beat [A] before it continues the prose chain on through Beats [E-Z]. Short runs of beats can go off on tangents that terminate at dead ends. This creates a much more complex structure than a simple chain. In this book we won't concern ourselves with this level of complexity. At this point you only need to understand that prose is constructed by linking together beats in a chain that may or may not be completely linear, as we can see by the previous diagram.

BEAT/LINK ASSIGNMENT

Perform your own beat/link analysis on the following prose sample. Identify what you believe are the individual beats. That is, try to find the smallest segments of prose that provide one piece of story information, one character perception, or one character activity as you perceive it as a reader. Then for each beat, try to find the previous beat that spawned its occurrence. That is, for each beat, try to find a previous beat to which it is logically linked or connected. To help figure that out, ask yourself the link test question: "Why aren't I confused by the appearance of this beat?"

You'll notice that I haven't provided an answer key or my own beat/link analysis for this assignment. That's because I want you to try the first few assignments in this book without the temptation of having my answers at your fingertips. I want to maximize your thought process while you're learning the fundamentals of the beat/link analysis. After the first few assignments, I'll provide you with my analyses for comparison.

As you work through your beat/link analysis, consider these two questions:

- Can the beats you identify be put into categories?

- Can the links you identify be put into categories?

By the time you get to the end of this book, you will be able to take any sample of prose from any author (professional or not) and identify the three types of prose in use and the individual beats and links. In doing so, you will be *amazed* at how much you can learn about the prose construction process from the works of masters and amateurs alike (that is, you can see specifically what to do and what not to do when constructing your own prose).

The NORTAV Method provides us with something we have never had before in our pedagogy: a common context for defining, discussing, learning, and analyzing prose construction techniques.

Isn't that exciting? I certainly think so!

PROSE SAMPLE

The following prose sample is taken from a vignette I wrote a few years back called *The Devil's Holiday*. This and other works of mine are available on my website: http://ajabbiati.com/.

> ... When Flueric reached the center of the square, he slipped between an elderly couple studying a crumpled map of the city and a silver-haired priest clutching a Bible to his chest.
>
> "*Scusi*, pardon me," Flueric said.
>
> He stepped onto a narrow granite rim that ran around the obelisk, and his view improved immensely. From here he could see over the heads of the crowd, beyond

Bernini's great façade, over the pillars and the saints that crowned the cornices of the court of St. Peter, all the way to the rooftop of the Sistine Chapel herself.

"Visiting?" the priest asked Flueric. "I can't quite place your accent."

Flueric looked down on the priest. Though he was clearly an older man, his smile was warm and childlike. His cheeks were freshly shaved, a spot of tissue still stuck to a nick on his neck. His eyes were cast to the side, pale, milky. The eyes of a blind man.

"In a manner of speaking," Flueric said.

"Have you seen the catacombs?" the priest asked. "I remember how amazed I was the first time I saw them."

"Yes," Flueric said. "It took me a while to find them, too. They used to bury the dead there in secret. Christians."

The priest nodded. "I haven't been there in over fifty years. My parents took me there when I was young. It feels like yesterday..."

WRITING EXERCISE

Go to your bookshelf and take down a novel you haven't read, preferably something published in the last few years. Open to a random page and read a small section until you can identify a point-of-view character and the general situation he/she is currently facing. As soon you identify a point-of-view character and his/her current situation, close the book. Now pick up where you left the story and construct the next 500 words of prose yourself. Do whatever you like with the characters, plot, setting, etc. Or introduce new information. Write whatever comes to mind. The narrative content is not important. What is important is that you attempt do this exercise by constructing your prose *as consciously as possible*, through the use of beats and links. Try not to fall into your dreamstate. This is not meant to replace your actual writing process. *This is an exercise.* If this feels strange, don't worry. The point here is for you to start thinking of prose not as one long blob, but rather as a chain of linked beats, and the best way to do that is to practice forging a chain of beats yourself, consciously, one beat at a time.

LET'S RECAP

Here in Chapter 2, my goal was to define the three types of prose, beats and links, the beat/link analysis, and explain more about how a unit of prose functions. You learned that:

- Prose is a distilled set of writing that portrays a story through a narrator and/or through a character's senses.

- Portraying a story through a narrator and/or through a character's senses results in three types of prose: Direct Character Experience (DCE), Narration, and Narrated Character Experience (NCE).

- Direct Character Experience, or DCE, reflects the moment-to-moment perceptions and activities of a character with little-to-no presence of a narrator.

- Narration is story information that is portrayed to the reader through a narrator. It reflects any information that does *not* pertain to the perceptions and activities of a character.

- Narrated Character Experience, or NCE, reflects the perceptions and activities of a character through a narrator.

- All three types of prose are constructed using small bits of story information, character perceptions, or character activities, called beats.

- Each beat is linked to a previous beat through some kind of relationship in order to form a chain of logic that leads the reader through the scene segment, scene, chapter, or novel.

- Beats can be linked one after another in a linear fashion, or they be linked in a non-linear fashion, with short tangents and side chains.

- A beat/link analysis can be performed on prose to identify the beats and describe how those beats are linked together into a chain.

We will build on the concepts I've just covered here. Make sure you understand everything in Chapter 2 before moving on to Chapter 3.

Remember: the NORTAV Method is not a silver bullet or a magic formula for constructing prose. It is a critical body of knowledge that every professional writer should understand. Your goal in this book is to learn this body of knowledge and apply it to your own unique writing process *in whatever way comes natural to you*.

Now let's move on to Chapter 3, where you will learn all about constructing Direct Character Experience, the first type of prose.

Chapter 3

DIRECT CHARACTER EXPERIENCE

Discovering the First Type of Prose

WHERE ARE WE IN THE BIG PICTURE?

Now that you understand a little about the three types of prose and how a unit of prose functions, we're going to spend the next three chapters of this book covering, in detail, how to construct each of the three types of prose. We'll start with the first type, called Direct Character Experience.

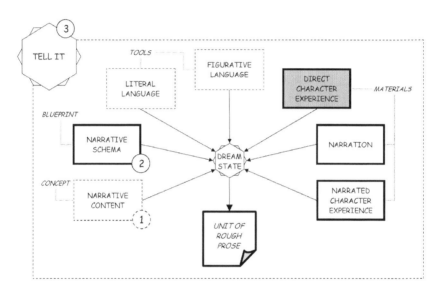

Direct Character Experience

WHAT IS DIRECT CHARACTER EXPERIENCE?

When a writer uses only the moment-to-moment perceptions and activities of a character to portray the story, with little-to-no sense of a narrator, we call this type of prose *Direct Character Experience*, or *DCE*. A writer uses DCE when she wants to put the reader deep into the senses of a character so that the reader experiences the illusion she is there, within or beside the character, experiencing the events of

> **Direct Character Experience** is prose that reflects the moment-to-moment perceptions and activities of a character with little-to-no sense of a narrator.

the story as the character experiences them. Some how-to books, workshops, and university programs teach writers to use a first-person narrator or the present tense to achieve this kind of intimacy. This is one of the inaccuracies of our pedagogy. Though both suggestions will help create some sense of intimacy, it is through the use of DCE that intimacy is truly achieved between a reader and a character, as illustrated by the following diagram:

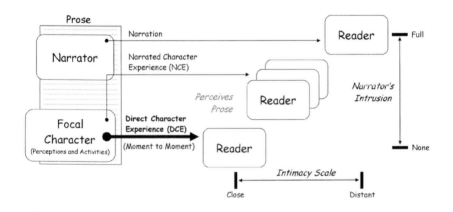

Direct Character Experience, Intimacy, and Narrative Intrusion

Keep in mind, there is always a narrator present in prose. However, the more the narrator is hidden, i.e. the less the narrator's presence intrudes into the prose, the more the reader experiences the illusion of perceiving the perceptions and activities of a character, moment-to-moment, along with the character.

A BIT ON NARRATIVE SCHEMAS

I mentioned that a narrative schema defines one or more unique styles of writing based upon a specific use of narrators, narrative intrusion, points of view, narrative tense, prose types, and other storytelling factors, and the pattern of their use throughout a work of fiction. We will fully cover this topic in Chapter 6. I do, however, want to stop for a brief moment and give you a little more information here about narrative schemas.

Writers will *always* use a one specific style of writing, purposefully, at any given point in a work of fiction, and will only change writing styles when there is a valid reason for doing so. A reader will notice when a writing style changes and will look for a reason for that change. If the reader can't find one, she'll become confused and the quality of the prose will deteriorate.

```
A NORTAV Tip:
Work purposefully in one and only one
    unique writing style at a time.
```

Imagine if a writer suddenly changed the narrative tense (one factor of a writing style) from past to present. A reader would immediately notice that change and look for the cause or reason for it. If she can't find one, she'll become confused. Or if the writer suddenly changed the point-of-view character (another factor of a writing style), the reader would immediately notice that change and expect it to have happened for a reason. Again, if she can't find a reason for the change, she'll become confused.

What you need to know before we continue is that prose types are also a factor of a writing style. Changing prose types or changing the use of a prose type can potentially cause a reader to notice a change in the writing style.

In this chapter I'm going to teach you how to construct one type of prose: DCE. The goal is to learn to work consistently in a writing style that uses *only* DCE. There are other writing styles that use other prose types or more than one prose type at a time, and we'll get to those in later chapters.

FOCAL CHARACTERS

Moving on, let's define another term. You know that DCE portrays a beat, scene segment, scene, chapter, or novel to the reader through the moment-to-moment perceptions and activities of a character. Our pedagogy refers to the character through which the reader experiences a beat, scene segment, scene, chapter, or novel as a *point of view* character. For the remainder of this book, we will try to avoid the term *point of view*. It has been overloaded with multiple meanings across different contexts, and as such it causes a lot of confusion. For now, forget the term *point of view*. Take it into the backyard and shoot it. Several times. We will stand on the shoulders of narratologists and adopt from those giants a much better term. We will call the character through which the reader experiences a beat, scene segment, scene, chapter, or novel, a *focal character*. Therefore it is the focal character's moment-to-moment perceptions and activities that are portrayed through DCE.

> A **Focal Character** is the character through which the reader experiences a beat, scene segment, scene, chapter, or novel.

DIRECT CHARACTER EXPERIENCE BEATS

In DCE there are five different types of beats that can be used to portray a focal character's moment-to-moment perceptions and activities. They are:

Observations: These are beats that describe what a focal character perceives through her five senses—sight, hearing, taste, touch, and smell.

Reactions: These are beats that describe the involuntary internal or external reactions of a focal character—fear, disgust, joy, lust, a jerk of the head, a stagger backwards, a scream, etc.

Thoughts: These are beats that describe the conscious or semi-conscious thoughts of a focal character—analyses, memories, musings, calculations, prior knowledge at the surface of a character's consciousness, etc.

Actions: These are beats that describe the voluntary physical activities performed by a focal character—walking, grabbing, running, sitting, looking, smelling, etc. Note the "acts of observing" (looking, smelling, listening, touching, tasting) are actions, not observations. What is actually seen or smelt or heard or felt or tasted is an observation.

Vocalizations: These are beats that describe the voluntary vocalizations produced by a focal character, such as speech, grunts, groans, etc. Note that dialogue is not a type of beat but rather an exchange of Vocalization beats (what a focal character says to someone) and Observation beats (what a focal character hears someone say).

BEAT/LINK ASSIGNMENT

In the last assignment you performed a beat/link analysis without knowing anything about the specific types of beats or links available to a writer. The point was to emphasize how a work of prose is actually constructed by having you try to discover on your own the small pieces of information (beats) and how they related to each other (links). For this assignment, perform a beat/link analysis on the prose sample below based on what you've learned so far about the five types of beats used in DCE. Don't expect your analysis to be perfect. We will spend the remainder of Chapter 3 learning about each of these five types of beats in detail. For this assignment, simply try to spot the focal character's observations, reactions, thoughts, actions, and vocalizations. Notate the start of each with a bracket containing the first letter of the beat type: [O], [R], [T], [A], or [V]. Locate and make a note of the relationships (links) that connect the beats into a prose chain. You can do this right in the book, or print/photocopy the sample and work with it separately.

Again, I have not provided an answer key for this assignment. I want you to concentrate on figuring this out without the benefit of a cheat sheet! After this assignment, though, I will begin providing my own analyses for comparison. When you are through with your beat/link analysis, consider these questions:

- Were you able to break the entire passage into beats?

- Was each beat clearly of one type, or could some have been represented by more than one type?

PROSE SAMPLE

The following prose sample is taken from a short story I recently published called *Lot-17*. It was written using a DCE-based writing style. Again, this and other published works of mine are available at http://ajabbiati.com/.

The focal character in this sample is Ann LaPlante.

> ... A late spring sun was sinking behind the trees, its red glow barely visible through branches laden with new growth. Ann LaPlante glanced at her husband as they walked along the trail. He looked awful. She couldn't

remember the last time Pete had smiled. An aura of worry surrounded him. It had been there ever since he'd learned of Lydia's plight. Ann could not bring herself to believe it completely, though there were some at church that had insisted it could happen. She would know for sure, though. In just a few hours.

Pete looked at her.

"We're pretty lucky, huh?" he said. "When Father Cordoba told us there was a vortex right here in Stony Creek, I was stunned. He says it's only a minor one, but still. I think it was God's will that we moved here."

"Yes," she said. She hoped it was God's will.

"We might've had to take Lydia to one of the more powerful vortexes. Mount Shasta. Or Sedona. Susan said Lydia would never have made it. She was relieved they only had to bring her here." Pete paused. "Ann... I want to thank you for understanding."

"Lydia's your daughter, Pete. What else could we do?"

"My daughter, yes. And Susan's. Not yours. You didn't have to—"

"I knew you had a daughter when we married."

"But Lydia was never part of my life. I never thought she would be."

"We've been through all this."

"I know," Pete said, "but we spent our life savings on this lot."

"We had to," Ann replied. "We couldn't get access to the property otherwise."

Her husband said nothing as the two reached the end of the trail. They were at the top of a small depression, a glen, filled with tall grass and rough boulders. A handful of tenacious white birch grew about the clearing. There was a shack in the center, a quaint one, Ann thought. It was in need of a fresh coat of paint, but it seemed in good repair. A pretty green glass window gleamed next to its weather-stained door. She liked the look of the place...

WRITING EXERCISE

Go back to your bookshelf and take down a novel you haven't read. Again, preferably something published in the last few years. Open to a random page and read a small section until you can identify a focal character and the general situation he/she is currently facing. Pick up where you left the story and construct the next 500 words of prose yourself. Write whatever comes to mind. Construct your prose *as consciously as possible*, through the use of Observation beats, Reaction beats, Thought beats, Action beats, and Vocalization beats. Make sure all beats have a link back to a previous beat. Your first beat should link back to the last beat you read in the story. Like the last exercise, try not to fall into your dreamstate. This is not meant to replace your actual writing process. *This is an exercise.* The point here is for you to start getting a feel for constructing the five different types of DCE beats.

LET'S RECAP

In this section, my goal was to provide you with an introduction to the first type of prose: Direct Character Experience.

You learned that:

- Direct Character Experience, or DCE, is prose that reflects the moment-to-moment perceptions and activities of a focal character with little-to-no sense of a narrator.

- DCE is used to create a sense of intimacy between the reader and the focal character.

- A DCE-based writing style uses only the DCE prose type.

- A writer will work purposefully in one and only one unique writing style at a time.

- A reader will notice any change in writing style and will expect to find a reason for that change.

- Focal characters are the characters through which the reader experiences a beat, scene segment, scene, chapter, or novel. In our old terminology, these characters were called "point of view" characters.

- We have abolished the term "point of view" and promise never to use it again (unless absolutely necessary).

- DCE is constructed by linking together five different types of beats that reflect a focal character's perceptions and activities. Those five types of beats are Observations, Reactions, Thoughts, Actions, and Vocalizations.

Now we will cover each type of DCE beat in detail, beginning with Observations.

Observation Beats

WHAT ARE OBSERVATION BEATS?

An *Observation beat* describes what a focal character perceives through her five senses—sight, hearing, taste, touch, and smell—as the story unfolds, moment to moment. Note that Observation beats can also reflect internal physical observations, such as feeling sick, feeling pain, feeling hot, feeling cold, etc.

> An ***Observation Beat*** is a description of what a focal character perceives through her five senses—sight, hearing, taste, touch, or smell—as the story unfolds, moment to moment.

HOW ARE OBSERVATION BEATS USED?

There are two ways in which observations are reflected in DCE. The first is when the focal character's observation is semi-conscious or incidental. In this case the writer tacks a small bit of the focal character's incidental observation onto a beat of another type. In other words, if a focal character is concentrating on performing an action, the writer may tack on small bits of the focal character's semi-conscious or incidental observations to the Action beat.

Let's look at an example of this. Keep in mind we are working with DCE, so there is always a focal character involved. The example reflects how a focal character is perceiving events through his five senses, *not* how a narrator is describing them to the reader from an outside perspective. Thus, try to put yourself inside the focal character.

In this example, a "boy" is the focal character and his attention is fixed on getting to the local candy store before it closes:

> The boy pulled his red, freshly-painted wagon down the busy street toward Mary's Munchies.

This is an Action beat (we will get to these soon enough), yet there are small bits of the focal character's incidental or semi-conscious observations in here ("red, freshly-painted," "busy"). Both of these incidental observations represent what the boy (the focal character) can see, but because the boy only takes in the sights semi-consciously or incidentally (i.e. he is not focused on these things), they are not beats and are not part of the prose chain itself, but rather are tacked on to add color and depth to the Action beat.

The technique of tacking on small, inconsequential bits of information to beats of a different type applies to all focal character perceptions and activities, not just observations. We create *incidental information* by adding adjectives, direct/indirect objects, and other short, modifying phrases to beats of different types. Incidental information is not notated in a beat/link analysis, although underlining it can sometimes be useful.

Incidental Information are bits of inconsequential information that are tacked onto beats of different types.

Getting back to observations, the second way to reflect observations in DCE is when the focal character is focused on her observation. Whenever a perception or activity is rendered as the point of the focal character's attention, it is considered a *focused beat*. A focused Observation beat (or simply "Observation beat" for short) is part of the prose chain.

> A **Focused Beat** is a beat representing
> a focal character's point of focus,
> which becomes part of the prose chain.

How much the focal character is focused on the perception or activity will affect how the beat is constructed. Generally, the more the focus, the more the detail. The less the focus, the less the detail.

> **A NORTAV Tip:**
> Construct DCE beats with more or less
> detail depending on the focal
> character's level of focus and the
> situation at hand.

Let's assume we have a focal character named Kevin. He's a police officer and is trying to keep a troubled girl, Betty, from committing suicide. Betty is in her bedroom. Kevin is outside her door in the hall-way. Suddenly he hears what sounds like the hammer of a gun being cocked. Adrenalin courses through him. The next set of beats might be:

> Kevin kicked open the door, which slammed against Betty's
> bedroom wall with a crash.

This is an Action beat followed by an Observation beat. The first half of the sentence describes Kevin's action (kicking open the door). The second half describes what Kevin sees (the door slamming against the wall) and what Kevin hears (the crash). Now, because Kevin is not focusing his attention completely on the door but rather focusing it on racing into the room to save the girl, the details of the Observation beat are kept to a minimum because he would not realistically perceive them in detail in this kind of situation.

Let's continue our example:

> Betty sat on the side of her bed. There was a .38 in her hand, black and deadly as a scorpion. She gazed up at Kevin, eyes brimming with tears.
>
> "Don't," she pleaded.

This Observation beat is comprised of multiple sentences. They describe what Kevin sees and hears after he kicks open the door. He is focused on taking all this in, so the Observation beat is longer (four sentences), but all the sentences are still relatively short and only contain a few details (".38," "deadly as a scorpion," "eyes brimming with tears"). Why? We are trying to describe what Kevin is experiencing through his senses as he would actually have experienced them in this situation. The pressure is on Kevin, so Kevin wouldn't have the time to notice the minutia of the setting, like the color of the bed sheets, the design of the wallpaper, the knickknacks on top of the bureau at the back of the room, etc. So even though Kevin is highly focused on the observation, the situation also has an impact on how the beat is constructed.

The technique of crafting beats according to the character, the character's focus, and the situation at hand applies to beats of all types.

NORTAV ASSIGNMENT

Since *NORTAV* stands for Narration, Observation, Reaction, Thought, Action, and Vocalization, and since those are the crux of what our beat/link analysis are meant to reveal (I will explain the *N* for Narration in Chapter 4), I will now refer to the beat/link analysis by its actual name: the NORTAV analysis.

In the last assignment, you did your best to locate the five different types of beats used in DCE. The point was to give you a preview of what performing a full NORTAV analysis is all about. For this assignment I want you to read the following sample of prose and try to find only the Observation beats. See if you can locate the focal character's semi-conscious or incidental observations. Just make a mental note of these, or, if you'd like, underline them. For the focal character's focused observations, notate them as Observation beats by inserting an [O] before the word that begins the beat. To make your commentary clearer, you can add a numeric identifier to each beat for reference purposes, such as [O4]. Since we will not be identifying all the beats in the sample, we'll need something to mark the end of each Observation beat, for clarity. Use a blank set of brackets [ ] to do this. If you can identify the link that leads to the Observation beat, do so. The goal here is to pay very close attention to the Observation beats in use. Try to identify and understand the techniques the author uses to construct each.

You can do your work right in this book, or print/photocopy out the sample and work with it separately. When you're done, compare your results with the NORTAV analysis I provide directly after the prose sample.

A quick note: Most of the samples used throughout the rest of this book were taken from the works of professional and often best-selling and/or award-winning authors. Many run up to 500 words. I believe it is only through context that you can truly see how prose is con-structed. Simply providing a series of short examples would not be nearly as effective.

Offering 500 words of hard-wrought prose for critical examination is a generous gift indeed. I again want to thank those very special authors who contributed their prose to this book.

PROSE SAMPLE: Guido Henkel's *Curse of Kali*

Allow me to introduce Guido Henkel. Guido is the author of the Jason Dark supernatural mystery series, which includes *Demon's Night*, *Heaven's on Fire*, *Dr. Prometheus*, *The Blood Witch*, *Terrorlord*, and the award-winning *Ghosts Templar*. The following prose sample is taken from his Jason Dark novel: *Curse of Kali*. You can find more information about Guido at `http://www.guidohenkel.com/`.

The focal character in the following DCE-based sample is Jason Dark.

> ... Jason Dark eyed a smaller, man-sized door that was set flush into the foreboding barn-size doors of the warehouse, allowing easy access for a single person. Without a word, he reached for the handle and pulled it open. For the length of a few heartbeats he stopped and simply listened. Only the soft lapping of the brackish water against the dock was audible, drowning out even the distant noise of the metropolis at large.
>
> He turned and looked at Siu Lin. Careful, now! He could clearly read her determined face in the bright moonlight.
>
> A thick fog rolled in from the river, its ethereal arms weaving in a sluggish dance, like ghostly wisps, eating away at the moon's light. Dark blacked out his lantern and took a careful step forward.
>
> The inside of the warehouse was dark, and only shadows allowed the eye to create an image of the interior. Without a word, Dark waved Siu Lin inside and closed the door, careful not to make an unnecessary sound. Together they stood in silence and listened. A foghorn blew somewhere in the distance, lonely and forlorn. Other than that, the warehouse was silent.
>
> Almost in unison, Dark and Siu Lin opened the blackout shades of their lanterns, allowing the soft glow of the kerosene flames to illuminate the room. Thirty feet above them, the slatted ceiling covered the cavernous structure. Stairs and walkways splashed the walls with

their wooden rag-tag construction. Large stacks of ship-ping crates and containers lined up in jumbled rows down the length of the entire warehouse, each announcing its far-away origins by stenciled-on designations. The rows disappeared into the darkness, interrupted only by smaller passages between different stacks.

Dark looked over his lantern and saw Siu Lin tilting her head as she took in the enormous structure. Time and again her dark eyes scanned the walls and walkways, be-fore she returned his gaze and nodded. "You lead."

As Dark took cautious steps, the sphere of light traveled with him, peeling ever new shapes and details out of the darkness. Two steps behind him, Siu Lin followed, silent as a snake on cotton balls. Walking backwards so she could see behind them, she brought up the rear, taking no chances for a surprise.

"I do not like this," she finally whispered. "Where's Baker?"

"Maybe he's late." Even as he said the words, however, Dark felt that the answer was more of an excuse, rather than any actual conviction on his part.

"Then who unlocked the door?"

"Let's just take a look around."

They proceeded another few yards down the main aisle into the warehouse, when Dark unexpectedly froze. Siu Lin nearly bumped into him and was ready to open her mouth, when she turned and saw what had stopped Dark dead in his tracks...

NORTAV ANALYSIS: Guido Henkel's *Curse of Kali*

What follows is my NORTAV analysis of Guido's prose sample. Compare it to your analysis. See where we agree and where we differ. If we differ, try to understand why we differ. Remember, performing a NORTAV analysis can be as much an art as a science. As you'll see, there are times when beats can be categorized in more than one way, depending on how the writer crafted the beat and how the reader perceives the beat. This is normal. So if our analyses differ, that's okay, provided you can articulate an appropriate reason for the difference.

Fair warning: This analysis will be longer than most, as it will contain quite a few concepts that need to be defined as we go. Take your time as you work through this analysis and make sure you grasp all the concepts. When reading my NORTAV analyses, be sure to reference back to my notated prose in order to benefit from the full impact of the explanation. That is, read a segment of notated prose, then read my subsequent analysis, then reread the notated segment and try to understand how my analysis applies and how it compares to your analysis.

Finally, please make sure you do your analysis *before* reading my analysis. Otherwise, the convention of placing the beat notation at the start of a beat rather than at the end of a beat can be somewhat coercive if you haven't yet formed your own opinion.

With that, let's begin.

> Jason Dark eyed [O1] a smaller, man-sized door that was set flush into the foreboding barn-size doors of the warehouse [ ], allowing easy access for a single person.

Here we have [O1], our first Observation beat. It is Jason Dark's observation of the door in front of him. This is a typical way of providing the reader with a description of setting using DCE. Our focal character, Jason, "eyes" something, and then we, the reader, are provided next with what he "eyed" through the use of an Observation beat. Remember, the acts of making a visual observation ("looking," "eyeing," "scanning," "searching," etc.) are not Observation beats; they are Action beats.

> Without a word, he reached for the handle and pulled it open. For the length of a few heartbeats he stopped and simply listened. [O2] Only the soft lapping of the brackish water against the dock was audible, drowning out even the distant noise of the metropolis at large. [ ]

Here we have [O2], our next Observation beat. Jason "listens" and then we are provided with a description of what he hears through an Observation beat. This is the same tactic Guido used before, where the Action beat (the "act of observing") directly precedes the Observation beat.

Two points of interest here.

First, in this context, the fact that Jason Dark is carefully sneaking into a suspicious area causes Guido to use these "act of observing" Action beats explicitly. He wants to draw attention to that act of observing. In other situations where the act of observing is less critical, many authors will skip the "act of observing" Action beat altogether and let the reader infer its existence (more on this in a moment). For example, if a character opens a door (Action beat), the next beat could simply be the description of what she sees (Observation beat). The reader doesn't need the "act of observing" Action beat in order to follow the prose chain. We get them here, though, because that act of observing is an important part of the situation at hand.

The second interesting point to note is that Guido doesn't use phrasings like "he saw" or "he heard" in his prose (at least not yet). He doesn't write "Jason looked across the room and saw a door that was part of another door..." This would cause the narrator's presence to intrude into the prose and cause the prose to slip into NCE, which we wouldn't want if we were trying to write in a DCE-based writing style. Said another way, adding narrative intrusions, or tags, like "saw" or "heard" within Observation beats is a form of narrative intrusion. It is the narrator telling us that the character sees or hears something, rather than letting us experience that observation directly along with the character. You want to limit your use of these kinds of tags when writing DCE Observations.

A NORTAV Tip:
When creating Observation beats in DCE, limit the use of tags such as "he saw," "he heard," "he smelled," to minimize the narrator's presence.

He turned and looked at Siu Lin. [?] Careful, now! He could clearly read her determined face in the bright moonlight. [ ]

You may have designated this [?] beat as an Observation beat in your NORTAV analysis. Guido sets up the same situation as before. He uses an "act of observing" action: "He turned and looked at Siu Lin." We expect to get an Observation beat next, but instead of describing how Jason directly perceives Siu Lin through his five senses, Guido gives us "Careful, now! He could clearly read her determined face in the bright moonlight." This is actually a Thought beat, not an Observation beat. What Guido is doing here is providing us with Jason's observation through Jason's thought, after the observation has occurred. We can almost "see" what Jason saw by understanding how Jason mentally interprets the missing Observation beat. Subtle?

Reread the two beats and put yourself deep into Jason's perspective. How do you perceive the second beat? You should perceive it as Jason mentally processing what he's just seen, even though we the readers haven't actually seen it. Jason comes to the conclusion that he has to be careful because Siu Lin's appearance (again, which we aren't actually given directly) is "determined." Though this *beat substitution* technique (using one beat to portray what is normally portrayed by a different type of beat) starts to get into advanced theory, I do want to point it out to you so you can recognize the technique when you see it. I'll do the same thing for a few more terms before this analysis is over.

> **Beat Substitution** is using one type of beat to portray something that is usually portrayed by another type of beat.

> [O3] A thick fog rolled in from the river, its ethereal arms weaving in a sluggish dance, like ghostly wisps, eating away at the moon's light. [ ]

Ah. Here Guido provides us with a perfect setup for defining another term. [O3] is a typical Observation beat. Jason observes the thick fog rolling in from the river. But what beat does this link back to? In order to follow the prose chain, we should know what beat caused Jason to observe this; however we are not given a specific "act of observing" beat that spawns this Observation beat. We infer that Jason "looked at" or "noticed" the thick fog simply from the context of the prose and the situation at hand.

I mentioned earlier that in some cases we don't need the "act of observing" Action beat that precedes an Observation beat. This is precisely one of those cases. Any time a beat is needed to complete the prose chain and it's not explicitly provided, it's considered an *implied beat.*

> An ***Implied Beat*** is a beat that is
> necessary to complete the prose chain
> but is not provided by the writer and
> therefore must be inferred
> by the reader.

Dark blacked out his lantern and took a careful step forward.

[O4] The inside of the warehouse was dark, [ ] and only shadows allowed the eye to create an image of the interior.

Speak of the devil. [O4] is another example of an Observation beat linked back to an implied "act of observing" Action beat. Jason steps forward. Then it's implied that he "looks." Then we are given the Observation beat describing what he sees. Notice the section of prose beginning with "and only shadows...." Did you notate this as part of [O4]? Is this really Jason's sensory observation? Doubtful. This could be an example of beat substitution, where Guido provides us with an impression of sensory detail (normally done with an Observation beat) through the use of a Thought beat. That is, this could be perceived as Jason realizing (realization is a form of thought) that he can only make out what's in the room based on the shapes of the shadows. It could also be argued that this is a narrator telling us "only shadows allowed the eye to create an image of the interior." If so, this would cast the entire Observation beat as NCE, and it does sound a little like something a voice-over narrator might say. So, is this a Thought beat or is it a beat of Narration? The truth is, this last part is ambiguous.

Which brings us to an important definition. As I've mentioned, performing NORTAV analyses is as much art as science. A writer constructs prose from the subconscious. She isn't consciously churning out prose that is narratively perfect in every detail as if it were lines of programming code. As such, sometimes there are ambiguities in the way beats are cast or perceived, as in this last example. There are often times when a beat could be perceived as more than one type of beat. When this occurs, we call it *beat ambiguity*.

> **Beat Ambiguity** is when a beat can be perceived as more than one type of beat.

Ambiguous beats should be notated according to the writing style currently in use. When using a DCE-based writing style, tie goes to the runner. In other words, if the choice is between a DCE Thought beat and a Narration beat, and the writer is working in a DCE-based writing style, then notate the ambiguous beat as a DCE Thought beat. If both choices happen to be DCE, (e.g. a Thought beat versus an Observation beat), simply make a gut call and move on. This is why I prefer to use the largest prose samples possible. Context is king when performing NORTAV analyses! Knowing the current prose type in use will help you accurately perform the analysis.

> **A NORTAV Tip:**
> When determining the type of an ambiguous beat, notate it based on the prose type currently in use.

The corollary here is that if you need to know the current prose type in use to perform an accurate analysis, you *really* need to be aware of the current prose type you are working with when you write. All through this sample Guido has been using DCE to put us deep into Jason's perspective. We would notate "and only shadows..." as a Thought beat.

As I've said, just try to grasp the general concept behind these definitions and move on. You can always come back to them later.

> Without a word, Dark waved Siu Lin inside and closed the door, careful not to make an unnecessary sound. Together they stood in silence and listened. [O5] A foghorn blew somewhere in the distance, lonely and forlorn. Other than that, the warehouse was silent. [ ]

By now you should be getting the hang of notating Observation beats, especially Observation beats crafted in this fashion. [O5] is a typical Observation beat brought on by (linked back to) the "act of observing" Action beat of "listened." Guido's slight use of "Other than that" almost made me notate the entire last sentence as a Thought beat, but I would consider the phrase "Other than that" to be an incidental thought tacked onto the larger Observation beat. Again, this is both art and science. Beats are notated based on how they are constructed *and* how they are perceived. You might perceive this one way, and I might perceive it another.

> Almost In unison, Dark and Siu Lin opened the blackout shades of their lanterns, allowing the soft glow of the kerosene flames to illuminate the room. [O6] Thirty feet above them, the slatted ceiling covered the cavernous structure. Stairs and walkways splashed the walls with their wooden rag-tag construction. Large stacks of shipping crates and containers lined up in jumbled rows down the length of the entire warehouse, each announcing its far-away origins by stenciled-on designations. The rows disappeared into the darkness, interrupted only by smaller passages between different stacks. [ ]

Here is another typical use of an implied "act of observing" Action beat leading to a subsequent Observation beat. Notice that compared to the previous Observation beats, [O6] is detailed and runs on for several sentences. Guido is crafting his beats such that they are realistic to Jason's perceptions and the situation at hand (as a professional writer will always do). The more Jason pays attention to his observations, the longer and more detailed they are rendered in the prose.

> Dark looked over his lantern and saw [O7] Siu Lin tilting her head as she took in the enormous structure. Time and again her dark eyes scanned the walls and walkways, before she returned his gaze and nodded. "You lead." [ ]

Here's another "act of observing" Action beat ("looked") and a subsequent Observation beat, [O7]. Notice the tag "saw" Guido has slipped in here. As I said, this definitely casts the beat into NCE, therefore this beat is considered non-conforming.

```
A Non-Conforming Beat is a beat that
        is not part of the writing
          style currently in use.
```

A *non-conforming beat* is a beat that is not part of the writing style currently in use. Since Guido has been consistently using a DCE-based writing style, and the reader has become accustomed to perceiving beats as DCE, the reader ignores or simply won't notice this slight deviation into NCE. Why is that?

Because even if beats are not part of the writing style in use, the reader will still perceive them as belonging to the current writing style provided the deviations are minor and occur infrequently.

When you encounter an infrequent, minor non-conforming beat, notate the beat according to the current writing style in use if it's likely not to cause the reader to detect a change in the writing style.

> **A NORTAV Tip:**
> Notate a non-conforming beat based on the current writing style in use if it is unlikely to cause the reader to detect a change in the writing style.

> **A NORTAV Tip:**
> Limit the use of ambiguous and non-conforming beats whenever possible.

If one were to use the NORTAV Method in one's editing/revision process, one could choose to revise any ambiguous and/or non-conforming beats if desired. A writer should always try to limit the use of ambiguous or non-conforming beats whenever possible.

> As Dark took cautious steps, [O8] the sphere of light traveled with him, peeling ever new shapes and details out of the darkness. Two steps behind him, Siu Lin followed, silent as a snake on cotton balls. Walking backwards so she could see behind them, she brought up the rear, taking no chances for a surprise.
>
> "I do not like this," she finally whispered. "Where's Baker?" [ ]

Here's another example of an implied "act of observing" Action beat and a subsequent Observation beat, [O8]. Keep in mind, Siu Lin's speech here is not dialogue or a Vocalization beat. Remember, Jason is the focal character. We experience all this through his senses. Therefore Siu Lin's speech is part of what Jason observes (hears), so it's included in the Observation beat.

"Maybe he's late." Even as he said the words, however, Dark felt that the answer was more of an excuse, rather than any actual conviction on his part.

[O9] "Then who unlocked the door?" [ ]

This is more of Siu Lin's speech, observed by Jason in Observation beat [O9].

"Let's just take a look around."

They proceeded another few yards down the main aisle into the warehouse, when Dark unexpectedly froze. Siu Lin nearly bumped into him and was ready to open her mouth, when she turned and saw what had stopped Dark dead in his tracks.

This last bit of prose is an example of why I think the NORTAV Method is so special. We can quickly describe exactly what Guido has done here in specific, concrete terms that we can all immediately understand and discuss.

Did you notice anything out of the ordinary in this bit of prose?

Remember links connect beats, one after another, in some logical order or fashion. In this case Guido has created suspense by arranging his beats out of the normal logical sequence one would expect. This is known as *beat reordering*.

> ***Beat Reordering*** is when a beat of prose is purposefully put out of order in the prose chain to achieve certain effects.

As I've mentioned, normally the "act of observing" Action beat leads to an Observation beat. After the Observation beat, the focal character might react to what she's observed (in a Reaction beat) or think about what she's observed (in a Thought beat). However, in this example, Guido has given us the "act of observing" Action beat, skipped the Observation beat, and went right to a Reaction beat. He will give us the Observation beat shortly, out of its normal sequence (and outside of this excerpt). This reordering of beats out of their normal sequence is a technique writers use to create certain effects. Here, the delaying of the Observation beat until after the Reaction beat is a way to manufacture suspense. You've probably seen this trick used before, but now you know how to explain it using the NORTAV Method! (We will cover the natural ordering of DCE beats at the end of this chapter.)

This ends our first NORTAV analysis. It might have seemed long and perhaps skirted the edge of complexity a bit, but I promise these analyses will get easier. In this analysis there were quite a few terms to define. Now that that's done, I'll only be adding a few more as we go.

WRITING EXERCISE

For this exercise, I want you to construct 50 DCE beats that could potentially lead (link) directly to an Observation beat. Invent different focal characters. Mix up the narrative tense (past, present) and the narrator (first-person or third-person, using our old terminology). These could be "act of observing" Action beats such as:

> [A] I gazed through a gap in the carnival fence.

> [A] Sheila sniffs at the odor wafting from the kitchen.

Or they could be regular Action beats that set up implied "act of observing" Action beats, such as:

> [A] Paul stepped out of the car.

> [A] I stuffed the Iron Maiden CD into the player.

Or they could be any other type of DCE beat you'd like to create, provided they can be used to set up an Observation beat. Once you have all your "leading" beats written, go back and write the subsequent Observation beat (or beats). Use paragraph breaks if needed. When you are done, you should have the start of 50 unique prose chains. Save your work so you can revisit these prose chains in the next exercise.

I'll do a couple and notate them for clarity as an example:

(1)   [A] Sheila sniffs at the odor wafting from the kitchen. [O] It reeks of dead meat and onions.

(2)   [A] Paul stepped out of the car. [O] Icy rain hit him hard and soaked his t-shirt in an instant. The wind howled. Leaves scattered across the driveway.

LET'S RECAP

In this section, my goal was to present you with the details of DCE Observation beats, and we covered a *lot* of information. Congratulations on working through it all! You learned that:

- An Observation beat describes what a focal character perceives through her five senses—sight, hearing, taste, touch, or smell— as the story unfolds, moment to moment.

- Incidental information are small, inconsequential bits of information that are tacked onto beats of a different type. Bits of incidental information are not part of the prose chain and are not notated in a NORTAV analysis, but they can be underlined for usefulness.

- A focused beat is a beat that reflects a focal character's focus or a narrator's main point or topic at hand, is part of the prose chain, and is notated in a NORTAV analysis.

- When constructing Observation beats, limit your use of narrative tags such as "he saw," "he heard," or "he smelled," as they will cause the writing style to shift to an NCE-based writing style.

- Beat substitution is when a writer uses one type of beat to portray something that is usually portrayed by another type of beat.

- An implied beat is a beat that is necessary to complete the prose chain but is not provided by the writer and therefore must be inferred by the reader.

- Beat ambiguity is when a beat of prose can be perceived as more than one type of beat.

- Ambiguous beats are notated based on the writing style currently in use.

- A non-conforming beat is a beat that is not part of the writing style currently in use.

- Non-conforming beats are notated based on the current prose type in use if the reader is not likely to notice a change in the writing style.

- Limit the use of any ambiguous or non-conforming beats whenever possible.

- Beat reordering is when a beat appears out if its natural sequence in the prose chain.

- And finally, we now refer to the beat/link analysis by its actual name: a NORTAV analysis.

Let's move on to the next type of DCE beat: Reactions.

Reaction Beats

WHAT ARE REACTION BEATS?

A *Reaction beat* describes the involuntary internal or external reactions of a focal character—fear, disgust, joy, lust, a jerk of the head, a stagger backwards, a scream, etc.—as the story unfolds, moment to moment.

> **A Reaction Beat** is a description of a focal character's involuntary internal or external reactions—fear, disgust, joy, lust, a jerk of the head, a stagger backwards, a scream—as the story unfolds, moment to moment.

HOW ARE REACTION BEATS USED?

Though reactions can be incidental, the predominance of reactions are rendered as focused beats simply because of the nature of what the beat is reflecting. Reactions are involuntary responses manifested in a focal character by some type of stimulus. This stimulus (in most situations) will usually capture the focal character's attention. For example, if a character was walking down a dark alley and someone jumped out of the shadows at him, he would most likely have a reaction that would command his complete focus.

That said, Reaction beats tend to be short, as involuntary reactions are often short, sometimes occurring within in the space of a heartbeat. For instance, a focal character might react to another character's action with a momentary grunt of disgust, a stab of envy, or a jolt of fear. Unlike Observation beats, which tend to come in the form of a description of the focal character's internal processing of sensations, there are a few ways Reaction beats can be rendered. Let's take a look an example. Here Penelope, our focal character, has come home from a long day at work. She unlocks her front door and steps into her living room.

> [O1] Everywhere, furniture was overturned. The draws of her computer desk were pulled out and scattered across the floor, along with all their contents. A long crack ran down the front of her TV screen. On the wall by the kitchen, the word *NARC* was scrawled in bold red letters.

> [R2] A surge of fear coursed through Penelope.

We have [O1], an Observation beat reflecting what she sees when she enters her living room. (We imply the "act of observing.") Then we have her involuntary reaction, [R2]. Notice [R2] is relatively short and rendered as a description of how she's responding internally to what she's seen. This is how a Reaction beat is normally formed in DCE, as it portrays what the focal character is experiencing internally for the reader. This is just like we do for Observation beats. Also notice that [R2] doesn't read "she felt a surge of fear course..." While it certainly could be worded like this, the use of a narrative tag like "she felt" in a Reaction beat is analogous to what we said about using tags like "she saw" or "she heard" in Observation beats. This is a form of narrative intrusion and would cause the prose type to shift into NCE.

> **A NORTAV Tip:**
> When creating Reaction beats in DCE, limit the use of narrative tags such as "he felt," etc.

Now let's look at the same example with a bit of a twist.

> [O1] Everywhere, furniture was overturned. The draws of her computer desk were pulled out and scattered across the floor, along with all their contents. A long crack ran down the front of her TV screen. On the wall by the kitchen, the word *NARC* was scrawled in bold red letters.

> [R2] Penelope's purse fell from her hand, and she gasped.

What's the different here?

In this case, Penelope's reaction is dropping the purse and gasping. At first this may look like another example of beat substitution, where an Action beat and a Vocalization beat appear to be standing in for a Reaction beat. Not true. In this case the focal character's action (dropping the purse) is involuntary, as is the vocalization (the gasp). Action beats and Vocalization beats are voluntary character activities. That is, the focal character consciously decides to perform them. Reactions beats are involuntary internal (mental) or external (physical/vocal) responses to stimuli. So, even though [R2] may appear like an Action beat and a Vocalization beat, it is actually two other ways, a physical way and a vocal way, to render a Reaction beat.

A last word on Reaction beats: They are probably the least used type of DCE beat. As you might imagine, the number of times you involuntarily react to something during the course of a normal day is minimal compared to the number of times you observe things, think about things, perform some kind of physical activity, or talk to someone. Of course fiction isn't usually concerned with a "normal" day, and often includes parts of a character's life where reactions are much more prevalent, but they still aren't as prevalent as the other types of beats. Use them with discretion, else your readers might think your characters are drama queens!

NORTAV ASSIGNMENT

In the last assignment, you tried to locate all the Observation beats in a sample written in a DCE-based writing style. The point was to give you a chance to focus on identifying one type of DCE beat. For this assignment I'm providing you with two shorter samples to work with, for, as I mentioned, Reaction beats appear less frequently in prose, and finding one example with enough Reaction beats to make the assignment worthwhile would be a bit troublesome. I want you to read the following two short samples of prose and try to find both the Observation beats and the Reaction beats. If you run across observations or reactions that are incidental, make a mental note of them or underline them if you wish. For focused Observation beats and Reaction beats, notate them by inserting an [O] or an [R] before the word that begins the beat. To make your commentary clearer, you can add a numeric identifier to each beat for reference purposes, such as [O4] or [R7]. For clarity, use a blank bracket [ ] to mark the end of each beat if necessary. If you can identify the links between beats, do so. The goal here is to pay very close attention to the Observation and Reaction beats. Try to identify and understand the techniques the author uses to construct each.

You can do your work right in this book, or print/photocopy out the sample and work with it separately. When you're done, compare your results with the NORTAV analysis I provide directly after the prose sample.

PROSE SAMPLE: Terri Reid's *Loose Ends* and *Good Tidings*

For this assignment, we'll work with the prose of one of Amazon's top-selling authors for the Kindle: Terri Reid. Terri is the creator of the Mary O'Reilly paranormal mystery series, which includes *Loose Ends*, *Good Tidings*, *Never Forgotten*, and *Final Call*. The following prose samples are taken from *Loose Ends* and *Good Tidings*. You can find more information about Terri at: http://terrireid.com/.

The focal character in both the following DCE-based samples is Mary O'Reilly.

From Loose Ends:

> ... Freezing, Mary shivered beneath a police-issued wool blanket in the front seat of the cruiser while Bradley reported the information to the Jo Davies County Sheriff's Department.
>
> "From the look of the slug, it's the same caliber of weapon that was used earlier this week in a similar shooting," he said.
>
> He listened for a moment and then looked directly at Mary as he spoke into the phone. "Yes, the intended victim is going to be placed under 24-hour surveillance. Yes, she has agreed to the surveillance."
>
> He raised his eyebrow, daring her to disagree. Mary sighed and nodded. Okay, she thought, someone trying to kill me twice, maybe I should give in a little.
>
> "Yes, her wound has been cared for," he said.
>
> Mary winced, remembering the sting of the antiseptic ointment Bradley had applied just before bandaging the two-inch scrape...

From Good Tidings:

> ... Mary sighed and blinked away the tears that filled her eyes. Although his death occurred more than 40 years ago, she was certain there were still family members who remembered a lost son every year at Christmas time and mourned for him.
>
> The phone rang and Mary jumped. "O'Reilly."

"Hey, how are you doing this morning?" Bradley asked. "How was your drive home?"

From her seat on the floor, she could glance out the window and just see her car positioned horizontally across the driveway. "Pretty uneventful," she lied.

Bradley chuckled. "So you parked like that on purpose?"

She jumped up and went to the window. Bradley's cruiser was at the curb. "Is this police harassment?" she asked.

"No, I called to inform you that today is 'Make Breakfast for your Favorite Cop Day,'" he responded, "Your favorite cop who has been up all night dealing with the damn snowstorm."

Mary chuckled. "Wow, I didn't realize," she said. "But there's no way I can make breakfast for my favorite cop today."

"Why not?"

"Because my dad's in Chicago," she said, "There's no way I could drive there in time for breakfast."

She sighed heavily. "So, I suppose I'll have to settle," she said, "Would you like some breakfast?"

Mary watched him hop out of the cruiser and make his way through the newly fallen snow to her porch.

"Well, since you asked," he said into the phone, just before rapping on the door.

Laughing, she opened it as she hung up the phone...

NORTAV ANALYSIS: Terri Reid's *Loose Ends* and *Good Tidings*

What follows is my NORTAV analysis of Terri's DCE-based sample from *Loose Ends*. Again, compare this to your analysis. See where we agree and where we differ. If we differ, try to understand why we differ.

> [O1] Freezing,

Here Terri opens with an Observation beat. [O1] contains a single word that describes Mary's internal observation. Remember, physical observations can be internal, so being in pain, being cold, being hot, being nauseated, are all Observation beats.

> [R2] Mary shivered beneath a police-issued wool blanket in the front seat of the cruiser

[R2] is Mary's involuntary reaction or response to being cold. Notice everything after the word "shivered." This is an incidental observation tacked onto [R2]. Mary isn't really paying attention to these observations, though they are surely at the edge of her perception. She's paying attention to the long observation that's about to follow.

> [O3] while Bradley reported the information to the Jo Davies County Sheriff's Department.
>
> "From the look of the slug, it's the same caliber of weapon that was used earlier this week in a similar shooting," he said.
>
> He listened for a moment and then looked directly at Mary as he spoke into the phone. "Yes, the intended victim is going to be placed under 24-hour surveillance. Yes, she has agreed to the surveillance."
>
> He raised his eyebrow, daring her to disagree.

[O3] is a long Observation beat describing what Mary is seeing and hearing. Remember, dialogue is not a type of beat. Here Bradley's half of the dialogue is something Mary hears during the course of this Observation beat.

> [R4] Mary sighed [ ] and nodded. Okay, she thought, someone trying to kill me twice, maybe I should give in a little.

When Bradley raises his eyebrow at Mary, Mary can't hold back an exasperated, involuntary sigh, represented by [R4]. Keep in mind, we use the [ ] to notate the end of a beat when it runs into beats we haven't covered in detail yet, as in this case. If you're feeling preco-cious, you can always take a stab at notating the beats we haven't yet covered in detail. (Hint: In this section, [R4] is followed by an Action beat and then a Thought beat.)

> [O5] "Yes, her wound has been cared for," he said.

Here Terri gives us more of Mary's observations in [O5]. Mary hears Bradley say this.

> [R6] Mary winced, [ ] remembering the sting of the anti-septic ointment Bradley had applied just before bandaging the two-inch scrape.

Here we get one final Reaction beat, [R6]. In [O5], Mary hears Bradley mention her newly-acquired wound. This Observation beat brings forth the recent memory of the pain she experienced, and she winces (reacts) involuntarily. Two things to note here. One, notice all the Reaction beats in this prose sample. They are short. We get "Mary shivered," "Mary sighed," and "Mary winced." As I said, that's to be expected. Reaction beats are short because that is how we react, in short, involuntary physical, vocal, or mental reactions. Second, notice the order of the beats in this last example. If we were performing a NORTAV analysis in the editing phase of our own writing and we came across this example, we might consider reordering this if we wanted to increase our intimacy with the reader (i.e. write in as pure DCE as possible). It's really the memory here that causes the reaction of wincing, not Bradley's mentioning of the fact. So something like the following rewrite would put the reader a tad closer to Mary, as the reader would experience the beats in the order that Mary would actually have experienced them:

> Remembering the sting of the antiseptic ointment Bradley had applied just before bandaging the two-inch scrape, Mary winced.

This is an artistic choice. There is no right or wrong answer here; it depends on the unique writing style established by the writer. As long as the writer is consistent, the reader will perceive the story consistently and not detect a change in the writing style.

A NORTAV Tip:
The goal of every writer is to use prose types to create a writing style that is consistent.

Now let's move on to the next sample.

Here is my NORTAV analysis of Terri's DCE-based sample from *Good Tidings*. Compare it to your analysis and note any differences.

> [R1] Mary sighed [ ] and blinked away the tears that filled her eyes. Although his death occurred more than 40 years ago, she was certain there were still family members who remembered a lost son every year at Christmas time and mourned for him.

This sample opens with a focused Reaction beat, [R1]. Mary sighs involuntarily.

[O2] The phone rang and

Here we have an Observation beat, [O2]. Mary hears a phone ring. Obvious stuff. Now let's use our link test question: Why are we not confused by the appearance of this beat? Especially when there is no preceding beat that this one links to? The answer is, though the phone call itself may be surprising, the fact that somewhere a phone has started to ring is not confusing to the reader. That happens all the time. There are certain beats that do not require a link back to a previous beat.

> An **Initiating Beat** is a beat that does not require a link back to a previous beat, for the reader knows intuitively why the beat exists and why it appears in the prose chain.

When a beat starts a new line in the prose chain and its appearance is intuitively obvious, it does not require a link back to a previous beat. It is inherently clear to the reader why the beat exists or why it has appeared. This type of beat is called an *initiating beat*.

[R3] Mary jumped. [ ] "O'Reilly."

Here Terri gives us Reaction beat [R3]. This is Mary's involuntary physical response to being surprised by the phone. Again, note how short these reactions are.

[O4] "Hey, how are you doing this morning?" Bradley asked. "How was your drive home?"

Here we get Observation beat [O4]. Mary hears Bradley ask these questions.

> From her seat on the floor, she could glance out the window and just see [O5] her car positioned horizontally across the driveway. [ ] "Pretty uneventful," she lied.

[O5] is another Observation beat. Mary sees her car in the driveway.

> [O6] Bradley chuckled. "So you parked like that on purpose?"

Here Terri gives us another Observation beat, [O6]. Mary hears Bradley laugh and ask a question.

> She jumped up and went to the window. {A7} [O8] Bradley's cruiser was at the curb. [ ] "Is this police harassment?" she asked.

[O8] is yet another typical focused Observation beat. Mary sees Bradley's cruiser outside. Notice this links back to an implied "act of observing" Action beat {A7}. We aren't actually told that Mary looks out the window. We infer this.

A NORTAV Tip:
Notate implied beats in a NORTAV analysis with the use of curly brackets { }.

Notice that I've marked the implied beat with curly brackets. This is how we notate any implied beats in a NORTAV analysis. So even though we haven't added Action beats to our NORTAV analyses yet, I think you've learned enough about this particular use of an implied beat so that we can start using the curly bracket { } notation.

Let's move on.

> [O9] "No, I called to inform you that today is 'Make Breakfast for your Favorite Cop Day,'" he responded, "Your favorite cop who has been up all night dealing with the damn snowstorm."

Here Terri gives us another typical Observation beat. In [O9], Mary hears Bradley say this over the phone.

> [R10] Mary chuckled. [ ] "Wow, I didn't realize," she said. "But there's no way I can make breakfast for my favorite cop today."

[R10] is a Reaction beat. Mary has a short, involuntary reaction (she chuckles) to what Bradley has just said.

> [O11] "Why not?"

[O11] is an Observation beat. Again, Mary hears Bradley say this over the phone.

> "Because my dad's in Chicago," she said, "There's no way I could drive there in time for breakfast."

> [R12] She sighed heavily. [ ] "So, I suppose I'll have to settle," she said, "Would you like some breakfast?"

[R12] is a Reaction beat. Mary has a quick, involuntary reaction based on what she herself has just said. As she's speaking it, she realizes she can't make it to her dad's, so she expresses her disappointment with a sigh.

Or is this really a fake or dramatic sigh?

If you thought the sigh was voluntary, you would not notate this as a Reaction beat, but rather as a Vocalization beat. Remember, this is as much an art as is it a science. There are times when smart people like you and me can notate the same beat differently and be equally justified in doing so.

> Mary watched him [O13] hop out of the cruiser and make his way through the newly fallen snow to her porch.

> "Well, since you asked," he said into the phone, just before rapping on the door. [ ]

And here Terri provides us with another example of an "act of observing" Action beat ("watched") and a subsequent focused Observation beat, [O13].

> [R14] Laughing, [ ] she opened it as she hung up the phone.

Finally, here is a last example of a Reaction beat. In [R14], Mary laughs at Bradley's jest from the previous beat. Since we assume she's genuinely laughing, we assume the laugh is involuntary, and therefore this is a Reaction beat.

Pop quiz: What would this beat be if she were faking her laughter?

And so we end our second NORTAV analysis.

By now you should be getting the hang of this. When examining prose that is meant to be intimate, moment-to-moment events reflecting a focal character's perceptions and activities, these DCE beats should start appearing to you naturally. In fact, the moment they started appearing to me was the moment the NORTAV Method was born. When that happened, the feeling was indescribably epiphanous. It wasn't a light bulb going off in my head; it was a nuclear explosion. I felt like Neo when he suddenly recognized the patterns in the Matrix. Once you understand and can spot these patterns of DCE beats in the work of published authors and in your own work, learning to use the rest of the prose types (Narration and Narrated Character Experience) becomes a simple matter of varying the theme.

By the way, the answer to the pop quiz is "a Vocalization beat."

WRITING EXERCISE

Take out your work from the previous exercise. To each of the 50 Observation beats in your prose chains, link a Reaction beat (or beats) that is (or could be) appropriate. Keep in mind, it does not yet have to be obvious to the reader why the character is reacting the way he/she is. When you are linking a Reaction beat to longer Observation beats, the character will most likely (but not always) be reacting to the last thing he/she observed in the prose chain. If you find that you simply can't come up with an appropriate Reaction beat to link to an Observation beat, feel free to modify the prose chain if that helps. If you still can't come up with an appropriate Reaction beat, create a new prose chain that you can work with. Use paragraph breaks if needed. When you are finished with this exercise you should have 50 prose chains that include a leading beat, an Observation beat (or beats), and a Reaction beat (or beats).

Again, I will do two and notate them for clarity as an example:

(1)   [A] Sheila sniffs at the odor wafting from the kitchen. [O] It reeks of dead meat and onions. [R] She nearly gags.

(2)   [A] Paul stepped out of the car. [O] Icy rain hit him hard and soaked his t-shirt in an instant. The wind howled. Leaves scattered across the driveway. [R] Goosebumps broke out on his arms and he shivered.

LET'S RECAP

In this section, my goal was to present you with the details of Reaction beats.

You learned that:

- A Reaction beat describes a focal character's involuntary internal or external reactions, such as fear, disgust, joy, lust, a jerk of the head, a stagger backwards, a scream, etc.

- Though reactions can be incidental, they are most often rendered as focused beats.

- A Reaction beat is often very short, reflecting the quick nature of reactions.

- A Reaction beat can be represented as a description of an involuntary internal sensation, as an involuntary physical action, or an involuntary vocalization.

- When constructing Reaction beats, limit the use of narrative tags such as "he felt" that would cause the beat to shift into NCE.

- An initiating beat is a beat that does not require a link back to a previous beat, for the reader knows intuitively why the beat exists or why it appeared in the prose chain.

- An implied beat is notated in a NORTAV analysis by the use of curly brackets, such as {A}.

Now let's tackle the next type of DCE beat: Thoughts.

Thought Beats

WHAT ARE THOUGHT BEATS?

A *Thought beat* describes the conscious or semi-conscious thoughts of a focal character—analyses, memories, realizations, musings, calculations, prior knowledge, etc.—as the story unfolds, moment to moment.

> A **Thought Beat** is a description of a focal character's conscious or semi-conscious thoughts— analyses, memories, realizations, musings, calculations, prior knowledge, etc.—as the story unfolds, moment to moment.

HOW ARE THOUGHT BEATS USED?

Thoughts can be incidental or rendered as focused beats. Thought beats portray what is happening within a focal character's mind, moment to moment, as she muses over events, plans out strategies, talks to herself (mentally), analyzes options, realizes things, or remembers events or knowledge from the past.

Let's look at an example. Our focal character will be a paramedic named Charlie. Charlie is in a cabin in the wilds of Colorado in January. Rose, his girlfriend, is late coming back from a hike in the woods. Charlie starts to get worried. He wonders where Rose could be as he stares out the cabin window at the base of a mountain.

> [O1] Thick, snow-covered evergreens, once his favorite tree, clambered up the lower slope.

Here we have an incidental thought ("once his favorite tree") that's tacked onto an Observation beat, [O1]. Charlie observes the mountain, but his thoughts are on Rose. He sees the mountain, he sees the forest, but his focus is on why Rose is late. The fact that evergreens were once his favorite tree is a small bit of incidental, semi-conscious thought that bubbles up to the surface of Charlie's consciousness while he observes the trees and worries about Rose. Let's continue with this example.

> [T2] Where could she be? She went into the forest over three hours ago. She hadn't planned on hiking too far up the mountain trail. She only wanted to go out for a breath of fresh Colorado air.

[T2] is a typical Thought beat. It's a direct rendering of what is going on within Charlie's mind. Here Charlie continues to worry about Rose. The beat follows his thought process as it happens, moment to moment. Notice there is no narrative tag like "Charlie worried" used in this example. When constructing Thought beats, you want to avoid the use of tags like "he thought," "he worried," or "he considered," if you can. These tags will cause the beat to shift into NCE and thus become non-conforming, or worse, cause the reader to notice a change in the DCE-based writing style. As with the other beats we've covered so far, when constructing DCE, the writer can get away with occasional deviations without making the reader feel the writing style has changed. As always, keep narrative tags to a minimum when working in a DCE-based writing style.

A NORTAV Tip:
When creating Thought beats, limit the use of narrative tags such as "he thought," "he worried," "he mused," etc.

Let's continue our example.

> Charlie stepped away from the window and began pacing the cabin's wide-planked floor. [T3] It was cold out there, but Rose had dressed warm. [T4] The temperature in the mountains of Colorado in the dead of winter often dips below zero. At zero degrees Fahrenheit a person can experience frostbite in only thirty minutes. [T5] She had on her thermal gear, so she should be all right. Still, it wasn't like Rose to be late.

This is where notating Thought beats can get a little tricky. After an initial Action beat (un-notated), we have a typical Thought beat, [T3]. [T5] is also a typical Thought beat. [T4] however is an example of how a focal character can dredge up some past knowledge to the surface of his consciousness, and yet might not necessarily consciously realize it's there. In this example, Charlie is a paramedic. He knows about things like frostbite. After he thinks about the cold and remembers Rose had dressed warm, his subconscious recalls some facts concerning what he knows about the situation.

Do these facts actually go through his mind or is this really the voice of the narrator chiming in? Read the example again and pay attention to how you perceive it.

A NORTAV Tip:
Use a triggered semi-conscious Thought beat to introduce background information to the reader.

In truth, [T4] is a bit ambiguous and could be perceived by the reader either way. Sometimes when you run into this situation in a NORTAV analysis, it can be tempting to notate these borderline conscious/semi-conscious Thought beats as Narration beats, for story information or "data dumps" often come to the reader straight from the narrator. As always, determine the writing style the writer is using. Check the context. If the writing style in use is DCE-based and there's a focal character that would know the information, and that focal character is in a position to have that information come to mind (i.e. the semi-conscious knowledge is somehow triggered, as in this case), the beat is a Thought beat. Else, it's probably a Narration beat. Writers often use this kind of borderline conscious/semi-conscious Thought beat to introduce background information to the reader. Check out some of Dan Brown's scene openings in *The Da Vinci Code*. He is a master of this technique.

NORTAV ASSIGNMENT

In the last assignment you tried to locate the Observation beats and Reaction beats in a DCE-based sample of prose. The point was to give you a chance to focus on identifying two of the five types of DCE beats. For this assignment I want you to read the following sample and try to find the Observation beats, the Reaction beats, and the Thought beats. If you run across observations, reactions, or thoughts that are incidental, make a mental note of them or underline them if you wish. For focused beats, notate them by inserting an [O], [R], or [T] before the word that begins the beat. To make your commentary clearer, you can add a numeric identifier to each beat for reference purposes, such as [O4], [R7], or [T10]. For clarity, use a blank bracket [ ] to mark the end of the beat if necessary. If you find an implied beat, notate it with curly brackets { }. If you can identify the links between beats, do so. The goal here is to pay very close attention to the Observation, Reaction, and Thought beats. Try to identify and understand the techniques the author uses to construct each.

You can do your work right in this book, or print/photocopy the sample and work with it separately. When you're done, compare your results with the NORTAV analysis I provide directly after the prose sample.

PROSE SAMPLE: Bob Mayer's *Atlantis: Book 1*

For this assignment, we'll work with the prose of NY Times best-selling author Bob Mayer. Bob, writing as Robert Doherty, is the creator of the extremely successful Atlantis and Area 51 series. Under his own name he's penned The Green Beret and Black Ops series and written such novels as *Chasing the Ghost* and *Duty, Honor, Country: A Novel of West Point and the Civil War*. The following sample is taken from *Atlantis: Book 1*. You can learn more about Bob and his work at his website: http://www.bobmayer.org/.

The focal character in the following DCE-based sample is Lieutenant Presson.

> ... Lieutenant Presson tapped his compass, then pressed the intercom switch. "Give me a bearing," he asked his radio operator, seated behind him.
>
> "This thing's going nuts, sir. Spinning in circles."
>
> "Damn," Presson muttered. He keyed his radio. "Any of you guys have a bearing?"
>
> The pilots of the four other TBM Avengers reported a similar problem with their compasses. Presson could sense the irritation and underlying fear in some of the voices. Flight 19 had been experiencing difficulties from take off and the other crews were in training with little flight experience.
>
> Presson looked out of his cockpit and saw only ocean. It was a clear day with unlimited visibility.

They should have been back at the airfield by now. Two hours ago they'd passed a small string of islands which he assumed were the Florida Keys. He wasn't as sure of that assumption now. This was his first training mission out of Fort Lauderdale Air Station. He had been recently transferred from Texas, and, as he stared at his wildly spinning compass, he wished he had paid more attention to their flight route.

He hadn't wanted this flight. He'd asked the Squadron Commander to replace him, but the request had been denied because Presson could give no good reason for his request. He hadn't voiced the real reason: to fly today would be a bad idea.

Well, it had been a bad idea, Presson thought to himself. And now he was beginning to question his judgment. Believing they had flown over the Keys, he'd ordered the flight to turn northeast toward the Florida Peninsula. But for the last 90 minutes, they had seen nothing but empty ocean below them. Could he have been mistaken? Could they have flown over some other islands and were they now well over the Atlantic, rather than the Gulf of Mexico like he had assumed? Where was Florida?

They had barely two hours of fuel left. He had to make an immediate decision whether to turn back, but now he couldn't depend on his compass for a westerly heading. He glanced at the setting sun over his shoulder and knew that west was roughly behind them, but a few degrees off either way, and if Florida was behind them, they could pass south of the Keys and really end up in the Gulf. But if his original assumption had been right, then Florida should be just over the horizon ahead.

Presson bit the inside of his mouth, drawing blood but the pain was unnoticed as he struggled with the problem, knowing the wrong decision would put them all in the sea...

NORTAV ANALYSIS: Bob Mayer's *Atlantis: Book 1*

What follows is my NORTAV analysis of Bob's prose sample. Again, compare this to your analysis. See where we agree, where we differ, and why we differ.

Lieutenant Presson tapped his compass, then pressed the intercom switch. "Give me a bearing," he asked his radio operator, seated behind him.

[O1] "This thing's going nuts, sir. Spinning in circles."

You may have notated the short phrase beginning with "his radio operator..." as an Observation beat. This is an incidental observation. It clues the reader in to Presson's semi-conscious/incidental observation while he's talking. After that we find a typical Observation beat, [O1], representing half of the dialogue exchange between Presson and his radio operator.

"Damn," Presson muttered. He keyed his radio. "Any of you guys have a bearing?"

{O2} [T3] The pilots of the four other TBM Avengers reported a similar problem with their compasses. [T4] Presson could sense the irritation and underlying fear in some of the voices.

Here we find a few things of interest. Notice the start of this section of prose. Presson curses, which could be a Reaction beat or a Vocalization beat, depending on whether it's voluntary or involuntary. The "muttering" gives it a voluntary feel, so we leave this as an un-notated Vocalization beat.

Presson then asks his men a question (an un-notated Vocalization beat). But where is the direct response of the men to Presson's question? Bob summarizes it in [T3] by implying the observation of the dialogue and using beat substitution. Instead of playing out all the individual responses, we instead get a semi-conscious/conscience Thought beat where Presson takes in what the men have just said and comes to the realization that all four are reporting a similar problem. Some might label this as a beat of NCE. And Bob may in fact have written it that way, as it does accomplish a summarization of the men's response that might appear to be coming from a narrator. Again, because we are deep within Presson's perceptions, and because Bob has already established a consistent DCE-based writing style, we notate this particular beat as Presson's thought after the implied Observation beat {O2}.

Remember, a reader will usually perceive ambiguous beats as belonging to the current writing style in use, so always determine the writing style as soon as possible and notate accordingly. Context is king when performing a NORTAV analysis! Note: You will want to remember this technique. Performing summations (which is something a writer often needs to do) in a DCE-based writing style is not easy, as focal character perceptions and activities are reflected moment to moment, not in summary. Summary is usually accomplished through a narrator. This technique of beat substitution happens to be one way—a very good way—to get the job done.

And finally, [T4] reflects Presson's analysis of the men's response.

> **A NORTAV Tip:**
> Use beat substitution to accomplish summarization when in writing in a DCE-based writing style.

[T5] Flight 19 had been experiencing difficulties from take off and the other crews were in training with little flight experience.

[T5] is a Thought beat, where Presson is remembering past events conjured up by the previous beat in the chain.

Presson looked out of his cockpit and [O6] saw only ocean. [T7] It was a clear day with unlimited visibility.

Here we begin with an initiating action ("act of observing") beat. The initiating beat includes an incidental observation "out of his cockpit" and is followed by Observation beat [O6].

Note that the use of the tag "saw" causes an inconsequential deviation here (i.e. renders the beat non-conforming). [T7] reflects Presson's realization based on what he sees in [O6]. In other words, Presson sees the ocean. He sees no clouds in the sky (inferred). Then he concludes that the day is clear and visibility is unlimited. You may have flagged this last beat as an Observation beat, but consider "with unlimited visibility." That's a conclusion, not a description of a sensory perception, therefore the beat is notated as a Thought beat. And again, one might legitimately notate [O6] and [T7] as a form of NCE. In this case, they are tad ambiguous, but since a DCE-based writing style has been established and these deviations are minor and infrequent, we choose the DCE option for notation.

[T8] They should have been back at the airfield by now. Two hours ago they'd passed a small string of islands which he assumed were the Florida Keys. He wasn't as sure of that assumption now. This was his first training mission out of Fort Lauderdale Air Station. He had been recently transferred from Texas, and, [ ] as he stared [O9] at his wildly spinning compass, [T10] he wished he had paid more attention to their flight route.

The first part of this section is a Thought beat, [T8], where Presson is analyzing the situation and remembering past events. Bob slips in an "act of observing" Action beat "as he stared" (un-notated) and then gives us [O9], an Observation beat that describes the compass spinning.

He follows this with [T10], a Thought beat depicting Presson's direct thought.

> [T11] He hadn't wanted this flight. He'd asked the Squadron Commander to replace him, but the request had been denied because Presson could give no good reason for his request. He hadn't voiced the real reason: to fly today would be a bad idea.

> [T12] Well, it had been a bad idea, Presson thought to himself. And now he was beginning to question his judgment. Believing they had flown over the Keys, he'd ordered the flight to turn northeast toward the Florida Peninsula. But for the last 90 minutes, they had seen nothing but empty ocean below them. Could he have been mistaken? Could they have flown over some other islands and were they now well over the Atlantic, rather than the Gulf of Mexico like he had assumed? Where was Florida?

> [T13] They had barely two hours of fuel left. He had to make an immediate decision whether to turn back, but now he couldn't depend on his compass for a westerly heading.

Here Bob gives us [T11], [T12], [T13], three Thought beats that follow Presson's chain of analysis as it runs through his mind, moment to moment.

You might be noticing that my commentaries are getting shorter. Now that you understand the basic concepts, I don't need to beat a dead horse (there's a pun on beats in there somewhere!) by explaining the same concepts over and over. As we continue with these analyses, I will try to use less and less redundant explanation.

With that, let's continue.

> He glanced [O14] at the setting sun over his shoulder and [T15] knew that west was roughly behind them, but a few degrees off either way, and if Florida was behind them, they could pass south of the Keys and really end up in the Gulf. But if his original assumption had been right, then Florida should be just over the horizon ahead.

This is straight DCE-based writing in action. We get an "act of observing" Action beat (un-notated), followed by [O14], the Observation beat it leads to, followed by [T15], a Thought beat that analyzes what the Observation beat implies.

> Presson bit the inside of his mouth, [O16] drawing blood but [?17] the pain was unnoticed as [T18] he struggled with the problem, knowing the wrong decision would put them all in the sea...

In this last section we get an Action beat (un-notated), followed by [O16], an Observation beat. Presson bites the inside of his mouth (Action beat) and then vaguely senses the blood in his mouth (Observation beat). Standard stuff. But what about [?17], the beat that follows? How did you notate this beat?

If you are writing about the perceptions of a character (using a DCE-based writing style), you cannot reveal things that are not part of that character's scope of perception. In other words, you can't have a focal character observe something he isn't able to observe, or think about something he is incapable of thinking about, etc. In this last beat, Presson's pain goes unnoticed. If this pain is truly unnoticed, then this beat is not DCE, but rather NCE, for only a narrator would able to report to the reader something unnoticed by the focal character. But, again, because Bob has established a DCE-based writing style, we can assume this is an incidental observation. That is, it is a bit of observation that Presson picks up on only semi-consciously.

Lastly, [T18] is a Thought beat.

WRITING EXERCISE

Take out your work from the previous exercise. To each of the 50 Reaction beats in your prose chains, link a Thought beat (or beats) that is (or could be) appropriate. The Thought beat (or beats) can be as short as a single word that runs through the character's mind, or as long a several paragraphs of memory or reasoning. Whatever works. If you find that you simply can't come up with an appropriate Thought beat (or beats) to link to a Reaction beat, feel free to modify the prose chain if that helps. If you still can't come up with an appropriate Thought beat, create a new prose chain that you can work with. Use paragraph breaks if needed. When you are finished with this exercise you should have 50 prose chains that include a leading beat, an Observation beat (or beats), a Reaction beat (or beats), and a Thought beat (or beats).

Again, I will do two and notate them for clarity as an example:

(1)   [A] Sheila sniffs at the odor wafting from the kitchen. [O] It reeks of dead meat and onions. [R] She nearly gags. [T] It has to be the worst stench she's ever come across, and she has come across some pretty heinous smells in her time as *The Daily Yowl*'s lead investigative reporter.

(2)   [A] Paul stepped out of the car. [O] Icy rain hit him hard and soaked his t-shirt in an instant. The wind howled. Leaves scattered across the driveway. [R] Goosebumps broke out on his arms and he shivered. [T] It was a long way to the house. Nearly two hundred yards. Paul

wished he had brought a jacket, or at least a sweater. It was late fall for Christ's sake. What was he thinking?

LET'S RECAP

Before we recap, I think it's time to pull out my standard reminder:

The NORTAV Method is not a silver bullet or a magic formula for constructing prose. It is a critical body of knowledge that every professional writer should understand. Your goal in this book is to learn this body of knowledge and apply it to your own unique writing process *in whatever way comes natural to you.*

In this section, my goal was to present you with the details of Thought beats. You learned that:

- A Thought beat describes the conscious or semi-conscious thoughts of a focal character—analyses, memories, realizations, musings, calculations, prior knowledge, etc.—as the story unfolds, moment to moment.

- Thoughts can be incidental or rendered as focused beats.

- When constructing Thought beats, limit your use of narrative tags such as "he thought," "he worried," "he mused," etc., that would cause the beat to shift into NCE.

- You can use a triggered semi-conscious Thought beat to portray background information to the reader.

- You can use Thought beats to represent what is usually portrayed in other beats (i.e. through beat substitution) as one way to accomplish summarization in DCE.

With that, we can move on to the next type of DCE beat: Actions.

Action Beats

WHAT ARE ACTION BEATS?

An *Action beat* describes the voluntary physical activities performed by a focal character—walking, grabbing, running, sitting, looking, smelling, etc. —as the story unfolds, moment to moment.

> An **Action Beat** is a description of a focal character's voluntary physical activities—walking, grabbing, running, sitting, looking, smelling, etc.—as the story unfolds, moment to moment.

HOW ARE ACTION BEATS USED?

Actions can be incidental or rendered as focused beats. Action beats reflect the voluntary activities performed by a focal character and, with the exception of Vocalization beats, are probably the easiest to identify. As you have already learned, identifying an Action beat can get tricky when an action performed by a focal character is involuntary. When that's the case, the action is identified as a Reaction beat. I've also mentioned that "acts of observing" (looking, smelling, listening, touching, tasting) are actions, not observations. What is actually seen or smelt or heard or felt or tasted are observations.

Even though Action beats are mostly straight forward, it will still do us some good to look at an example. Our focal character for this example will be Emily.

[A1] Emily spotted the assassin, [O2] just as he shouldered his way onto the crowded sidewalk.

Here [A1] is an "act of observing" Action beat. Emily actively uses her senses (sight) to search for the assassin. When she sees the assassin slip into the crowd, we get [O2], an Observation beat.

> [O3] People were rushing toward Washington Square like a river of human flesh. [T4] She had only a split second to make a decision. [A5] Emily yanked her .45 from beneath her jacket and sprinted across the street.

Here we get the typical Action beat. Emily sees the crowd moving toward Washington Square in [O3], realizes she has only a split second to decide what to do in [T4], and then she takes action in [A5]. She grabs her gun (one part of the Action beat) and sprints across the street (the other part of the Action beat). Now, why are these two actions notated as one Action beat and not two?

As I've mentioned, notating beats is as much art as it is science. How to group words, phrases, clauses, and sentences into beats is up to the person performing the analysis. If there are several beats of the same type that run in sequence (as in this case), and there is no need to identify any of these beats individually to perform some aspect of the analysis, then for simplicity the beats can be collected together into a single beat. We call this "collection beat" a *compound beat*. If one of the beats in a compound beat is individually and specifically used in the analysis (perhaps in identifying a link to a subsequent beat), then break apart the compound beat and notate separately.

Let's get back to Emily.

A **Compound Beat** is a beat that combines multiple beats of the same type for simplicity in performing a NORTAV analysis.

[O6] A horn blared, and [R7] she jumped backwards. [O8] A cab zipped past, its driver shaking a fist at her. [A9] Emily glared at the cabbie.

Here we have [O6], an initiating Observation beat, followed by [R7], a Reaction beat. Emily hears the horn blare and jumps backward to get out of the way. This action is involuntary, and thus we identify the beat as a Reaction beat, not an Action beat. We then have [O8], an Observation beat, followed by [A9], an Action beat.

Finally, notice I haven't mentioned anything about narrative tags in Action beats. That is because the action itself can be perceived by the reader as the focal character's experience or a narrative tag. Think about that for a moment. With an Observation, Reaction, or Thought beat, a writer can identify and separate the narrative tag and the experience, as in the observation: "He saw a big red ball." Here, "he saw" is the narrative tag and "a big red ball" is the observation. With Action beats, however, the narrative tag and the experience are often one in the same, as in "He ran to the store." We can perceive "he ran" as the narrator telling us what the focal character is doing (a tag), just like "he saw." However, because the tag is also the character's action, we can also perceive "he ran" as if we were inside or beside the focal character. This means Action beats by nature are ambiguous. They can be perceived as either DCE or NCE, depending on the current writing style in use. So, like with ambiguous beats, notate all Action beats based on the writing style currently in use.

NORTAV ASSIGNMENT

In the last assignment you tried to locate the Observation beats, Reaction beats, and Thought beats in a sample written in a DCE-based writing style. The point was to give you a chance to focus on identifying three of the five types of beats in DCE. For this assignment, I want you to read the following sample and try to find the Observation beats, the Reaction beats, the Thought beats, and the Action beats. If you run across observations, reactions, thoughts, or actions that are incidental, make a mental note of them or underline them if you wish. For focused beats, notate them by inserting an [O], [R], [T], or [A] before the word that begins the beat. To make your commentary clearer, you can add a numeric identifier to each beat for reference purposes, such as [O4], [R7], [T10], or [A13]. For clarity, use a blank bracket [ ] to mark the end of the beat if necessary. If you find an implied beat, notate it with curly brackets { }. If you can identify the links between beats, do so. The goal here is to pay very close attention to the Observation, Reaction, Thought, and Action beats. Try to identify and understand the techniques the author uses to construct each.

You can do your work right in this book, or print/photocopy the sample and work with it separately. When you're done, compare your results with the NORTAV analysis I provide directly after the prose sample.

PROSE SAMPLE: Blake Crouch's *Shining Rock*

For this assignment we'll turn to the prose of best-selling author Blake Crouch. Blake has written several thrillers, including *Desert Places*, *Locked Doors*, *Abandon*, and *Snowbound*. His novel *Serial*, co-authored with J. A. Konrath, has sold over 350,000 copies. The following sample is taken from Blake's short story *Shining Rock*. You can learn more about Blake and his work at http://www.blakecrouch.com/.

The focal character in the following DCE- based sample is Roger.

> ... He walked off the trail and crouched down in the grass. Five yards ahead lay the edge of the rhododendron thicket. Roger thought he recalled that piece of red a hundred feet or so up the gentle slope, though he couldn't be sure.
>
> For a while, he lay on the ground, just listening.

The grass swayed, blades banging dryly against one another.

Rhododendron leaves scraped together.

Something scampered through the thicket.

This was his thirteenth summer coming to Shining Rock, and he found that most of their time here had vanished completely from memory—more impression than detail. But a few of their trips remained clear, intact.

The first time they'd come and accidentally discovered this place, the twins were only six years old, and Michelle had lost her front teeth to this gap while she and Jennifer wrestled and rolled in a meadow one sunny afternoon, cried her heart out, afraid the tooth fairy wouldn't pay for lost teeth.

There had been the trip seven years ago where he and Sue had to fake happy faces for the girls, crying at night in their tent, while fifteen hundred miles away, in a laboratory in Minneapolis, a biopsy cut from the underside of Sue's left breast was screened for a cancer that wasn't there.

Three years back, he'd been anxiously awaiting news on an advertising campaign he'd pitched, which if chosen, might have netted him half a million dollars, remembered trying not to dwell on the phone call he'd make once they left these mountains, knowing if he got a yes, what that would mean for his family. He'd pulled over once they reentered cell phone coverage at an overlook outside of Asheville. Walked back toward the car a moment later, eyes locked with Sue's, shaking his head.

But looking at the time they'd spent here as a whole,

forest instead of tree, it felt a lot like his life—so many good times, some pain, and it had all raced by faster than he could've imagined.

Roger crawled to the thicket's edge and started up the hill, the flashlight and the Glock shoved down the back of his fleece pants.

After five minutes, he stopped to catch his breath.

He thought he'd been making a horrible racket, dead leaves crunching under his elbows as he wriggled himself under the low branches of the rhododendron shrubs. But he assured himself it wasn't as much noise as he thought. To anyone else, to Donald, it probably sounded like nothing more than the after-hour scavenging of a raccoon.

Roger was breathing normally again and had rolled over on his stomach to continue crawling when he spotted the outline of a tent twenty yards uphill. The moon shone upon the rain fly, and in the lunar light, he could only tell that it was dark in color.

He pulled the gun out of his waistband...

NORTAV ANALYSIS: Blake Crouch's *Shining Rock*

What follows is my NORTAV analysis of Blake's prose sample. As always, compare this to your analysis. Note where we agree, where we differ, and if we differ, why we differ.

Remember, these analyses will contain less and less explanation as we cover the same ground over and over, so in many cases I'll simply note the types of beats used in each section and move on.

[A1] He walked off the trail and crouched down in the grass

{A2} [O3] Five yards ahead lay the edge of the rhododendron thicket. [T4] Roger thought he recalled that
piece of red a hundred feet or so up the gentle slope,
though he couldn't be sure.

Here Blake gives us [A1], an initiating Action beat, {A2}, an implied
Action beat ("act of observing"), then [O3], an Observation beat.
Finally, we get [T4], a Thought beat that includes a narrative tag
"Roger thought," which will probably be ignored by most readers as
Blake has already begun to establish a DCE-based writing style.

[A5] For a while, he lay on the ground, [A6] just listening.

Here [A5] is a good example of another way to accomplish summation
when using a DCE-based writing style. Blake takes a typical Action
beat ("...he lay on the ground...") and extends it with a very short
narrative phrase "For a while..." While technically not DCE, this bit of
incidental narrative information doesn't make the reader feel the
writing style has changed because it summarizes only a very short
period of time. That is, we feel like we're waiting right there along with
Roger. If Blake were to span a longer period of time, such as "For two
days," this would not work without making the reader feel the narrator's presence. That is, we would no longer sense the beat as a delayed,
moment-to-moment beat, but rather as something that is "told" to us
by a narrator.

> **A NORTAV Tip:**
> Use infrequent incidental narrative
> information that spans short periods
> of time to summarize a beat of DCE so
> that the reader will not detect a
> change in the DCE-based writing style.

When working in a DCE-based writing style, keep narrative summations like these limited in time. And like the use of some narrative tags ("he thought," "she felt," etc.), keep the use of these types of narrative summarizations to a minimum in order to maintain a consistent DCE-based writing style.

The second beat, [A6], is, of course, an "act of observing" Action beat.

> [O7] The grass swayed, blades banging dryly against one another.
>
> Rhododendron leaves scraped together.
>
> Something scampered through the thicket.

[O7] is a typical compound Observation beat, spawned by the previous Action beat. It is actually three separate Observation beats, but we lump them together into a compound beat for simplicity.

> [T8] This was his thirteenth summer coming to Shining Rock, and he found that most of their time here had vanished completely from memory—more impression than detail. But a few of their trips remained clear, intact.
>
> The first time they'd come and accidentally discovered this place, the twins were only six years old, and Michelle had lost her front teeth to this gap while she and Jennifer wrestled and rolled in a meadow one sunny afternoon, cried her heart out, afraid the tooth fairy wouldn't pay for lost teeth.
>
> There had been the trip seven years ago where he and Sue had to fake happy faces for the girls, crying at night in their tent, while fifteen hundred miles away, in a laboratory in Minneapolis, a biopsy cut from the

underside of Sue's left breast was screened for a cancer that wasn't there.

Three years back, he'd been anxiously awaiting news on an advertising campaign he'd pitched, which if chosen, might have netted him half a million dollars, remembered trying not to dwell on the phone call he'd make once they left these mountains, knowing if he got a yes, what that would mean for his family. He'd pulled over once they reentered cell phone coverage at an overlook outside of Asheville. Walked back toward the car a moment later, eyes locked with Sue's, shaking his head.

But looking at the time they'd spent here as a whole, forest instead of tree, it felt a lot like his life—so many good times, some pain, and it had all raced by faster than he could've imagined.

[T8] is a very long compound Thought beat triggered by the previous Observation beat. The familiar sight has caused Roger to recall these memories.

Notice Blake doesn't simply dump this information on us willy-nilly through the use of an intrusive narrator. He finds an opportunity in the storyline where the focal character can be reminded of these events. Then he uses that opportunity to trigger the memories so the reader can experience them along with Roger. In doing so, the reader is provided the information she needs, she's kept intimate with Roger, and as such she feels closer to Roger as a character.

[A9] Roger crawled to the thicket's edge and started up the hill, the flashlight and the Glock shoved down the back of his fleece pants.

[A10] After five minutes, he stopped to catch his breath.

The first beat, [A9], is a typical Action beat. Now notice the phrase starting with "the flashlight…" I perceive this as an incidental observation. It's a small bit of semi-conscious observation tacked onto [A9]. One could perceive this as a focused Thought beat if one assumes Roger is mentally "checking off" the existence of these items, making sure they are where they are supposed be. Either way would work, depending on how you perceive it.

The second beat, [A10], is another Action beat. Notice this is another example of a quick summary that is still perceived as DCE. The phrase beginning with "to catch…" is a little tricky and starts to push the beat a little more towards NCE. But, again, because Blake has established a consistent DCE-based writing style, we perceive these small deviations as part of Roger's perception. In this case, I would perceive this short phrase as an incidental thought.

> [T11] He thought he'd been making a horrible racket, dead leaves crunching under his elbows as he wriggled himself under the low branches of the rhododendron shrubs. But he assured himself it wasn't as much noise as he thought. To anyone else, to Donald, it probably sounded like nothing more than the after-hour scavenging of a raccoon.

Here [T11] is a typical Thought beat. It's also an example of beat substitution, as we get more of a sense of Roger's observations (what he has been hearing) rendered after the fact through his thoughts.

> [?12] Roger was breathing normally again and had rolled over on his stomach to continue crawling when [A13] he spotted [O14] the outline of a tent twenty yards uphill. The moon shone upon the rain fly, and in the lunar light, he could only tell that it was dark in color.

How did you notate [?12]? Here we have definitely entered the realm of NCE. Technically, the way this is written, we don't experience this beat through Roger's senses, moment to moment. This is a narrator telling us of Roger's perceptions and activities as they had occurred moments before the "act of observing" Action beat [A13]. Thus, this is a non-conforming beat of NCE. But, since we are so deep in Roger's experience, and since Blake has been using a consistent DCE-based writing style, we tend to perceive this beat as something Roger is realizing or reflecting on, nearly moment to moment. When the writer does a good job of maintaining a consistent DCE-based writing style like Blake does here, even this kind of non-conforming beat can be perceived as DCE.

As I've said, the goal of every writer is to establish a unique writing style and to use it consistently. The more consistent the use, the more the reader will ignore or gloss over infrequent ambiguous or non-conforming beats. If the writer switches between writing styles, the transition should be handled smoothly and with reason. This keeps the reader's experience smooth and clear, like a well-edited movie. Jumping between writing styles for no reason (or using a writing style inconsistently) will give the reader a clunky, zoom-in, zoom-out, schizophrenic experience. We will get more into this in Chapter 6.

The last beat in this section, [O14], is an Observation beat.

[A15] He pulled the gun out of his waistband...

And we end with [A15], a typical Action beat.

WRITING EXERCISE

Take out your work from the previous exercise. To each of the 50 Thought beats in your prose chains, link an Action beat (or beats) that is (or could be) appropriate. You can add a simple, semi-conscious Action beat like the scratching of a chin, or you could link together several Action beats in a series. Whatever works. If you find that you simply can't come up with an appropriate Action beat (or beats) to link to a Thought beat, feel free to modify the prose chain if that helps. If you still can't come up with an appropriate Action beat, create a new prose chain that you can work with. When you are finished with this exercise you should have 50 prose chains that include a leading beat, an Observation beat (or beats), a Reaction beat (or beats), a Thought beat (or beats), and an Action beat (or beats).

Again, I will do two and notate them for clarity as an example:

(1)   [A] Sheila sniffs at the odor wafting from the kitchen. [O] It reeks of dead meat and onions. [R] She nearly gags. [T] It has to be the worst stench she's ever come across, and she has come across some pretty heinous smells in her time as *The Daily Yowl*'s lead investigative reporter.

[A] She pulls a tazer out of her purse.

(2)   [A] Paul stepped out of the car. [O] Icy rain hit him hard and soaked his t-shirt in an instant. The wind howled. Leaves scattered across the driveway. [R] Goosebumps broke out on his arms and he shivered. [T] It was a long way to the house. Nearly two hundred yards. Paul wished he had brought a jacket, or at least a sweater. It was late fall for Christ's sake. What was he thinking? [A] He shoved his hands in his pockets.

LET'S RECAP

In this section, my goal was to cover the details of Action beats. You learned that:

- An Action beat describes the voluntary physical activities performed by a focal character—walking, grabbing, running, sitting, looking, smelling, etc. —as the story unfolds, moment to moment.

- Actions can be incident or rendered as focused beats.

- Action beats can be perceived as both the narrative tag and the direct character experience, and thus can be perceived as either NCE or DCE. Notate Action beats based on the writing style currently in use.

- For simplicity, you can collect a sequence of beats of the same type into a single compound beat, provided none of the individual beats are used specifically in the NORTAV analysis.

- You can use small infrequent bits of incidental narrative information that span short periods of time to summarize a DCE beat without the reader feeling the writing style has changed.

And now let's move on to the last type of DCE beat: Vocalizations.

Vocalization Beats

WHAT ARE VOCALIZATION BEATS?

A *Vocalization beat* describes the voluntary vocal sounds produced by a focal character—speech, grunts, groans, etc. —as the story unfolds, moment to moment.

> A **Vocalization Beat** is a description of the voluntary vocal sounds produced by a focal character—speech, grunts, groans, etc.—as the story unfolds, moment to moment.

HOW ARE VOCALIZATION BEATS USED?

Vocalizations can be incidental or rendered as focused beats. Vocalization beats reflect the voluntary vocalizations performed by a focal character and are certainly the easiest type of DCE prose beat to identify, as they are usually quoted and attributed to the focal character. As you have already learned, identifying a Vocalization beat can get troublesome when the vocalization performed by a focal character is involuntary. When this is the case, the vocalization is identified as a Reaction beat. I've also mentioned that dialogue is not a type of beat, but rather a "conversation" represented by the exchange of a focal character's Vocalization beats (what she says to another character) and her Observation beats (what she hears the other character say). Let's take a look at a quick example. Here, Bill is our focal character.

[R1] Bill snorted and [A2] slapped a hand on his knee.

[V3] "That, sir, is the funniest thing I've ever heard."

[O4] Charlie Watson shook with laughter. The old timer finished stuffing his pipe and lit it with a bright red lighter.

[O5] "Uh, yup," Charlie grunted as he bit down on the stem of his pipe. "That's 'bout how it happened. Swear, 'twas."

[V6] "I believe you." [V7] Bill let out an exaggerated sigh. [V8] "Mr. Watson, I'd love to stay and chat, but I've got a train to catch."

Here we have an example that covers just about every aspect of identifying Vocalization beats. Notice the first Reaction beat, [R1]. Though this is a vocalization of Bill's, it is considered a Reaction beat because it is Bill's involuntary response to something that has just occurred (hearing Mr. Watson's funny story). This Reaction beat leads to [A2], a typical Action beat (slapping his knee). Then we have [V3], a Vocalization beat (Bill speaks). Notice there is no Vocalization beat tag ("he said," "he commented," "he replied," etc.) used here. Can you guess why?

A NORTAV Tip:
When creating Vocalization beats in a DCE-based writing style, limit the use of narrative tags such as "he said," "he mused," etc.

Very good! Vocalization beat tags are narrative intrusions, just like "he saw," "he felt," "he mused," etc. When working in a DCE-based writing style, use them for clarification purposes if you must, but keep them to a minimum so that the reader will not feel the writing style has shifted to NCE. Some instructors believe you shouldn't use "dialogue" tags at all, or you should limit them to simple, direct tags like "he said," "he asked," or "he replied." These instructors give all sorts of reasons, but they really don't put their reasoning into any context other than that of their own personal preferences. With the NORTAV Method, we have a context, so let me tell you what and what not to do concerning "dialogue" tags within the context we've established.

I've already told you, when working in a DCE-based writing style, limit your use of narrative tags. All these tags distance the reader slightly from the focal character. They are narrative intrusions and could make the reader feel the writing style has changed. But, if you want or need to use a tag to keep the dialogue clear as to who is speaking to whom at any given moment, put a "tag" on the speech of the character to whom the focal character is speaking. In other words, put the "tag" within the focal character's Observation beat.

> **A NORTAV Tip:**
> If tags are required to keep dialogue clear, first use tags to describe a non-focal character's speech within the focal character's Observation beat, then use simple tags like "he said" within the focal character's Vocalization beat.

Notice "grunted" in [O5]. This is perceived by the reader not as a narrative tag or intrusion but rather as a description of how Bill observes Charlie Watson's speech. In other words, "grunted" is not a narrative intrusion at all, but rather it is part of Bill's internal observation of the manner in which Charlie Watson is speaking.

Subtle? Perhaps. But it's an important distinction, so make sure you understand the difference before moving on.

In short, when working with dialogue, keep the narrative tags on focal character Vocalization beats to a minimum, and if you use a tag, keep it limited to "he said," "he asked," "he replied," and other such simple, direct tags. As some instructors have correctly pointed out, the reader will gloss over these small, simple, direct narrative intrusions as if they weren't there, which keeps the reader from feeling the DCE-based writing style has changed. For tagging the speech of non-focal characters (within a focal character's Observation beat), you can get away with more tags and more descriptive tags, as these aren't perceived by the reader as tags at all, but rather as descriptions of how the focal character is perceiving the non-focal character's speech.

Let's move on to [V6], [V7], and [V8], the last three Vocalization beats in the example. [V6] is a typical Vocalization beat where Bill speaks. [V7] is a Vocalization beat where Bill vocalizes a voluntary, purposeful sigh. [V8] is a last Vocalization beat where Bill speaks again.

And that is about all there is to understanding Vocalization beats.

NORTAV ASSIGNMENT

In the last assignment, you tried to locate the Observation beats, Reaction beats, Thought beats, and Action beats in a DCE-based sample of prose. The point was to give you a chance to focus on identifying four of the five types of DCE beats. For this assignment, I want you to read the following sample and try to find *all* the different types of DCE beats: Observation beats, Reaction beats, Thought beats, Action beats, and Vocalization beats. If you run across perceptions or activities that are incidental, make a mental note of them or underline them if you wish. For focused beats, notate them by inserting an [O], [R], [T], [A], or [V] before the word that begins the beat. To make your commentary clearer, you can add a numeric identifier to each beat for reference purposes, such as [O4], [R7], [T10], [A13], or [V16].You shouldn't need to use a blank bracket [ ] to mark the end of a beat, for you should be able to identify all the beats in the following prose sample. If you find an implied beat, notate it with curly brackets { }. If you can identify the links between beats, do so. The goal here is to pay very close attention to the use of all DCE beats. Try to identify and understand the techniques the author uses to construct each.

You can do your work right in this book, or print/photocopy the sample and work with it separately. When you're done, compare your results with the NORTAV analysis I provide directly after the prose sample.

PROSE SAMPLE: Gemma Halliday's *Hollywood Confessions*

For this assignment, we'll work with the prose of award-winning author Gemma Halliday. Gemma is the creator of the Hollywood Headlines mystery series, which includes *Hollywood Scandals* and *Hollywood Secrets*. Gemma is also the creator of the multi-book mystery series High Heels. The following prose sample is taken from Gemma's latest Hollywood Headline novel *Hollywood Confessions*. You can find more information about Gemma and her work at her website: http://www.gemmahalliday.com/.

The focal character in this "first-person" DCE-based sample is Allie Quick.

> ... Marco beamed like a proud papa. "So, what can I do for you, dahling? We're on a tight schedule today, but for you I could bump someone."
>
> "I appreciate the sentiment, Marco, but I'm actually here for..." I leaned in and whispered, "a little information."
>
> He closed his heavily lined eyes and shook his head in the negative. "Sorry, dahling, no can do. You know my lips are sealed. What would happen if I tongue-wagged about every celebutant who came through here? I'd be out on my hot little fanny, that's what."

I grinned. "You know that would never happen. Fernando couldn't function without you."

Marco pursed his lips. Then nodded. "Well, that's true."

"Listen, I just need a confirm or deny over a new hair color."

He shook his head again. "Sorry. I have taken the celebrity hairdresser's oath. 'What happens in the salon stays in the salon.'"

"Hmmm." I narrowed my eyes. "What if I made it worth your while?"

He raised one drawn-in eyebrow at me. "Worth my while?"

"I happen to have an informant that happens to follow the club scene very closely. And happens to know where one very desirable celebrity is planning on partying this very evening."

Marco leaned in. "I'm intrigued. A-lister?"

I shrugged. "At least a B-plus."

"Who?"

I looked over both shoulders, trying to match his level of drama as I leaned in and whispered, "Adam Lambert."

"Shut the front door!" Marco said, almost spilling his glitter on the marble floor. "Where?"

"I'll tell you...if you can tell me a little something."

He narrowed his eyes at me. "Ooh, you are wicked, girl.

Fine. You cracked me." He paused, looked over both shoulders for prying ears then nodded, setting finger to the side of his nose. "Come into my office, dahling."

He turned and led the way through the salon. I followed him past buzzing drying stations and flying straight razors until we hit a door at the back. He opened it, doing an exaggerated over the shoulder again, and led the way inside.

I followed, trying not to smirk as I saw we were in a supply closet. Very cloak-and-dagger.

"So, what do you want to know?" he asked in a low whisper.

"Jennifer Wood. Is it true Pippi Mississippi has a new hair color?"

"Ah." He steepled his fingers. "She was in here the other day."

"And?"

"And America's favorite blonde teeny bopper?"

"Yes?"

"Now a redhead."

Bingo. "I don't suppose you got any pictures of her?"

He looked offended. "I don't suppose I did! What do you think I am, some sort of gossip?" Heaven forbid. "But," he said.

"But?"

"Fernando did take a snapshot for his wall of fame."

Double bingo.

"I'll throw in Adam's home address if you get me a copy."

Marco squealed like a second grader. "Done!" Then he scuttled off to find the picture in question...

NORTAV ANALYSIS: Gemma Halliday's *Hollywood Confessions*

What follows is my NORTAV analysis of Gemma's prose sample. As always, compare this to your analysis. Note where we agree, and if and why we differ. (Surely our differences are becoming less frequent at this point, right?) Keep in mind, these analyses will get shorter and shorter as we cover the same ground over and over. As you are now familiar with the standard use of all five DCE beats, I'll only provide commentary for beats that are tricky or used in a somewhat non-standard or interesting way.

[O1] Marco beamed like a proud papa. "So, what can I do for you, dahling? We're on a tight schedule today, but for you I could bump someone."

[V2] "I appreciate the sentiment, Marco, but I'm actually here for..." [A3] I leaned in and whispered, [V4] "a little information."

[O5] He closed his heavily lined eyes and shook his head in the negative. "Sorry, dahling, no can do. You know my lips are sealed. What would happen if I tongue-wagged about every celebutant who came through here? I'd be out on my hot little fanny, that's what."

[R6] I grinned. [V7] "You know that would never happen. Fernando couldn't function without you."

Notice [R6]. I notated this as a Reaction beat, as I felt this was Allie's involuntary reaction to the situation. If this was a sly, purposeful grin on her part, how would you notate it? As an Action beat, of course!

[O8] Marco pursed his lips. Then nodded. "Well, that's true."

[V9] "Listen, I just need a confirm or deny over a new hair color."

[O10] He shook his head again. "Sorry. I have taken the celebrity hairdresser's oath. 'What happens in the salon stays in the salon.'"

[V11] "Hmmm." [A12] I narrowed my eyes. [V13] "What if I made it worth your while?"

[O14] He raised one drawn-in eyebrow at me. "Worth my while?"

[V15] "I happen to have an informant that happens to follow the club scene very closely. And happens to know where one very desirable celebrity is planning on partying this very evening."

[O16] Marco leaned in. "I'm intrigued. A-lister?"

[A17] I shrugged. [V18] "At least a B-plus."

[O19] "Who?"

[A20] I looked over both shoulders, [T21] trying to match his level of drama as [A22] I leaned in and whispered, [V23] "Adam Lambert."

Notice [T21]. Here Gemma slips a little into NCE. This beat is most likely Allie the narrator, at the time of the telling of the story, describing how Allie the character was feeling at the time of the events of the story.

However, since we are in such tightly written DCE, that is, since Gemma has established a consistent DCE-based writing style, the reader still perceives this ambiguous/non-conforming beat as part of Allie's thought process as it was happening at the time of the story.

> [O24] "Shut the front door!" Marco said, almost spilling his glitter on the marble floor. "Where?"
>
> [V25] "I'll tell you...if you can tell me a little something."
>
> [O26] He narrowed his eyes at me. "Ooh, you are wicked, girl. Fine. You cracked me." He paused, looked over both shoulders for prying ears then nodded, setting finger to the side of his nose. "Come into my office, dahling."
>
> [O27] He turned and led the way through the salon. [A28] I followed him [O29] past buzzing drying stations and flying straight razors until we hit a door at the back. He opened it, doing an exaggerated over the shoulder again, and led the way inside.

There's something interesting going on in [O29]. Notice where the narrator's pronoun of self-reference changes from "I" to "we." This happens when the perceptions or activities portrayed by a beat are the combination of the focal character's perceptions and activities and another character's perceptions and activities. In this case, this beat describes what both Allie and Marco are experiencing. When this happens, the reader ends up perceiving the beat through a *group focal character*. As you might expect, grouping together perceptions and activities of multiple characters distances the reader from the primary focal character, as the reader experiences the events through a group rather than through a single entity. And, the mere fact that it's grouped gives the reader a sense of the narrator's presence. Too much of this might make the reader feel the writing style has changed to NCE. Of course, this situation can come up often, so how does one best handle it when trying to write in a DCE-based writing style?

> A **_Group Focal Character_** represents two or more characters acting as the focal character for a beat of prose.

You handle it just like Gemma does here. You minimize the number of beats portrayed through a group focal character. Take a look at [O27]. Every beat from here until [A30] could have been portrayed through a group focal character. In other words, Gemma could have written: "We turned and headed through the salon..." etc. Instead she keeps the two character's perceptions and activities as separate as possible, staying within Allie's perceptions and activities to the maximum extent, and only casts a couple of small-yet-necessary spots into a grouping through the use of the pronoun "we." Thus, the reader perceives it all as DCE and doesn't detect a change in the writing style.

> [A30] I followed, [T31] trying not to smirk as I saw we were in a supply closet. [T32] Very cloak-and-dagger.

Notice [T31]. There is a tag ("I saw") in the Thought beat here. This might have caused you to notate this portion of [T31] as an "act of observing" Action beat, followed by an Observation beat. If you did, that's fine. I notated it as part of [T31], for the use of "saw" here really means "realized," which casts the entire statement as a Thought beat (which, incidentally, uses beat substitution to include Allie's observations).

> [O33] "So, what do you want to know?" he asked in a low whisper.

> [V34] "Jennifer Wood. Is it true Pippi Mississippi has a new hair color?"

> [O35] "Ah." He steepled his fingers. "She was in here the other day."

[V36] "And?"

[O37] "And America's favorite blonde teeny bopper?"

[V38] "Yes?"

[O39] "Now a redhead."

[T40] Bingo. [V41] "I don't suppose you got any pictures of her?"

[O42] He looked offended. "I don't suppose I did! What do you think I am, some sort of gossip?" [T43] Heaven forbid. [O44] "But," he said.

[V45] "But?"

[O46] "Fernando did take a snapshot for his wall of fame."

[T47] Double bingo.

[V48] "I'll throw in Adam's home address if you get me a copy."

[O49] Marco squealed like a second grader. "Done!"

Then he scuttled off to find the picture in question.

And that ends the analysis. At this stage in your learning process, you should be able to understand these analyses simply by following the notations through the prose sample.

WRITING EXERCISE

Take out your work from the previous exercise. To each of the 50 Action beats in your prose chains, link a Vocalization beat that is (or could be) appropriate. You can add a short, simple Vocalization beat such as a purposeful grunt of displeasure, or you could create a longer Vocalization beat. Whatever works. If there isn't a second character in your prose chain, you can assume one is present (where appropriate) so that the focal character has someone to speak to. If you find that you simply can't come up with an appropriate Vocalization beat to link to a Thought beat, feel free to modify the prose chain if that helps. If you still can't come up with an appropriate Vocalization beat, create a new prose chain that you can work with. When you are finished with this exercise you should have 50 prose chains that include a leading beat, an Observation beat (or beats), a Reaction beat (or beats), a Thought beat (or beats), an Action beat (or beats) and a Vocalization beat (or beats).

Again, I will do two and notate them for clarity as an example:

(1)   [A] Sheila sniffs at the odor wafting from the kitchen. [O] It reeks of dead meat and onions. [R] She nearly gags. [T] It has to be the worst stench she's ever come across, and she has come across some pretty heinous smells in her time as *The Daily Yowl*'s lead investigative reporter.

[A] She pulls a tazer out of her purse and gestures to her cameraman.

[V] "Let's go, Sam," she says.

(2)   [A] Paul stepped out of the car. [O] Icy rain hit him hard and soaked his t-shirt in an instant. The wind howled. Leaves scattered across the driveway. [R] Goosebumps broke out on his arms and he shivered. [T] It was a long way to the house. Nearly two hundred yards. Paul wished he had brought a jacket, or at least a sweater. It was late fall for Christ's sake. What was he thinking? [A] He shoved his hands in his pockets.

[V] "This better be worth it."

If you have been doing the exercises all along (shame on you if you haven't!), you now have the opening lines (or middle lines or ending lines) to 50 different short stories or novels!

Congratulations!

Save them for future projects or use them as prompts when you need something to kick-start your muse.

LET'S RECAP

In this section, my goal was to present the details of Vocalization beats.

You learned that:

- A Vocalization beat describes the voluntary vocal sounds produced by a focal character—speech, grunts, groans, etc. —as the story unfolds, moment to moment.

- Vocalizations can be incidental or rendered as focused beats.

- Involuntary vocalizations are reactions.

- Dialogue is a "conversation" represented by the exchange of a focal character's Vocalization beats (what she says to another character) and her Observation beats (what she hears the other character say).

- Narrative tags within Vocalization beats should be kept to a minimum, and when used they should be kept simple and direct, such as "he said," "he answered," "he replied," etc., for the reader will gloss over or ignore these.

- Tags describing a non-focal character's speech are not narrative intrusions at all, can be more frequent and more descriptive, and are included within the focal character's Observation beat.

- A group focal character represents two or more characters acting as the focal character for a beat, which should be minimized in DCE.

And that concludes our discussion of the five types of DCE beats. In the next section we will look at the ordering of DCE beats.

DCE and the Ordering of Beats

THE NATURAL RESPONSE SEQUENCE

As you know, beats of DCE are linked together using a logical relationship (unless the beat is an initiating beat). We call this type of link, simply, a *logical link*.

> A **Logical Link** is a link that ties together two beats through the use of a logical relationship.

This is the standard way all beats are connected to form a prose chain. The logical relationship could be a serial relationship (i.e. the beats form a series of events), some kind of cause and effect relationship, a set pattern, a set topic, or any relationship the writer can think of, provided the reader can understand that relationship explicitly or intuitively. The reader's ability to understand the relationship between each beat is what enables the reader to follow the prose chain from beginning to end.

When linking beats using nearly any type of logical relationship, there is no required order or sequence in which beats must occur. That is, any type of DCE beat can be linked to any other type of DCE beat in any order, provided the logic is clear.

Take a look at the following diagram. In this random sequence, an Action beat leads to a Thought beat, which leads to another Action beat, which leads to a Vocalization beat, which leads to an Observation beat, and so forth. Provided there is some kind of logical relationship between each beat, the order or sequence of the beats is irrelevant.

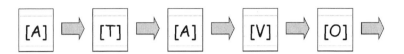

A Random Order of DCE Beats

For fun, try to create an example of DCE that follows the above sequence. Here's my attempt:

[A1] Zoe dragged herself up the front steps.

[T2] It had been three long years since she'd been home. She wondered if much had changed.

[A3] She pushed open the screen door.

[V4] "Anyone home?"

[O5] A strange, unfamiliar silence wafted over her.

In this example we have a series of events that portray a focal character's return to her home. We have no problem following the beats as they lead from one to the next. The first beat is an initiating beat. It is the first beat in the example, and therefore we don't expect there to be a relationship back to a previous beat. We accept it as a new concept. When we arrive at [T2], we understand intuitively that these are the thoughts playing through Zoe's mind as she walks reluctantly up the front steps. It makes simple, logical sense based on what we know of the situation, and therefore we make the conceptual leap from [A1] to [T2] with no difficulty. When Zoe opens the screen door in [A3], we accept this as yet another logical step. She could have done any number of things here, not just open the door. She could have stopped to think. She could have looked out over the neighborhood. She could have done anything provided it fit into the situation set up by the writer. Next, we find another logical step as we jump to [V4]. In [O5] we have another example of an initiating beat. Here Zoe herself is not moving the prose chain forward, but rather something is interrupting into the prose chain (a strange silence), and of course we aren't confused because, once more, it makes perfect sense given the situation.

This is all material we've covered, so the logical link should be nothing new to you at this point.

In truth all links are logical links, but there is one special kind of logical link that we need to look at a bit closer, as it will indeed force a specific order or sequence on DCE beats. We touched on this briefly already, but now we'll look at this concept in a little more detail.

> A **Stimulus/Response Link** is a link
> that ties together two beats through a
> stimulus/response relationship.

When the logical link between two beats is a *stimulus/response link*, that is, when the focal character is responding or reacting directly to a beat that is acting as a type of stimulus, then any responding beats will occur in a natural response sequence.

Take a look at the following diagram:

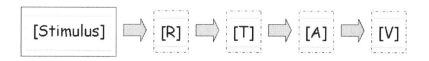

The Natural Response Sequence

Here we see a beat that is acting as a stimulus on a focal character. This beat can be of any type (though more often than not it's an Observation beat). In response to that stimulus, the focal character can (optionally) react, think, act, or vocalize. If she responds directly using any or all of these beats, they will appear in the order shown in the above diagram, that is: [R], [T], [A], [V]. This *natural response sequence* is based on the order in which an actual human being will most often respond to a stimulus. In fiction, focal characters will react to a stimulus before they think about it. They will think about a stimulus before they perform an action in response to it (remember, some actions are reactions, and those must happen at the start of the sequence), and they will vocalize a response after all these other responses have or could have occurred. Prose that reflects this natural order will appear more realistic and therefore more professional to the reader.

> The **Natural Response Sequence** is the
> order of optional beats
> ([R],[T],[A],[V])
> through which a focal character may
> respond directly to a stimulus.

Now, does the natural response sequence look familiar? It should. It is the sequence you just constructed over the last five writing exercises. Theoretically I could have chosen any sequence for the exercises, but I chose this order to get you to start working with the natural response sequence while you learned about each type of DCE beat. If you look back at your 50 prose chain examples, you should find, at a minimum, the Observation beats are acting as a stimulus for the subsequent Reaction beats. The rest of the beats may also be linked in a stimulus/response fashion, or you may have moved on to something beyond a direct response to the Observation beat(s) and therefore used logical links. It depends on what you did with the exercises. (For more information on the natural response sequence, check out Jack Bickham's masterpiece *Scene and Structure*.)

Let's look at an example that uses the natural response sequence.

[A1] Kate readied her weapon and kicked open the door.

[O2] Quentin Price lay dead on the floor, a bullet hole between his eyes.

[R3] Her mouth dropped open.

[T4] Rod Stapleton had arrived before her! And he'd finished off Quentin for good.

[A5] She clicked the Glock's safety to the on position.

[V6] "Dammit."

We'll start with the link between [A1] and [O2]. Is [O2] the focal character's direct response to [A1]? No. It's more of an effect caused by the occurrence of [A1]. Kate isn't responding directly to [A1], she simply is in a position to observe the results of [A1].

What about the link between [O2] and [R3]? Is [R3] the focal character's direct response to [O2]? Yes. It is Kate's involuntary response (her reaction) to what she sees in [O2].

If you look closely, you'll see that [R3], [T4], [A5], and [V6] are all responses to the stimulus beat [O2] presented in the natural response sequence. If you fiddle around with this example, you will find that removing any one of the optional response beats [R3], [T4], [A5], or [V6] will not impact the professionalism of the prose. It may change the meaning or emphasis of the sample, but it won't change the quality. Conversely, if you reordered any of the optional response beats, you will notice a variation or degradation in the quality of the prose. In most cases, the prose becomes muddier and harder for the reader to parse. In at least one case, however, the writer can reorder the response beats to manufacture a certain sense of suspense.

Can you guess how? If you go back to our NORTAV analysis of Guido Henkel's *Curse of Kali* and reread the section on beat reordering, you will have your answer. By moving the reaction beat before the stimulus beat [O2], you will start to see the drama or suspense that can be created.

For example:

> [A1] Kate readied her weapon and kicked open the door.
>
> [R3] Her mouth dropped open.
>
> [O2] Quentin Price lay dead on the floor, a bullet hole between his eyes.
>
> [T4] Rod Stapleton had arrived before her! And he'd finished off Quentin for good.
>
> [A5] She clicked the Glock's safety to the on position.
>
> [V6] "Dammit."

Warning: Many critics, as well as Jack Bickham, consider this a cheap way to manufacture suspense. Whether or not you agree, it is certainly a technique you will want to use sparingly, else your prose might slip into the land of the melodramatic.

NORTAV ASSIGNMENT

In past assignments you tried to locate each type of DCE beat and, if possible, the links between the beats in a DCE-based sample of writing. For this assignment do the same, but I also want you focus specifically on identifying any stimulus/response links and any occurrence of the natural response sequence. For incidental perceptions and activities, make a mental note of them or underline them if you wish. For focused beats, notate them by inserting an [O], [R], [T], [A], or [V] before the word that begins the beat. To make your commentary clearer, you can add a numeric identifier to each beat for reference purposes, such as [O4], [R7], [T10], [A13], or [V16]. If you find an implied beat, notate it with curly brackets { }. The goal here is to pay very close attention to the stimulus/response links and the natural response sequence. Try to identify and understand the techniques the author uses to construct each.

You can do your work right in this book, or print/photocopy the sample and work with it separately. When you're done, compare your results with the NORTAV analysis I provide directly after the prose sample.

PROSE SAMPLE: Dean Wesley Smith's *Jukebox Gifts*

For this assignment, we'll work with the prose of best-selling author Dean Wesley Smith. Highly regarded in traditional and independent publishing circles, Dean has written over ninety novels and more than a hundred short stories. His novels include *Laying the Music to Rest* and *The Hunted*. With his wife Kristine Kathryn Rusch, he co-authored *The Tenth Planet* trilogy and *The 10th Kingdom*. The following prose sample is taken from Dean's short story *Jukebox Gifts*. You can learn more about Dean at http://www.deanwesleysmith.com/.

The focal character in this "first-person" DCE-based sample is Stout.

> ... The stereo behind the bar was playing soft Christmas songs as I clicked the lock to the front entrance of the Garden Lounge and flicked off the outside light. I could feel the cold of the night through the wood door and the heat of the room surrounding me. I took a deep breath. Christmas Eve was finally here.

I could see the entire lounge and the backs of my four best friends sitting at the bar. I had never been much into decorating with Christmas stuff and this year was no different. My only nod to the season was small Christmas candles for each table and booth. Some customer had tied a red ribbon on one of the plants over the middle booth and the Coors driver had put up a Christmas poster declaring Coors to be the official beer of Christmas. The candles still flickered on the empty tables, but the rest of the bar looked normal. Dark brown wood walls, dark brown carpet, an old oak bar and friends. The most important part was the friends. My four best friends' lives were as empty as mine. Tonight, on the first Christmas Eve since I bought the bar, I was going to give them a chance to change that. That was my present to them. It was going to be an interesting night.

"All right, Stout," Carl said, twisting his huge frame around on his bar stool so that he could face me as I wound my way back across the room between the empty tables and chairs. "Just what's such a big secret that you kick out that young couple and lock the door at seven o'clock on Christmas Eve?"

I laughed. Carl always got right to the point. With big Carl you always knew exactly where you stood.

"Yeah," Jess said from his usual place at the oak bar beside the waitress station, "What's so damned important you don't want the four of us to even get off our stools?" Jess was the short one of the crowd. When he stood next to Carl the top of Jess's head barely reached Carl's neck. Jess loved to play practical jokes on Carl. Carl hated it.

"This," I said as I pulled the custom-made felt cover off

the old Wurlitzer jukebox and, with a flourish, dropped the cloth over the planter and into the empty front booth. My stomach did a tap dance from nerves as all four of my best customers whistled and applauded, the sound echoing in the furniture and plant-filled room.

David, my closest friend in the entire world, downed the last of his scotch-rocks and swirled the ice around in the glass with a tinkling sound. Then, with his paralyzed right hand, he pushed the glass, napkin and all, to the inside edge of the bar. "So after hiding that jukebox in the storage room for the last ten months, we're finally going to get to hear it play?"...

NORTAV ANALYSIS: Dean Wesley Smith's *Jukebox Gifts*

What follows is my NORTAV analysis of Dean's prose sample. As always, compare this to your analysis and note any differences.

[O1] The stereo behind the bar was playing soft Christmas songs [A2] as I clicked the lock to the front entrance of the Garden Lounge and flicked off the outside light. [O3] I could feel the cold of the night through the wood door and the heat of the room surrounding me. {T4}[R5] I took a deep breath. [T6] Christmas Eve was finally here.

We start with an Observation beat, [O1], and an Action beat, [A2], that occur simultaneously. These link logically (as a series of events) to the next beat, [O3]. Things get interesting as we get to the next couple beats. Notice {T4} and [R5]. This is an implied Thought beat and a Reaction beat. How do we know there is an implied Thought beat here? Stout is taking a deep breath in reaction to the realization (an implied semi-conscious thought) that what he's been waiting for is finally about to occur. Thus, the unwritten {T4} is acting as a stimulus to [R5], and then to [T6], where Stout puts his realization into conscious thought. Notice the order of beats here. We have an implied stimulus beat leading to a Reaction beat and then to a Thought beat, which follows the natural response sequence.

> [O7] I could see the entire lounge and the backs of my four best friends sitting at the bar. [T8] I had never been much into decorating with Christmas stuff and this year was no different. My only nod to the season was small Christmas candles for each table and booth. Some customer had tied a red ribbon on one of the plants over the middle booth and the Coors driver had put up a Christmas poster declaring Coors to be the official beer of Christmas. The candles still flickered on the empty tables, but the rest of the bar looked normal. Dark brown wood walls, dark brown carpet, an old oak bar and friends. The most important part was the friends. My four best friends' lives were as empty as mine. Tonight, on the first Christmas Eve since I bought the bar, I was going to give them a chance to change that. That was my present to them. It was going to be an interesting night.

[T6] leads logically (following the series of events) to the next beat, [O7]. [O7] leads to a compound Thought beat, [T8]. Notice how the sight of the best friends triggers (stimulates) the Thought beat? The link between these two beats is a stimulus/response link.

> [O9] "All right, Stout," Carl said, twisting his huge frame around on his bar stool so that he could face me as [A10] I wound my way back across the room between the empty tables and chairs. [O11] "Just what's such a big secret that you kick out that young couple and lock the door at seven o'clock on Christmas Eve?"

[O9] is an initiating Observation beat, and [A10] is a simultaneous Action beat. [O11] is the continuation of Stout's observation that began in [O9].

[R12] I laughed. [T13] Carl always got right to the point. With big Carl you always knew exactly where you stood.

Here [R12] is a Reaction beat that is linked back to [O11] through a stimulus/response link, as is the subsequent [T13]. [R12] and [T13] follow the natural response sequence.

[O14] "Yeah," Jess said from his usual place at the oak bar beside the waitress station, "What's so damned important you don't want the four of us to even get off our stools?" [T15] Jess was the short one of the crowd. When he stood next to Carl the top of Jess's head barely reached Carl's neck. Jess loved to play practical jokes on Carl. Carl hated it.

In this section we have an initiating Observation beat [O14], followed by Thought beat [T15]. Again, [O14] is acting as a trigger, which causes Stout to think about Jess for a moment in [T15].

[V16] "This," I said as [A17] I pulled the custom-made felt cover off the old Wurlitzer jukebox and, with a flourish, dropped the cloth over the planter and into the empty front booth. [R18] My stomach did a tap dance from nerves as [O19] all four of my best customers whistled and applauded, the sound echoing in the furniture and plant-filled room.

Here the beats [V16] and [A17] are also tied back to [O14] through a stimulus/response relationship. Notice the sequence of [T15], [V16], and [A17]. They follow the natural response sequence almost perfectly. The last two beats occur simultaneously and thus they are not technically out of order, however, were the two written in reverse order, even though they would remain simultaneous, the reader might sense them a little more intimately than the order presented here. One way is not better than the other. Again, it depends on the writing style that has been established.

Moving on, this section ends with a Reaction beat, [R18], and an Observation beat [O19]. This is the same technique Dean just employed. We have [O19] acting as a stimulus beat for the Reaction beat [R18], yet they are presented as happening simultaneously and in reverse order to the natural response sequence.

What's happening here is that Dean is using his unique writing style *consistently*, the mark of every professional writer.

> [O19] David, my closest friend in the entire world, downed the last of his scotch-rocks and swirled the ice around in the glass with a tinkling sound. Then, with his paralyzed right hand, he pushed the glass, napkin and all, to the inside edge of the bar. "So after hiding that jukebox in the storage room for the last ten months, we're finally going to get to hear it play?"

And finally we end with an initiating Observation beat [O19].

WRITING EXERCISE

Each of your 50 prose chains starts with a "leading" beat and an Observation beat. The Observation beat is acting as a stimulus beat for the subsequent Reaction beat and perhaps other beats in the prose chain. For this exercise I want you to construct eight new prose chains using the natural response sequence. This time, however, I don't want you to use an Observation beat as the stimulus beat. I want you to create two examples of a natural response sequence using each of the other four types of DCE beats as a stimulus beat. In other words, two chains should be a focal character's complete response (Reaction beat, Thought beat, Action beat, and Vocalization beat) to his or her own "stimulating" Reaction beat. Two should be the response to his or her own "stimulating" Thought beat. Two should be the response to a "stimulating" Action beat. And two should be the response to a "stimulating" Vocalization beat. Stimulus beats are usually Observation beats, so coming up with viable examples for these other types of "stimulating" beats might be tricky and take a bit of extra thought, but it shouldn't be impossible. In some cases you may need a leading beat or two to set up the situation. Do your best.

Again, I will do two and notate them for clarity as an example:

(1) [T(stimulus)] She was going to be late. [R] A soft groan escaped her lips. [T] Another interview blown! That was two in one week. [A] She kicked off the covers.

[V] "Damn it all to hell."

(2) [V (stimulus)] "Shut up!"

[R] I slap a hand over my mouth. [T] I have never blown up at anyone like this before, especially not a fellow teacher. [A] I drop my hand back in my lap and pretend to smooth the wrinkles from my skirt.

[V] "Melanie, I'm sorry. I shouldn't have said that."

LET'S RECAP

By now you should understand that:

- A logical link is a link that connects together two DCE beats through any logical relationship.

- DCE beats can be arranged in any order when connected using a logical link.

- The stimulus/response link is one particular type of logical link that represents a "stimulus/response" relationship between two beats.

- A stimulus/response link causes DCE beats to occur in a natural response sequence.

- The natural response sequence, ([R], [T], [A], [V]), is the order in which beats will occur such that they accurately reflect how a focal character would respond to a stimulus.

In the last section of this chapter I want to cover some of the challenges you may face when working with a DCE-based style of writing.

Challenges to Using a DCE-Based Writing Style

SUMMARIES

DCE reflects the moment-to-moment perceptions and activities of a focal character. This makes dealing with non-moment-to-moment perceptions and activities difficult in a DCE-based writing style. You've already run into two strategies for handling summaries. First, you could imply the perception and activity beats you wish to summarize and then reflect back on them "in summary" in a Thought beat. Or you could tack on a short bit of narrative direction to a beat, like "for a few seconds" to accomplish a summary, provided the time spanned is very short and the technique is used infrequently.

A third way to handle summary in a DCE-based writing style is to use a scene break to skip over the perceptions and activities you wish to summarize, and let the context of the story imply the occurrence of the unwritten perceptions and activities. For instance, a focal character can walk into a movie theater at the end of one scene and walk out of the theater at the start of the next scene. You don't need to play out the focal character observing the movie moment to moment or even in summary.

FLASHBACKS

In a DCE-based writing style, handing flashbacks can be tricky. You basically have two options. First, you can use context and a scene break like you can when dealing with summaries. For instance, a character could "remember" something about a specific event from the past at the end of one scene, and the next scene could be that event played out moment to moment. Implemented correctly, the reader will understand the shift in time. Else, the only alternative is to handle the flashback entirely within the memory of the focal character. That is, the focal character has to think back and remember the entire past event. For short events, this is relatively simple:

[A1] Davenport started at the photo. [O2] He was smiling, standing next to Lucas Brown at the gate of Camp Carson. [T3] He had spent that entire summer at Carson, swimming in the lake, toasting marshmallows, and chasing girls with Lucas.

In this short example, Davenport, the focal character, remembers (flashes back to) a past event in [T3]. The example starts in the past tense and shifts to the past perfect ("he had spent"). This flashback could continue for as long as the writer wanted to provide the reader with information from the past, but remaining in the shifted tense for too long becomes tiresome, both for the writer and for the reader.

For longer flashbacks the choice then is to start the flashback in the shifted tense, and then shift back to the normal tense once the flashback has taken hold.

For instance:

[A1] Jerry pulled up to the package store. [T2] Ten months, and not a drink. And here he was, about to fall off the wagon. Again. The last time had been a catastrophe. [T3] He had been at The Ole' Waterin' Hole. Marjorie had just dumped him. He could still recall the bartender that night.

[T4] "What'll it be, Mack?" he had said, sarcasm dripping from his voice.

[T5 or V5?] "Whiskey, and leave the bottle," I grunted.

[T6 or O6?] The bartender gave me a long disgusted glare, reached for the Wild Turkey, and poured me a shot.

[T7 or A7?] I downed it without hesitation and gestured for another.

Notice the tense shifts back at beat [T5 or V5?]. This creates the impression that the focal character has transitioned from recalling the events to *reliving* the events. This is fine and in fact works far better for longer flashbacks handled within a focal character's memory. Now notice the notation. Because we have embedded a past perception within a current perception, we now have a problem. In a NORTAV analysis, should we notate these embedded beats as Jerry's thought at the current time of the story? Or should we notate them as Jerry's perceptions and/or activities from the past, as there is no longer any sense of the current-time thought going on here?

In a NORTAV analysis, we do both. We track both levels of time so it's perfectly clear how the writer is constructing the prose. Here is how we would notate the previous sample:

> [A1] Jerry pulled up to the package store. [T2] Ten months, and not a drink. And here he was, about to fall off the wagon. Again. The last time had been a catastrophe. [T3] He had been at The Ole' Waterin' Hole. Marjorie had just dumped him. He could still recall the bartender that night.
>
> [T4] "What'll it be, Mack?" he had said, sarcasm dripping from his voice.
>
> [T-V5] "Whiskey, and leave the bottle," I grunted.
>
> [T-O6] The bartender gave me a long disgusted glare, and reached for the Wild Turkey.

Note that a writer does not have to stop at one level of embedded flashback. If in this example Jerry had been drinking at the bar (in the first flashback) and then flashbacked to an even earlier time (or to an imagined future time), one could track that in a NORTAV analysis simply by adding another level to the notation, such as [T-T-O9], etc.

Complicated?

Of course.

And if it's complicated to notate, you can be sure it's complicated to keep straight and accurate when you're creating the prose. This is precisely the kind of complexity writers are forced to learn on their own, subconsciously, through trial and error. At least now you have the NORTAV Method to help you consciously learn (and notate) this type of flashback!

THE ABSTRACT FOCAL CHARACTER

Finally, when working in a DCE-based writing style, you may encounter a situation where you wish to show the reader some particular event but you have no feasible focal character to place at the scene. In other writing styles you could simply use the narrator to tell the reader about the event. In a DCE-based writing style you must maintain the illusion that there is no narrator. Your choice then is to establish a fly-on-the-wall perspective (to use an old term).

A fly-on-the-wall perspective uses no sense of a focal character and no sense of a narrator. It is a way of portraying a scene to the reader as if she were experiencing the events through a "fly on the wall." The reader sees, hears, and/or smells the events of the story through the senses of some unknown, abstract entity on the scene. How can we accomplish this in a DCE-based writing style?

The writer can use an abstract focal character.

An *abstract focal character* is an invisible, un-commenting entity through which the reader can experience the events of a scene. Meaning, the writer will portray the events of a scene through the Observation beats (sight, sound, and smell only) of an abstract focal character. Adding taste and touch observations would convey the impression to the reader that there is an actual focal character at the scene. Adding any other type of DCE beat (Reactions, Thoughts, Actions, Vocalizations) would do the same.

> An ***Abstract Focal Character*** is an invisible, un-commenting entity through which the reader can experience the events of the story.

So when establishing a fly-on-the-wall perspective using a DCE-based writing style, use an abstract focal character and limit the content of the beats to the abstract focal character's sight, sound, and smell observations. Note: These observations should be presented as objectively as possible. Some incidental narrative information in addition to the observation is fine. But don't let commentary or opinion or conclusions work their way into the Observation beats, else the reader will feel the observations are coming from an actual focal character or narrator.

LET'S RECAP

By now you should understand that:

- To accomplish summary in a DCE-based writing style, imply the perceptions and activities you wish to summarize and then reflect back on them "in summary" in a Thought beat.

- To accomplish summary in a DCE-based writing style, tack on short bits of infrequent narrative direction, like "for a few seconds," to a beat.

- To accomplish summary in a DCE-based writing style, use context and a scene break to skip over the perceptions and activities you wish to summarize.

- To accomplish a flashback in a DCE-based writing style, use context and a scene break to transition to a new scene written as a flashback.

- To accomplish a flashback in a DCE-based writing style, shift the tense back to the normal tense when rendering a long flashback through a focal character's thoughts (memories).

- Notate a flashback beat that has had its tense shifted back to the normal tense by adding levels to the notation ([T-09], etc.) as it will make the analysis clearer.

- An abstract focal character is an invisible, un-commenting entity through which a reader can experience the events of the story.

- Use an abstract focal character and its objective sight, sound, and smell observations, with occasional objective incidental narrative information, to accomplish a fly-on-the-wall perspective in a DCE-based writing style.

WHY NOT STOP HERE?

You have now learned everything you need to construct prose using a DCE-based writing style. If you really wanted to stop your learning process here, you could. Plenty of professional authors have built solid careers using only a DCE-based writing style. If you feel absolutely must, skip the other two types of prose and move on to Chapter 6.

But you don't want to do that.

Why limit yourself to using only one type of prose and, therefore, only one basic writing style? I suspect that if you've made it this far you want to become the best writer you can be. And that means you want to learn everything there is know about the craft of writing. And that means you want to learn how to construct all three types of prose to create as many different writing styles as possible.

Am I right?

I thought so!

We will build on the concepts I've just covered here. Make sure you understand everything in Chapter 3 before moving on to Chapter 4.

Remember: the NORTAV Method is not a silver bullet or a magic formula for constructing prose. It is a critical body of knowledge that every professional writer should understand. Your goal in this book is to learn that body of knowledge and apply it to your own unique writing process *in whatever way comes natural to you.*

Now let's move on to Chapter 4, where you will learn all about the second type of prose: Narration.

Chapter 4

NARRATION

Discovering the Second Type of Prose

WHERE ARE WE IN THE BIG PICTURE?

Now that you understand what prose is and how it functions, and how to construct the first type of prose (DCE), we will move on to the second type of prose: Narration.

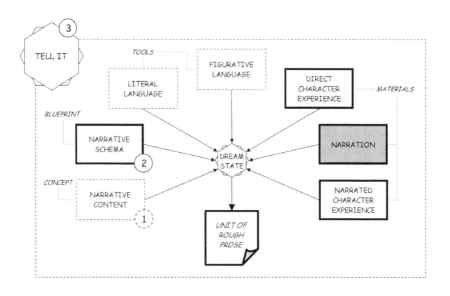

Narration

WHAT IS NARRATION?

In Chapter 3 you learned how to construct the first type of prose: Direct Character Experience. When using DCE, the writer portrays the moment-to-moment perceptions and activities of a focal character with little-to-no sense of a narrator's presence. In doing so, the reader intimately experiences the story through or beside a focal character.

Next, we're going to cover the second type prose: Narration.

> **Narration** is prose that originates from a narrator and does *not* reflect the perceptions and activities of a focal character.

Narration could be considered the opposite of Direct Character Experience. Where DCE reveals little-to-no sense of a narrator, Narration is information perceived by the reader as coming directly from the narrator of the story. Where DCE is used to reflect the perceptions and activities of a focal character, Narration is used to portray anything that is *not* a focal character's perceptions or activities. Again, Narration is prose that originates from a narrator and does *not* reflect the perceptions or activities of a focal character. And, as one would expect, Narration maximizes the distance between the reader and any focal characters, as illustrated by the following diagram:

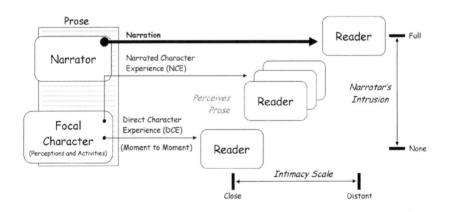

Narration, Intimacy, and Narrative Intrusion

Now you might be asking yourself, if Narration is prose that does not reflect the perceptions and activities of a focal character, what does it reflect? Good question. Narration can reflect anything, which is why it is easier to define it by what it isn't. Narration can be the small stage directions a narrator uses to help keep the reader aware of the current time and place of a story. Narration can be background information on the setting, historical information, or biographical information about a character. Narration can be scientific facts or philosophies. In short, because Narration can represent so many different things, it is far too broad to define specifically by the nature of its content. Narration, once more, can portray *any* information to the reader that does *not* reflect the perceptions or activities of a focal character.

A BIT MORE ON NARRATIVE SCHEMAS

Remember, a narrative schema defines one or more unique styles of writing and the pattern of their use throughout a work of fiction. In a Narration-based writing style, the only prose type in use is Narration. The goal of a Narration-based writing style to remove any sense of a focal character's experience, direct or narrated. That said, few if any works of fiction are written using only a Narration-based writing style. Stories have characters and characters experience things. So there will almost always be a writing style in a work of fiction that includes some form of focal character perceptions and activities (DCE or NCE). In most narrative schemas that include Narration in some form, either the Narration is being mixed with another prose type (as we will see in the next chapter) to form a single mixed-prose type writing style, or the writer is alternating between a Narration-based writing style and other writing styles and there is a pattern in the narrative schema that defines how the writing styles are being used. In this chapter we will look at the pure Narration-based writing style only. We will get into mixing and alternating prose types and writing styles in the next two chapters.

A FEW EXAMPLES OF NARRATION

To begin, let's take a look at some famous examples of Narration and

Narration-based writing styles from years past. We'll start with the opening to Alexander Dumas's classic swashbuckler *The Three Musketeers*:

> On the first Monday of the month of April, 1625, the market town of Meung, in which the author of Romance of the Rose was born, appeared to be in as perfect a state of revolution as if the Huguenots had just made a second La Rochelle of it. Many citizens, seeing the women flying toward the High Street, leaving their children crying at the open doors, hastened to don the cuirass, and supporting their somewhat uncertain courage with a musket or a partisan, directed their steps toward the hostelry of the Jolly Miller, before which was gathered, increasing every minute, a compact group, vociferous and full of curiosity.
>
> In those times panics were common, and few days passed without some city or other registering in its archives an event of this kind. There were nobles, who made war against each other; there was the king, who made war against the cardinal; there was Spain, which made war against the king. Then, in addition to these concealed or public, secret or open wars, there were robbers, mendicants, Huguenots, wolves, and scoundrels, who made war upon everybody. The citizens always took up arms readily against thieves, wolves or scoundrels, often against nobles or Huguenots, sometimes against the king, but never against cardinal or Spain. It resulted, then, from this habit that on the said first Monday of April, 1625, the citizens, on hearing the clamor, and seeing neither the red-and-yellow standard nor the livery of the Duc de Richelieu, rushed toward the hostel of the Jolly Miller. When arrived there, the cause of the hubbub was apparent to all.

This is a long section of Narration presented to the reader by the narrator of the story. The narrator is simply establishing the scene by providing the reader with information on the setting and on the state of affairs in Spain in 1625. There is no focal character here at all, thus the prose is by definition Narration.

If this isn't clear yet, read the sample again. In your mind's eye, can you "hear" the words as if they were coming from a voice-over narrator, as you might in a movie? Can you feel how this writing style is different than a DCE-based writing style where you "experience" the prose through or beside a focal character?

Now let's move on to another sample. Here are the opening lines to Jules Verne's *Around the World in 80 Days*:

> Mr. Phileas Fogg lived, in 1872, at No. 7, Saville Row, Burlington Gardens, the house in which Sheridan died in 1814. He was one of the most noticeable members of the Reform Club, though he seemed always to avoid attracting attention; an enigmatical personage, about whom little was known, except that he was a polished man of the world. People said that he resembled Byron—at least that his head was Byronic; but he was a bearded, tranquil Byron, who might live on a thousand years without growing old.
>
> Certainly an Englishman, it was more doubtful whether Phileas Fogg was a Londoner. He was never seen on 'Change, nor at the Bank, nor in the counting-rooms of the "City"; no ships ever came into London docks of which he was the owner; he had no public employment; he had never been entered at any of the Inns of Court, either at the Temple, or Lincoln's Inn, or Gray's Inn; nor had his voice ever resounded in the Court of Chancery, or in the Exchequer, or the Queen's Bench, or the Eccle-

siastical Courts. He certainly was not a manufacturer; nor was he a merchant or a gentleman farmer. His name was strange to the scientific and learned societies, and he never was known to take part in the sage deliberations of the Royal Institution or the London Institution, the Artisan's Association, or the Institution of Arts and Sciences. He belonged, in fact, to none of the numerous societies which swarm in the English capital, from the Harmonic to that of the Entomologists, founded mainly for the purpose of abolishing pernicious insects.

What is different here than the Narration you encountered in the Dumas sample? In this sample there is a potential focal character, Phileas Fogg. If there is a potential focal character, is this still Narration? The answer is yes. Can you see why? Here the narrator is providing the reader with information about Phileas Fogg, but the information is not Fogg's perceptions or activities. This is information concerning his personality and background. Reread the sample. Do you experience anything through or beside Fogg? No. Therefore the prose is Narration.

Clear? Great!

Now let's talk a little about the narrators themselves.

THE OMNISCIENT NARRATOR

In a Narration-based writing style, the reader experiences the story as information that is being "told" to her by a storyteller. These storytellers come in two varieties: The omniscient narrator and the character narrator. The *omniscient narrator* is a narrator that is not a character in the story, one who has access to any and all information pertaining to the story world, the story events, and the story characters. This type of narrator is "god-like." He or she can choose to reveal as much or as little information regarding the story world, the story events, and the story characters as he or she deems appropriate. In the Dumas and

Verne stories, you will find both these narrators are omniscient. They are not characters in their respective tales but rather each is an all-knowing, god-like entity that relates the tale to the reader. For ease and consistency, we refer to omniscient narrators using the gender pronoun that matches the author's gender. Thus, both Dumas's and Verne's omniscient narrators would be considered masculine and referenced as "he/his/him." Omniscient narrators are not, however, the authors themselves. Though some may assume the narrator to be the author, narrators can have can have their own opinions, agendas, mannerisms, and reliability, separate from the author. If you're interested in learning more about the theory behind this (and many other aspects of this book), you could start by reading Manfred Jahn's excellent webbook: *Narratology: A Guide to the Theory of Narrative*, located at: `http://www.uni-koeln.de/~ame02/pppn.htm/`.

> An **Omniscient Narrator** is a narrator that is not a character in the story and who has access to any and all information pertaining to the story world, the story events, and the story characters.

THE CHARACTER NARRATOR

Unlike the omniscient narrator, the *character narrator* is a character in the story. As a character in the story, this kind of narrator does not have god-like access to all the information pertaining to the story world, the story events, and the story characters. The character narrator can only reveal information that the character him- or herself would realistically have access to. For instance, if the narrator of a story is the character Sally, then Sally can only tell the reader about information she is privy to as the narrator or information she was privy to as a character in the story. That is all. She cannot reveal to the reader anything that is outside her scope of knowledge, which includes the inner thoughts and perceptions of any character except for herself (unless she makes it clear how she would know what was happening inside another character's head!).

> A **Character Narrator** is a narrator that is a character in the story and who only has access to the information pertaining to the story world, story events, and story characters he or she would realistically know.

Let's look at another famous sample of a Narration-based writing style, this time with a character narrator. Here are the opening lines to Mark Twain's *Adventures of Huckleberry Finn*, narrated by the character Huck.

> You don't know about me without you have read a book by the name of The Adventures of Tom Sawyer; but that ain't no matter. That book was made by Mr. Mark Twain, and he told the truth, mainly. There was things which he stretched, but mainly he told the truth. That is nothing. I never seen anybody but lied one time or another, without it was Aunt Polly, or the widow, or maybe Mary. Aunt Polly—Tom's Aunt Polly, she is—and Mary, and the Widow Douglas is all told about in that book, which is mostly a true book, with some stretchers, as I said before.
>
> Now the way that the book winds up is this: Tom and me

found the money that the robbers hid in the cave, and it made us rich. We got six thousand dollars apiece—all gold. It was an awful sight of money when it was piled up. Well, Judge Thatcher he took it and put it out at interest, and it fetched us a dollar a day apiece all the year round—more than a body could tell what to do with. The Widow Douglas she took me for her son, and allowed she would sivilize me; but it was rough living in the house all the time, considering how dismal regular and decent the widow was in all her ways; and so when I couldn't stand it no longer I lit out. I got into my old rags and my sugar-hogshead again, and was free and satisfied. But Tom Sawyer he hunted me up and said he was going to start a band of robbers, and I might join if I would go back to the widow and be respectable. So I went back.

Notice two things about the sample.

First, the "voice" of the character narrator should be obvious, as it so often is in character narrated stories. Because the narrator is also a character, the reader will often see the character's personality and traits reflected in the Narration, as it is here through Huck's dialect and lack of proper education. Second, notice the character narrator's use of the self-referencing "I." You may be thinking that omniscient narrators are only used in third-person point-of-view narratives and that character narrators are only used in first-person point-of-view narratives. While true, the fact is every narrator will refer to him- or herself as "I," regardless of whether the narrator is a character in the story or not. Check out Charles Dicken's *A Christmas Carol* and you'll find a great example of an omniscient narrator who will at times use the self-referencing "I."

When you encounter a narrator referring to him- or herself as "I," don't assume the narrator is a character narrator, and don't assume you are dealing with a first-person point-of-view narrative.

> **A NORTAV Tip:**
> All narrators will refer to him- or herself as "I," regardless of whether the narrator is a character in the story or not.

NARRATION BEATS

Unlike Direct Character Experience, which has five different types of beats, Narration has only one type of beat, called a *Narration beat*. A Narration beat is a single unit of story information that does not reflect a focal character's perception or activity. Narration can be incidental or rendered as focused beats. Incidental narrative information appears as small pieces of information (sometimes as small as a single word) that add color, depth, or direction to the prose chain. Focused Narration beats command the attention of the reader and represent the narrator's main point or topic.

> A **Narration Beat** is a single unit of story information that does *not* reflect a focal character's perception or activity.

Notating Narration beats in a NORTAV analysis works the same way as we saw with DCE beats. Things do get more complicated, however, when you are dealing with large chunks of Narration like we saw in the previous Dumas, Verne, and Twain samples. When you encounter large chunks of Narration, you can break them down into individual Narration beats based on the same principle we used to collect DCE beats of the same type into compound beats, only in reverse. In other words, we can break large chunks of Narration into individual Narration beats based on how those beats are logically linked together to form a prose chain.

Narration beats are simply one more unique type of beat used to construct prose. In fact, the Narration beat is the last basic type of beat used in constructing prose, making a grand total of six basic beats in all: N-O-R-T-A-V! (And now you should fully understand the acronym. Pat yourself on the back of you wish.)

LINKING NARRATION BEATS

So how does one link together Narration beats? All Narration beats are connected using logical links. As we are not dealing with the perceptions and activities of a focal character, stimulus/response links don't apply. Narration comes from the perspective of the storyteller, and the storyteller (usually) will not respond to stimuli in the story. Thus, when the writer is using only Narration, the beat chain would, obviously, appear as follows:

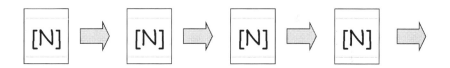

Order of Narration Beats

To illustrate how Narration is constructed as a linked series of Narration beats, let's notate the Verne sample.

[N1] Mr. Phileas Fogg lived, in 1872, at No. 7, Saville Row, Burlington Gardens, the house in which Sheridan died in 1814. [N2] He was one of the most noticeable members of the Reform Club, though he seemed always to avoid attracting attention; an enigmatical personage, about whom little was known, except that he was a polished man of the world. [N3] People said that he resembled Byron—at least that his head was Byronic; but he was a bearded, tranquil Byron, who might live on a thousand years without growing old.

[N4] Certainly an Englishman, it was more doubtful whether Phileas Fogg was a Londoner. He was never seen on 'Change, nor at the Bank, nor in the counting-rooms of the "City"; no ships ever came into London docks of which he was the owner; he had no public employment; he had never been entered at any of the Inns of Court, either at the Temple, or Lincoln's Inn, or Gray's Inn; nor had his voice ever resounded in the Court of Chancery, or in the Exchequer, or the Queen's Bench, or the Ecclesiastical Courts. He certainly was not a manufacturer; nor was he a merchant or a gentleman farmer. His name was strange to the scientific and learned societies, and he never was known to take part in the sage deliberations of the Royal Institution or the London Institution, the Artisan's Association, or the Institution of Arts and Sciences. He belonged, in fact, to none of the numerous societies which swarm in the English capital, from the Harmonic to that of the Entomologists, founded mainly for the purpose of abolishing pernicious insects.

As always, keep in mind this is as much art as it is science. You may find another way to break this up into individual Narration beats that is equally as valid. That's fine, as long as each beat represents one premise or idea or topic, and each premise or idea or topic leads logically from one to the next in a way the reader can follow explicitly or intuitively.

Here's the thought process behind how I broke up this sample into individual narration beats: In [N1], the narrator establishes the existence of Phileas Fogg. This leads to [N2], a general statement about who Fogg was. Next, in [N3], we get a little about what Fogg looked like. In [N4] we get a longer description that expands on [N2], giving us more detail about Phileas, specifically the fact that he was definitely English but not necessarily a Londoner. Any reader should be able to follow the logic Verne uses here to connect the beats. He is introducing us to a character, and thus we follow right along as the narrator discusses a series of different aspects of the character, in ever increasing levels of detail.

If we simplified each of these beats into "topic sentences," we can better see how Verne's logic works:

[N1] Mr. Phileas Fogg lived in 1872.

[N2] He was an enigmatical personage, about whom little was known.

[N3] People said that he resembled Byron.

[N4] Certainly an Englishman, it was more doubtful whether Phileas Fogg was a Londoner.

Does this manner of linking information sound familiar? It should. Breaking apart Narration into Narration beats in a NORTAV analysis or constructing Narration beats in your own fiction follows the same principles you have probably already used to write essays in school. When your Language Arts teacher taught you to construct your essays by using an introductory paragraph, multiple paragraphs that expand on the introduction (each with its own topic sentence), and a concluding paragraph, she was giving you a simplified blueprint on how to logically link together a series of information so the reader can follow along and understand your writing. We use this same basic principle to link together beats of Narration.

When performing a NORTAV analysis (or simply as an observant reader), you will want to identify the narrator as soon as possible. Explicitly understanding the narrative schema used in a work (which includes prose types, narrator, focal characters, patterns, etc.) makes the fiction easier to analyze and follow and often allows the observant reader to pick up on things an average reader wouldn't. As a writer, it is imperative that you know every aspect of the narrative schema you are working with at every given moment. You must know who your narrator is and when the narrator is addressing your reader directly. You must know when you are allowing the reader to fall into the illusion of experiencing the story within or beside a focal character. You must know when you are allowing the narrator to tell the reader about a focal character's perceptions and activities. As a writer, you are the director of the movie that is running through the reader's mind's eye. You have to know when and how to use each of the cameras (prose types) at your disposal. We will get more into this in Chapter 6.

NORTAV ASSIGNMENT

In previous assignments you tried to locate the DCE beats in a sample of prose. Now I want you to read the following sample and try to locate the Narration beats. For focused Narration beats, notate them with an [N]. If you run across narrative information that is incidental, make a mental note of it or underline it if you wish. As always, you can add a numeric identifier to each beat for reference purposes. Describe the logic that connects each beat of the prose chain. You can do your work right in this book, or print/photocopy the sample and work with it separately. Compare your results with the NORTAV analysis I provide directly after the prose sample.

PROSE SAMPLE: Arthur Conan Doyle's *The White Company*

For this analysis we will look at an excerpt from *The White Company*, a classic novel by Arthur Conan Doyle. For more information about Arthur Conan Doyle and his work, you can visit Project Gutenberg at http://www.gutenberg.org/.

This excerpt of a Narration-based writing style contains an omniscient narrator and no focal character.

... The great bell of Beaulieu was ringing. Far away through the forest might be heard its musical clangor and swell. Peat-cutters on Blackdown and fishers upon the Exe heard the distant throbbing rising and falling upon the sultry summer air. It was a common sound in those parts—as common as the chatter of the jays and the booming of the bittern. Yet the fishers and the peasants raised their heads and looked questions at each other, for the angelus had already gone and vespers was still far off. Why should the great bell of Beaulieu toll when the shadows were neither short nor long?

All round the Abbey the monks were trooping in. Under the long green-paved avenues of gnarled oaks and of lichened beeches the white-robed brothers gathered to the sound. From the vine-yard and the vine-press, from the bouvary or ox-farm, from the marl-pits and salterns, even from the distant iron-works of Sowley and the outlying grange of St. Leonard's, they had all turned their steps homewards. It had been no sudden call. A swift messenger had the night before sped round to the outlying dependencies of the Abbey, and had left the summons for every monk to be back in the cloisters by the third hour after noontide. So urgent a message had not been issued within the memory of old lay-brother Athanasius, who had cleaned the Abbey knocker since the year after the Battle of Bannockburn.

A stranger who knew nothing either of the Abbey or of its immense resources might have gathered from the appearance of the brothers some conception of the varied duties which they were called upon to perform, and of the busy, wide-spread life which centred in the old monastery. As they swept gravely in by twos and by threes, with bended heads and muttering lips there were few who did not bear upon them some signs of their daily toil. Here were two with wrists and sleeves all spotted with the ruddy grape juice. There again was a bearded brother with a broad-headed axe and a bundle of faggots upon his shoulders, while beside him walked another with the shears under his arm and the white wool still clinging to his whiter gown. A long, straggling troop bore spades and mattocks while the two rearmost of all staggered along under a huge basket o' fresh-caught carp, for the morrow was Friday, and there were fifty platters to be filled and as many sturdy trenchermen behind them. Of all the throng there was scarce one who was not labor-stained and weary, for Abbot Berghersh was a hard man to himself and to others...

NORTAV ANALYSIS: Arthur Conan Doyle's *The White Company*

What follows is my NORTAV analysis of Doyle's prose sample. As always, compare this to your analysis. Note where we agree, where we differ, and if we differ, why we differ.

[N1] The great bell of Beaulieu was ringing. Far away through the forest might be heard its musical clangor and swell. [N2] Peat-cutters on Blackdown and fishers upon the Exe heard the distant throbbing rising and falling upon the sultry summer air. [N3] It was a common sound in those parts—as common as the chatter of the jays and the booming of the bittern. [N4] Yet the fishers and the peasants raised their heads and looked questions at each other, for the angelus had already gone and vespers was still far off. [N5] Why should the great bell of Beaulieu toll when the shadows were neither short nor long?

We begin with Narration beat [N1]. Here Doyle introduces the setting by describing a ringing bell. This leads to Narration beat [N2], where peat-cutters and fishers hear the sound. In [N3] we get more information about the sound. In [N4] we see the people's reaction to the sound, and in [N5] we get an explanation of the people's reaction in the form of a question.

Now, normally I would have notated this entire section as a single compound Narration beat that describes the sound and effects of a ringing bell. But this is a good example of how some Narration can appear as character perceptions and activities, so I notated the beats in greater detail to make a point. [N1] almost reads like an Observation beat. [N2] almost reads like an "act of observing" Action beat that is out of its normal order. [N3] could almost be a Thought beat, describing what the peat-cutters and fishers are thinking. [N4] might be another Action beat and [N5] a Thought beat.

Are these beats experienced through a focal character? No. We don't really experience any of this through the peat-cutters and fishers, even though the narrator is somewhat describing their observations, actions, and thoughts. In this sense, the people described here are not focal characters. They are so abstracted they aren't characters at all, but rather more a part of the general setting. Thus, since there is no focal character, the prose type is Narration.

A NORTAV Tip:
If a narrator presents perceptions and activities to the reader that do not come from a focal character, then those perceptions and activities are considered Narration.

Subtle? Read the section again and pay close attention to how you perceive it as a reader. I perceive this as a narrator telling me about the scene and setting at hand, which includes the populace. I don't perceive any perceptions and activities through any characters.

> [N6] All round the Abbey the monks were trooping in. Under the long green-paved avenues of gnarled oaks and of lichened beeches the white-robed brothers gathered to the sound. From the vine-yard and the vine-press, from the bouvary or ox-farm, from the marl-pits and salterns, even from the distant iron-works of Sowley and the outlying grange of St. Leonard's, they had all turned their steps homewards. It had been no sudden call. A swift messenger had the night before sped round to the outlying dependencies of the Abbey, and had left the summons for every monk to be back in the cloisters by the third hour after noontide. So urgent a message had not been issued within the memory of old lay-brother Athanasius, who had cleaned the Abbey knocker since the year after the Battle of Bannockburn.

Next we have Narration beat [N6]. The sound of the bell leads us to this next piece of story information, where we have a group of monks gathering at an abbey in response to the sound. Towards the end of the beat Doyle presents us with old lay-brother Athanasius.

Here we get the first indication of someone who could be a focal character, but we are not yet given any of his perceptions or activities. We get a subtle impression that the brother is trying to remember if there has been such an urgent message before, but it has been abstracted far above the sense of a direct thought. At this point in the sample, it reads like background information about Athanasius, not Athanasius's current perceptions and activities.

So, like we saw with Phileas Fogg in the Verne analysis, this remains Narration.

> **A NORTAV Tip:**
> Like with a DCE-based writing style,
> limit the use of any ambiguous or
> non-conforming beats in a Narration-
> based writing style.

That said, prose that skirts the border of NCE and Narration can sometimes cause the writing to become less clear. It can make the reader think there is a focal character in play, and if there isn't, the reader may become confused. Like we do when working in a DCE-based writing style, limit the use of ambiguous or non-conforming beats when working with a Narration-based writing style.

[N7] A stranger who knew nothing either of the Abbey or of its immense resources might have gathered from the appearance of the brothers some conception of the varied duties which they were called upon to perform, and of the busy, wide-spread life which centred in the old monastery. As they swept gravely in by twos and by threes, with bended heads and muttering lips there were few who did not bear upon them some signs of their daily toil. Here were two with wrists and sleeves all spotted with the ruddy grape juice. There again was a bearded brother with a broad-headed axe and a bundle of faggots upon his shoulders, while beside him walked another with the shears under his arm and the white wool still clinging to his whiter gown. A long, straggling troop bore spades and mattocks while the two rearmost of all staggered along under a huge basket o' fresh-caught carp, for the morrow was Friday, and there were fifty platters to be filled and as many sturdy trenchermen behind them. Of all the throng there was scarce one who was not labor-stained and weary, for Abbot Berghersh was a hard man to himself and to others.

Finally, [N6] leads to Narration beat [N7], where we are given a more detailed description of the monks. So, at a high level, Doyle opens with the sound of a bell ringing through the land, which begins to gather the monks to the abbey, and then we end the excerpt with a description of the monks themselves, and, potentially, are introduced to one particular monk who may become a focal character as the work continues. One concept leads to the next, which leads to the next. And, even though there are places within this excerpt where Doyle presents us with possible focal characters and some background perceptions and activities, this is all still Narration.

Remember, Narration represents anything that is not a focal character's perceptions and activities. Conversely, if a beat is perceived in any way as coming from a focal character, and it reflects in any way that focal character's perceptions or activities, the beat is *not* Narration.

WRITING EXERCISE

For this exercise, I want you to invent a person, a place, an object, and an event. For each, construct a prose chain of at least four Narration beats that describe some non-physical aspect about that person, place, object, and event. (Physical descriptions can be mistaken for focal character observations, so we will avoid those for this exercise). Mix up the narrative tense (past, present) and the narrator (omniscient or character). Note, there may not be anything in your prose sample that will indicate if your narrator is a character in the story or not. That's fine.

Here is one example of a Narration-based writing style, notated for clarity. It includes a narrator describing the characteristics of an object to the reader:

> [N] The Starcruiser XJ7-32 was far superior to its only competitor, the Galaxy Z-Hopper out of Sector 9. [N]

With its extra holding bay, the Cruiser could carry ten percent more cargo than the Hopper. [N] Where the Hopper could make light speed in under 3.4 photellas, a fine feat, the Cruiser came in at an astounding 2.8. [N] Not only was the Cruiser a faster ship, it cost a mere half of what Kartron Corp was charging for the Hopper. Kartron was saddled with the higher labor costs in Sector 9, where the only workers available were humans and klyborgs. M.U.R.K, a private company that had yet to join the Imperial Commerce Guild, benefited from the cheaper labor in Sector 12, where Fundas worked for as little as seven kronobytes a day.

LET'S RECAP

By now you should understand that:

- Narration portrays anything that does *not* reflect the perceptions and activities of a focal character.

- A Narration-based writing style maximizes the distance between the reader and any focal character(s).

- There are two kinds of narrators: an omniscient narrator and a character narrator.

- Omniscient narrators are not characters in the story, are "god-like," and can choose to portray any aspect of the story world, story events, or story characters to the reader.

- Character narrators are characters in the story, are not "god-like," and can only portray the aspects of the story world, story events, or story characters to the reader that the character narrator would realistically know.

- Both types of narrators will refer to themselves with the self-referencing "I."

- A Narration beat is a single unit of story information that does not pertain to a focal character's perception or activity.

- Narration can be incidental or rendered as focused beats.

- Focused Narration beats reflect the narrator's main point or topic at hand.

- Incidental narrative information adds color, depth, or direction to the prose chain.

- Narration beats are always connected by logical links.

- When working in a Narration-based writing style, try to limit the use of ambiguous or non-conforming beats.

We will build on the concepts I've just covered here. Make sure you understand everything in Chapter 4 before moving on to Chapter 5.

Remember: the NORTAV Method is not a silver bullet or a magic formula for constructing prose. It is a critical body of knowledge that every professional writer should understand. Your goal in this book is to learn that body of knowledge and apply it to your own unique writing process *in whatever way comes natural to you*.

Now let's move on to Chapter 5, where you will learn about the third and final type of prose: Narrated Character Experience.

Chapter 5

NARRATED CHARACTER EXPERIENCE

Discovering the Third Type of Prose

WHERE ARE WE IN THE BIG PICTURE?

Now that you understand what prose is and how it functions, and how to construct two types of prose (DCE and Narration), we will move on to the third and final type of prose, called Narrated Character Experience.

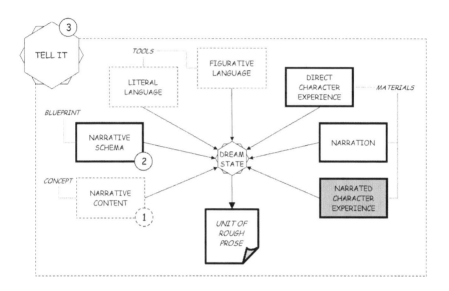

Narrated Character Experience

WHAT IS NARRATED CHARACTER EXPERIENCE?

When using a DCE-based writing style, the writer portrays the moment-to-moment perceptions and activities of a focal character with little-to-no sense of a narrator's presence. In doing so the reader intimately experiences the story through or beside a focal character. When using a Narration-based writing style, the writer portrays anything that is not a focal character's perception or activity to the reader, through an omniscient or character narrator. In doing so, the reader is distanced from the focal character(s) of the story. *Narrated Character Experience*, or *NCE*, is prose that reflects the perceptions and activities of a focal character through an omniscient or character narrator.

> **Narrated Character Experience** is prose that reflects the perceptions and activities of a focal character through an omniscient or character narrator.

NCE is a cross between DCE and Narration. As we can see from the following diagram, an NCE-based writing style creates a certain level of intimacy between the reader and a focal character, but that level of intimacy depends on how much the narrator intrudes into the prose. The less the intrusion, the more intimate the prose. The more the intrusion, the less intimate the prose.

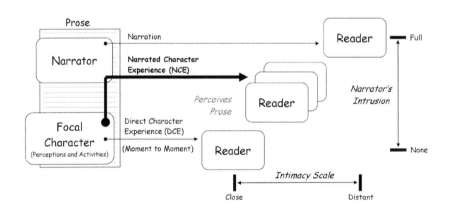

Narrated Character Experience, Intimacy, and Narrative Intrusion

Now, if NCE is a cross between DCE and Narration, how does that work?

An NCE beat can be created by adding Narration to a beat of DCE. It can be created simply by phrasing a DCE beat in a way that gives the reader the impression that the beat is coming from a narrator, and not something that is being experienced within or beside a focal character. It can be created by ordering DCE beats in a sequence that does not follow the actual sequence in which the events occurred at the time of the story. In other words, only a narrator telling of events after the fact can portray them in a different order in which they actually occurred.

That said, NCE has no new basic types of beats, per se. NCE beats do, however, fall into three categories, each of which can be notated specifically in a NORTAV analysis.

Let's look at each category in turn.

DIRECT NCE BEATS

The first category of NCE represents beats of direct narrated perceptions or activities, or *Direct NCE*. This category includes beats of individual focal character observations, reactions, thoughts, actions, and vocalizations that are portrayed to the reader through a narrator.

One way to create a beat of Direct NCE is to merge Narration with an individual beat of DCE. We have seen a few examples of this already. When a writer adds narrative tags like "he saw," "he heard," "he felt," "he grunted," to individual beats of DCE, she has just rendered the DCE beat through a narrator, and has thus created a beat of Direct NCE.

> **Direct NCE** are beats of individual focal character observations, reactions, thoughts, actions, and vocalizations that are portrayed to a reader through a narrator.

Also, we saw that adding narrative directives such as "the next day," "five minutes later," "when they arrived at the store," etc., to individual beats of DCE also casts the beat through a narrator and thus changes the beat to Direct NCE.

Direct NCE beats don't have to contain Narration. Sometimes a writer can cast a perception or activity as Direct NCE with the addition of a single word or a particular phrasing that gives the reader a gut feel or sense that the beat is originating from a narrator and not from the focal character directly. There are a myriad of ways a writer can cast observations, reactions, thoughts, actions, and vocalizations such that the narrator's presence is revealed to the reader, subtly or explicitly. Regardless of how the narrator is revealed, we end up with five types of Direct NCE beats: Narrated Observations, Narrated Reactions, Narrated Thoughts, Narrated Actions, and Narrated Vocalizations. In a NORTAV analysis we notate them as [No], [Nr], [Nt], [Na], and [Nv], respectively.

Here is an example of two Direct NCE beats:

> [Nt1] For months Sheila thought about the divorce,
> [No2] and she had felt perpetually sick to her stomach.

Notice first how each perception or activity can still be identified individually. Also notice how each beat is cast in a way that reveals a narrator. [Nt1] contains a narrative directive and a narrative tag ("For months," "Sheila thought"). [No2] also contains a narrative tag ("She felt") and it's rendered as a perception that has already occurred ("had felt"), which gives us a gut feel that this beat is coming from the narrator, not the focal character.

Because Direct NCE beats are still identifiable as individual perceptions and activities, they tend to follow the same pattern or logic when linking them together as beats of DCE. Direct NCE beats often follow the natural response sequence. Thus, Direct NCE beats keep the reader close to the focal character, though not quite as close as DCE.

MIXED NCE BEATS

The second category of NCE represents beats of mixed narrated perceptions and activities, or *Mixed NCE*. Beats of this category of NCE are created by mixing together two or more focal character perceptions or activities in such a way as to make it impossible (or impracticable) to break them out into individual beats.

> ***Mixed NCE*** are beats that represent a mix of focal character perceptions or activities which cannot easily be broken into individual beats.

When perceptions and activities are mixed together, the reader somewhat loses the sense that the perceptions and activities are happening individually, moment to moment, and begins to experience them more as something that is being told to them by a narrator. Like Direct NCE, Mixed NCE may or may not include Narration. With Mixed NCE, the reader is pushed a little further away from the focal character than when using beats of DCE or Direct NCE. Beats of Mixed NCE may or may not follow the natural response sequence. Any beat created by mixing together two or more perceptions or activities is called a Mixed NCE beat. In a NORTAV analysis, we notate all Mixed NCE beats as [Nm].

Here is an example of a Mixed NCE beat:

[Nm] Sheila alternated between thoughts of the divorce and bouts of nausea.

Notice how this beat cannot easily be broken into individual perceptions and activities. We can still recognize the individual perceptions and activities (thoughts of divorce, observations of nausea), but we can't break them out into linked, moment-to-moment beats. Thus, as I said, Mixed NCE pushes the reader a little further away from the focal character than beats of DCE and Direct NCE.

CONSOLIDATED NCE BEATS

The third and final category of NCE represents beats of consolidated narrated perceptions and activities, or *Consolidated NCE*. Beats of this category of NCE are created by abstracting or rolling up focal character perceptions or activities in such a way that the reader can sense the individual perceptions and activities, but they aren't revealed explicitly in the prose. They have been rolled up into a higher level concept. Consolidated NCE may or may not include Narration as well.

> *Consolidated NCE* are beats
> that represent a roll up of focal
> character perceptions or activities,
> where the individual perceptions
> and activities are sensed but
> not revealed explicitly.

When consolidating perceptions and activities, the reader loses any sense of the perceptions and activities happening individually, moment to moment. Thus the reader is pushed even further away from the focal character than when using beats of DCE, Direct NCE, or Mixed NCE. When consolidating perceptions and activities, the beats may or may not follow the natural response sequence. Any beat created by consolidating a focal character's perceptions or activities is called a Consolidated NCE beat. In a NORTAV analysis, we notate a Consolidated NCE beat as [Nc].

Here is an example of a Consolidated NCE beat:

[Nc] For months she suffered over the divorce.

Notice we no longer have any specific references to individual perceptions and activities, but we still get a sense they are occurring, and could probably guess at them if we had to.

MORE ON NARRATIVE SCHEMAS

Remember, a narrative schema defines one or more unique styles of writing and the pattern of their use throughout a work of fiction. You know that in a DCE-based writing style, a writer will use only DCE prose to create a single style of writing in which the reader will always feel as if she is within or beside a focal character. In a Narration-based writing style, a writer will use only Narration to create a single style of writing in which the reader will never feel as if she is within or beside a focal character.

An NCE-based writing style is different.

In an NCE-based writing style, the writer will use beats of NCE, but the writer can also include beats of DCE or Narration in the prose. In an NCE-based writing style a reader can feel within or beside a focal character one moment and feel as if she's listening to the voice of a narrator the next. Or the reader can feel somewhere in between. How a writer mixes beats of DCE or Narration with NCE can result in *many, many* different styles of writing, each producing a different sense of intimacy. The result is that the NCE-based writing style is the most versatile writing style. In fact, it is the style most often used by writers. Few if any writers will work in an absolutely pure DCE- or Narration-based writing style for the length of an entire work of fiction.

When working with an NCE-based writing style, it is up to the writer to create their own particular style and then *use it consistently*. For example, a writer may decide to use mostly DCE and a smattering of Consolidated NCE beats to establish a specific, intimate NCE-based writing style. Were she to use this style for any length of time and then suddenly introduce a block of Narration, the reader would sense the writing style has changed (possibly to a Narration-based writing style) and will look for an explicit reason for the change. Again, if there isn't one, the reader will become confused. Or, the writer may decide to use mostly Narration with a smattering of Consolidated NCE beats. Were she to use this un-intimate style for any length of time and then suddenly introduce a block of DCE, the reader would sense the writing style has changed (possibly to a DCE-based writing style) and will look for an explicit reason for the change.

When working with an NCE-based writing style in a NORTAV analysis, you might suspect that we would notate beats of DCE as DCE, beats of NCE as NCE, and beats of Narration as Narration. Almost, but not quite. In an NCE-based writing style, all beats of DCE are notated as Direct NCE. Why? Because as long as there is some recurring presence of a narrator within the prose, the reader will sense, even if only slightly, that all perceptions and activities are being rendered through a narrator. Thus, all DCE beats are perceived and notated as Direct DCE because, even though they do not contain a sense of the narrator, the narrator's presence lingers due to the existence of the surrounding NCE or Narration beats.

Note: Every unique NCE-based writing style will establish its own feel. Some styles will feel like the narrator is talking to the reader the entire time. Some styles will feel as if the narrator only pokes his head in every once in a while, just enough to keep the reader from falling into the focal character for too long. Some styles will fall somewhere in between. Again, when using an NCE-base writing style, the goal is to establish one particular feel and to keep that particular feel consistent.

Now that we know we can encounter multiple prose types in a single writing style, always read through a sample first to determine the writing styles and prose types in use when performing a NORTAV analysis. Once you know what prose types are in use and how the writer's style is operating (i.e. the narrative schema), go back and notate the individual beats accordingly.

> **A NORTAV Tip:**
> When performing a NORTAV analysis,
> always read through a sample first to
> determine the narrative schema in
> use. Then go back and notate
> the individual beats.

Sometimes it may take quite a few reads to determine the narrator, prose types, and how the prose types are being used. This is normal. Writing isn't easy, nor is performing a NORTAV analysis. The more you do each, however, the easier each becomes.

THE NCE-BASED WRITING STYLE AND THE ABSTRACT FOCAL CHARACTER

In an NCE-based writing style, you will never use an abstract focal character. An abstract focal character is used when you want to portray a scene with no sense of a narrator and no sense of a focal character, i.e. through a "fly on the wall." In an NCE-based writing style a narrator's presence is nearly always detectable. If you have a narrator and want to portray a scene to the reader in which there is no focal character, switch to a Narration-based writing style (using the same narrator, of course). What's the difference?

At first you might think the prose would look identical to that created through an abstract focal character within a DCE-based writing style, except that instead of notating everything as sight, sound, and smell Observation beats, you would notate everything as beats of Narration. While this can be true, when working with a Narration-based writing style a writer can add commentary, opinion, and conclusions to the prose because now there is an entity that can make them (i.e. the narrator). An abstract focal character cannot provide commentary, opinion, or conclusions; it is an invisible, un-commenting entity.

NORTAV ASSIGNMENT

Since NCE-based writing styles can be so varied, you will be performing four NORTAV analyses in this chapter in order to see how different professional writers work with different NCE-based writing styles. Take as much time as you need to work through each of these analyses. For the following NCE-based samples, I want you to notate any DCE *and* Direct NCE beats as [No], [Nr], [Nt], [Na], [Nv]; Mixed NCE beats as [Nm]; and Consolidated NCE beats as [Nc]. Notate any Narration beats as [N]. If you run across bits of information that are incidental, make a mental note of them or underline them if you wish. As always, you can add a numeric identifier to each beat for reference purposes. When it isn't intuitively obvious, document why you notated a beat as a certain type. When it isn't intuitively obvious, document the link between beats. You can do your work right in this book, or print/photocopy the sample and work with it separately. Compare your results with the NORTAV analyses I provide directly after each prose sample.

PROSE SAMPLE: Lawrence Block's *Keller in Dallas*

For the first part of this assignment we'll work with the prose of best-selling author Lawrence Block. Lawrence has been publishing fiction for over fifty years. Most famous for his Matthew Scudder private investigator series, his other novels include *A Drop of the Hard Stuff* and *Hit Man*, first in his John Keller mystery series. The following prose sample is taken from Lawrence's short story *Keller in Dallas*. You can find more information about Lawrence and his work at his website: http://lawrenceblock.wordpress.com/.

This NCE-based writing sample contains an omniscient narrator and a focal character, Keller.

> ... The young man, who would have looked owlish even without the round eyeglasses, unfolded a piece of paper and laid it on the counter in front of Keller. "The certificate

of expertization for Obock J1," he said. "Signed by Bloch and Mueller."

He might have been a Red Sox fan invoking Ted Williams, and Keller could understand why. Herbert Bloch and Edwin Mueller were legendary philatelists, and their assertion that this particular stamp was indeed a genuine copy of Obock's first postage due stamp, designated J1 in the Scott catalog, was enough to allay all doubt.

Keller examined the stamp, first with his unaided eye, then through the magnifier he took from his breast pocket. There was a photograph of the stamp on the certificate, and he studied that as well, with and without magnification. Bloch and Mueller had sworn to its legitimacy in 1960, so the certificate itself was almost half a century old, and might well be collectible in and of itself.

Still, even experts were sometimes careless, and occasionally mistaken. And now and then someone switched in a ringer for an expertized stamp. So Keller reached for another tool, this one in the inside pocket of his jacket. It was a flat metal oblong, designed to enable the user to compute the number of perforations per inch on the top or side of a stamp. Obock J1 was imperforate, which rendered the question moot, but the perforation gauge doubled as a mini-ruler, marked out in inches along one edge and millimeters along the other, and Keller used it to check the size of the stamp's overprint.

That overprint, handstamped on a postage due stamp initially issued for the French Colonies as a whole, had the name of the place—Obock—in black capitals. On the original stamp, the overprint measured 12-1/2 mm. by 3-3/4mm. On the reprint, a copy of which reposed in Keller's own collection, each dimension of the overprint was half a millimeter smaller.

And so Keller measured the overprint on this stamp, and found himself in agreement with Mr. Bloch and Mr. Mueller. This was the straight goods, the genuine article. All he had to do to go home with it was outbid any other interested collectors. And he could do that, too, and without straining his budget or dipping into his capital.

But first he'd have to kill somebody...

NORTAV ANALYSIS: Lawrence Block's *Keller in Dallas*

What follows is my NORTAV analysis of Lawrence's prose sample. As always, compare this to your analysis and note any differences.

[No1] The young man, who would have looked owlish even without the round eyeglasses, unfolded a piece of paper and laid it on the counter in front of Keller. "The certificate of expertization for Obock J1," he said. "Signed by Bloch and Mueller."

Lawrence opens with [No1], where an omniscient narrator is telling the reader about Keller's observation. If this sample were written in a DCE-based writing style, the reader might perceive this as Keller's direct observation with a bit of Keller's incidental thought tacked on ("who would have looked owlish even without the round eyeglasses"). This is not an incidental thought, however, as the context will show. Lawrence will soon establish a definitive NCE-based writing style, and thus we end up perceiving and notating beats accordingly.

As an opening line, the reader does not yet know what the narrative schema is, which is why the reader has to take in more context in order to discover the prose type, the narrator, the focal character, etc. As I've said, context is king. It is always easier to figure out the narrative schema first, and then try to break up the sample and notate its individual beats.

> [Nt2] He might have been a Red Sox fan invoking Ted Williams, and Keller could understand why. Herbert Bloch and Edwin Mueller were legendary philatelists, and their assertion that this particular stamp was indeed a genuine copy of Obock's first postage due stamp, designated J1 in the Scott catalog, was enough to allay all doubt.

[No1] triggers this Narrated Thought beat, [Nt2], through a stimulus/response link. (For simplicity, you can indicate logical links by notating that one beat "leads" to the next, and stimulus/response links by notating that one beat "triggers" the next.)

A NORTAV Tip:
In a NORTAV analysis, use "leads" to indicate a logical link and "triggers" to indicate a stimulus/response link.

Notice the narrative intrusion: "and Keller could understand why." Here the narrator is explaining Keller's thought to the reader. Still, even though these intrusions are relatively minor, the reader should start to feel the presence of a recurring narrator along with the focal character, and therefore start to get a sense of the NCE-based writing style.

> [Na3] Keller examined the stamp, first with his unaided eye, then through the magnifier he took from his breast pocket. [No4] There was a photograph of the stamp on the certificate, [Na5] and he studied that as well, with

and without magnification. [Nt6] Bloch and Mueller had sworn to its legitimacy in 1960, so the certificate itself was almost half a century old, and might well be collect- ible in and of itself.

[Nt2] leads to compound Narrated Action beat [Na3]. [Na3] then leads to [No4], which is a Narrated Observation beat with little sense of narrative intrusion. [No4] leads to [Na5], which is another Narrated Action beat. [Na5] triggers [Nt6], as the action here directly spawns the narrated thought.

[Nt7] Still, even experts were sometimes careless, and occasionally mistaken. And now and then someone switched in a ringer for an expertized stamp. [Na8] So Keller reached for another tool, this one in the inside pocket of his jacket. [No9] It was a flat metal oblong, [Nt10] designed to enable the user to compute the number of perforations per inch on the top or side of a stamp. Obock J1 was imperforate, which rendered the question moot, but the perforation gauge doubled as a mini-ruler, marked out in inches along one edge and mil- limeters along the other, and [Nc11] Keller used it to check the size of the stamp's overprint.

[Nt7] is a Narrated Thought beat that continues logically from [Nt6]. [Nt7] leads to [Na8]. Notice the subtle narrative intrusion here. The phrasing of the beat, using "So" and "this one" gives us the feel that the narrator is explaining Keller's action to us, rather than us experiencing it directly through Keller. Here we can see how even a single word or two can change DCE beats into Direct NCE.

[Na8] then leads to [No9], which triggers the Narrated Thought beat [Nt10], following the natural response sequence. One might notate the link between [Na8] and [No9] as a stimulus/response link. This is a matter of the reader's perception and preference. I usually consider the links between "acts of observing" beats, or beats that set up any type of observation, as being logical because they feel more "cause and effect" rather than "stimulus/response." [Nc11] follows logically from [Na8]. Here we get a beat of consolidated narrated perceptions and activities, as the reader perceives this beat as several different types of unmentioned perceptions and activities all happening at once. That is, Keller uses actions and thoughts and observations to check the size of the stamp's overprint. For me, it is here the NCE-based writing style is firmly established.

> [Nt12] That overprint, handstamped on a postage due stamp initially issued for the French Colonies as a whole, had the name of the place—Obock—in black capitals. On the original stamp, the overprint measured 12-1/2 mm. by 3-3/4mm. On the reprint, a copy of which reposed in Keller's own collection, each dimension of the overprint was half a millimeter smaller.

[Nc11] triggers [Nt12]. Note there is a lot of "observing" going on in this Narrated Thought beat. Like in DCE, beat substitution can also occur in NCE. So, the reader is getting the visual sense of the observation through a subsequent thought as Keller mulls over what he's just seen.

> [Na13] And so Keller measured the overprint on this stamp, and [Nt14] found himself in agreement with Mr. Bloch and Mr. Mueller. This was the straight goods, the genuine article. All he had to do to go home with it was outbid any other interested collectors. And he could do that, too, and without straining his budget or dipping into his capital.

[Na13] continues, or repeats, the action contained in the Consolidated NCE beat [Nc11]. You can see how this beat also helps to establish the narrative schema in use. The actual examination of the stamp happens in [Nc11]. In [Na13] the narrator is repeating himself as part of the storytelling style before continuing on to [Nt14]. This kind of repetition only works as a form of Narration and thus we explicitly experience the narrator's presence, hence the prose is NCE. Characters can't actually repeat the same event twice, unless they can travel back and forth in time!

In [Nt14] we have the narrator telling us what Keller was thinking after the examination of the stamp. We also start getting a sense that the narrator is passing through some of Keller's mannerisms, as the thoughts represented here appear very much as if they had come directly from Keller. Again, this is a stylistic choice Lawrence makes (many authors use this technique) in order to create more intimacy. That is, it gives the Narrated Thought beat more of a DCE feel.

> [Nt15] But first he'd have to kill somebody.

Finally, [Nt15] continues the train of thought from [Nt14].

PROSE SAMPLE: John Locke's *Follow the Stone*

Next we'll work with the prose of best-selling author John Locke. John was the first self-published author to hit the number one spot on Amazon/Kindle and has sold over a million ebooks. He is the creator of the Donovan Creed and Emmett Love series, which include the novels *Lethal People*, *A Girl Like You*, and *Saving Rachel*, amongst others. The following prose sample is taken from the Emmett Love novel *Follow the Stone*. You can find more information about John and his work at http://donovancreed.com/.

This NCE-based writing sample contains a character narrator and a focal character, both of whom are Emmett Love.

> ... I held the reins low while we walked, so Major could stretch his neck and toss his head if it pleased him. We'd done thirty miles over steep Ozark trails, and he was

gettin' pissed. He'd earned his sorghum hours ago and knew it. But I was determined to camp on the banks of the Gasconade, and we were eight miles shy.

I rubbed Major's neck. "Soon," I said.

He blew a loud snort, which I won't bother translatin'.

It was late September, 1860, and we were north of Devils Rock, Missouri, where the air's cool to the nostril this time of year, and scented with honeysuckle. A stand of short leaf pine lined the right side of the trail and ran deep as the eye could see. Limestone cliffs and mud bluffs dotted with pink dogwood towered above us on the left. A soft breeze pushed us eastward, mile after weary mile.

It was nearin' dusk when I saw the five small stones on the path.

I pulled back on the reins and slid off Major's back and tied him to a pine bough. He took the opportunity to chew what grass he could pull from the pine needles.

Shrug had arranged the stones as he always did, North, South, East and West, with the fifth stone pointin' in the direction he was headin'. I was annoyed [No] to see the fifth stone at the north-west point. Shrug knew I loved fishin' the Gasconade, and since he, too, had a passion for Nade perch, I was perplexed he would knowin'ly head the wrong way. But Shrug was the best scout in the territory, always had a reason for his actions, so I quietly cursed and climbed back on my horse and followed the stone.

Ten minutes into the ride we hit a clearin', where I found

a circle of stones that ringed a single footprint, the cause of our detour.

It was a woman's shoe print.

I was so stunned I nearly fell off my horse.

I looked around. It was so crazy uncommon to find a woman's shoe print in this part of the wilderness, I wondered if perhaps Shrug had played a trick on me. I climbed off Major's back and knelt down beside the shoe print and studied it carefully while thinkin' a talkin' horse, a tree that lays eggs, a flyin' pig—would make more sense. And yet...

It was real.

I looked around again, this time for a stone that'd show me where he went. There was none. I'm no skilled tracker, but I managed to follow the lady's shoe prints to the edge of the forest. I had no idea how old the prints were, but I figured 'em fresh, or Shrug wouldn't a' changed course. Maybe he'd find her and bring her back alive. More likely, he'd find evidence she'd been carried off by a pack of wolves or a bear...

NORTAV ANALYSIS: John Locke's *Follow the Stone*

What follows is my NORTAV analysis of John's prose sample. As always, compare this to your analysis and note any differences.

[Na1] I held the reins low while we walked, [Nt2] so Major could stretch his neck and toss his head if it pleased him. We'd done thirty miles over steep Ozark trails, and he was gettin' pissed. He'd earned his sorghum hours ago and knew it. But I was determined to camp on the banks of the Gasconade, and we were eight miles shy.

John begins with [Na1], a Narrated Action beat, where Emmett Love tells us about an action that he performed at the time the story was taking place. It leads to the Narrated Thought beat [Nt2]. Here we are told what Emmett was thinking at the time. The two beats are connected with the conjunction "so," which begins to give us a sense of the narrator's presence. In DCE we might simply get these beats separately, in the order in which the focal character experienced them. With the use of "so," we are getting the second beat not as a sequential perception but rather as an explanation of why the first beat occurred. We saw this in Lawrence's sample as well. Subtle? Perhaps, but at this point you should to be able to read and analyze prose at this level of detail.

[Na3] I rubbed Major's neck. [Nv4] "Soon," I said.

Here we have Narrated Action beat [Na3] leading to Narrated Vocalization beat [Nv4].

[No5] He blew a loud snort, which I won't bother translatin'.

[Nv4] leads to [No5], a Narrated Observation beat. In [No5] we have Emmett the narrator addressing the reader directly with the phrase "which I won't bother translatin'." First, the direct narrative intrusion here firmly establishes the fact they we are dealing with an NCE-based writing style. Second, notice how John keeps Emmett's dialect the same in the narrative intrusion as in his perceptions and activities. This is the same technique Twain used in the Huck Finn sample back in Chapter 4.

[No6] It was late September, 1860, and we were north of Devils Rock, Missouri, where the air's cool to the nostril this time of year, and scented with honeysuckle. A stand of short leaf pine lined the right side of the trail and ran deep as the eye could see. Limestone cliffs and mud bluffs dotted with pink dogwood towered above us on the left. [Nc7] A soft breeze pushed us eastward, mile after weary mile.

Next, [No5] leads to another Narrated Observation beat, [No6]. Notice the start of this beat. Here we enter an ambiguous area between NCE and Narration. Is the narrator telling us about something that is not a focal character perception and activity, or is this all part of the narrated observation, where the narrator is describing the setting (including the thought of the date) as it was observed by Emmett? In other words, is Emmett the narrator giving us the date, or is Emmett the character thinking about the date, consciously or semi-consciously, as he takes in the setting? As John has established an NCE-based writing style that is somewhat intimate, we notate the ambiguous beat as NCE because that is how we are conditioned to perceive it. That is, we've become used to experiencing things more through the focal character than through the narrator.

[No6] then leads to a beat of Consolidated NCE, [Nc7], which includes impressions of an action and an observation, along with some narrative summary.

[No8] It was nearin' dusk when I saw the five small stones on the path.

Here Narrated Observation beat [No8] logically follows [No7].

[Na9] I pulled back on the reins and slid off Major's back and tied him to a pine bough. [No10] He took the opportunity to chew what grass he could pull from the pine needles.

Next, [No8] leads to Narrated Action beat [Na9], which in turn leads to Narrated Observation beat [No10].

[Nt11] Shrug had arranged the stones as he always did, North, South, East and West, with the fifth stone pointin' in the direction he was headin'. [Nm12] I was annoyed to see the fifth stone at the north-west point. [Nt13] Shrug knew I loved fishin' the Gasconade, and since he, too, had a passion for Nade perch, I was perplexed he would knowin'ly head the wrong way. But Shrug was the best scout in the territory, always had a reason for his ac-tions, [Nv14] so I quietly cursed and [Na15] climbed back on my horse and followed the stone.

[No10] leads to [Nt11], a Narrated Thought beat. This beat uses some beat substitution, as it is Emmett's thoughts continuing to provide the reader with a description of what he saw back in [No8]. This beat triggers a response in [Nm12], which is a beat of Mixed NCE (a reac-tion, a narrative tag, and an observation), and [Nt13], a Narrated Thought beat. [Nt11] also ultimately triggers the Narrated Vocalization beat [Nv14] and the Narrated Action beat [Na15]. This sequence of beats roughly follows the natural response sequence. Remember, NCE beats don't have to follow the natural response sequence as closely as DCE, for in NCE a narrator is "telling" us of the events. We are not technically experiencing these events in the exact order as they happened, moment to moment, as we would in pure DCE-based writing style.

[Nc16] Ten minutes into the ride we hit a clearin', [Nm17] where I found a circle of stones that ringed a single footprint, the cause of our detour.

[Nc16] logically follows [Na15]. This is a beat of Consolidated NCE. We get the sense that it is an action and perhaps an observation, but they have been rolled up to a higher level concept. If you noted this beat as a Narrated Action beat, that would also be fine. [Nc16] leads to [Nm17], a beat of Mixed NCE. Here [Nm17] includes explicit elements of observation and thought and perhaps narrative information, but they are merged in a way that makes it difficult to notate separately.

[Nt18] It was a woman's shoe print.

Here the narrator is giving us Emmett's realization in the Narrated Thought beat [Nt18].

> [Nr19] I was so stunned I nearly fell off my horse.

[Nt18] triggers the Narrated Reaction beat [Nr19].

> [Na20] I looked around. [Nt21] It was so crazy uncommon to find a woman's shoe print in this part of the wilderness, I wondered if perhaps Shrug had played a trick on me. [Na22] I climbed off Major's back and knelt down beside the shoe print and studied it carefully [Nt23] while thinkin' a talkin' horse, a tree that lays eggs, a flyin' pig—would make more sense. And yet...
>
> It was real.

[Nt18] also triggers [Na20], a Narrated Action beat. Next we have [Nt21]. This Narrated Thought beat could be logically linked back to [Na20], or it could have been triggered by [Nt18] and narrated slightly out of order. For our purposes here, it really doesn't matter which way you notate it. Either works. Go with how you perceive it. Next comes Narrated Action beat [Na22] and Narrated Thought beat [Nt23]. These both come in logical sequence, one after the other.

> [Na25] I looked around again, [Nt26] this time for a stone that'd show me where he went. [No27] There was none. [Nt28] I'm no skilled tracker, but [Na29] I managed to follow the lady's shoe prints to the edge of the forest. [Nt30] I had no idea how old the prints were, but I figured 'em fresh, or Shrug wouldn't a' changed course. Maybe he'd find her and bring her back alive. More likely, he'd find evidence she'd been carried off by a pack of wolves or a bear.

Here we have a series of quick beats, one leading to the next. The previous beat [Nt23] leads to Narrated Action beat [Na25]. [Na25] leads to Narrated Observation beat [No27], followed by [Nt28], [Na29], and [Nt30]. This is all straight forward NCE-based writing.

When we look at the overall NCE style John uses in this sample, we get the sense that his tendency is to work with an intimate style of writing. Meaning, he mixes a lot of DCE with some NCE to create an experience that is less intimate then pure DCE-based writing, but more intimate than most NCE-based writing styles. Very different than Lawrence's sample, which was less intimate, as it used much less DCE (if any). In both cases, however, the writers keep their particular styles consistent.

PROSE SAMPLE: Barry Eisler's *Paris is a Bitch*

Now let's move on to the prose of best-selling author Barry Eisler. Barry's thrillers have won the Gumshoe Award and the Barry Award and have been included on many "Best Of" lists over the years. He is the creator of the John Rain series, which includes the novels *Rain Fall*, *Killing Rain*, *The Detachment*, and several others. The following prose sample is taken from Barry's John Rain short story *Paris is a Bitch*. You can find more information about Barry and his work at his website: http://www.barryeisler.com/.

This NCE-based writing sample contains a character narrator and a focal character, both of whom are John Rain.

… And now, satisfied that I had a way out if I needed one, I sat in the back of the restaurant on one of the old wooden chairs, enjoying the sounds of French and German and English, all pleasantly scrambled by the close walls and the dark, beamed ceiling; enveloped by the smells of bœuf à la bourguignonne and soupe à l'oignon and petites bouchées d'escargots sauce roquefort; and savoring the sight of the beautiful, deceptively elegant blonde across from me, who, if we could find a way past our professional tensions and make common cause of something better, I thought might actually be the best thing that had ever happened to me.

Delilah smiled and asked me in French, "What are you thinking?"

She was wearing a simple, cream-colored silk wrap dress with tasteful but still tantalizing décolletage, and the candle on the table between us was casting distracting shadows. I let my eyes linger where they wanted to linger, then smiled lasciviously and said, "About what I might want for dessert."

She smiled back. "Well, for that, you have to see the menu."

"I'll have to take my time with that. If it all looks good enough, I might even order more than one."

She raised an eyebrow. "You think you can handle that much?"

I looked into her blue eyes. "I don't know. I'll have to taste it and see."

She gave me a challenging look, the kind that would make weak men wilt and strong men wild. "Then come back to my apartment. We'll see if your eyes are bigger than your stomach. But..."

"Yes?"

"You can't stay tonight. I have to leave early tomorrow."

"Where are you going?" I said, immediately irritated at

myself for asking a question to which I already knew the answer. Or rather, the response.

"John. Why do you ask me that? You know I can't tell you."

"How long will you be gone?"

"And I can't tell you that, either. As you know."

I felt a stupid petulance taking hold of me and tried, without much success, to shrug it off. I shouldn't have pressed, but I said, "A day? A month? How long this time?"

She sighed. "Longer than a day, less than a month. I think."

I looked away, nodding. "You think."

An American in an expensive blazer and with perfectly groomed three-day facial stubble was blathering into his mobile phone at the table next to us. I hadn't noticed until just then, having been focused more on whether Delilah and I were speaking quietly enough not to be overheard than with whether anyone else was talking too loudly. I looked over, and his girlfriend touched his arm to let him know his phone monologue was annoying someone. He glanced at me but didn't change his volume. My irritation with Delilah was looking for an outlet, and I considered snatching the phone out of his hand, breaking it in two, shoving one half down his throat...

NORTAV ANALYSIS: Barry Eisler's _Paris is a Bitch_

What follows is my NORTAV analysis of Barry's prose sample. As always, compare this to your analysis and note any differences.

[Nt1] And now, satisfied that I had a way out if I needed one, [Na2] I sat in the back of the restaurant on one of the old wooden chairs, [Nm3] enjoying the sounds of French and German and English, all pleasantly scrambled by the close walls and the dark, beamed ceiling; enveloped by the smells of bœuf à la bourguignonne and soupe à l'oignon and petites bouchées d'escargots sauce roquefort; and savoring the sight of the beautiful, deceptively elegant blonde across from me, [Nt4] who, if we could find a way past our professional tensions and make common cause of something better, I thought might actually be the best thing that had ever happened to me.

Barry starts with a Narrated Thought beat, [Nt1]. This leads to [Na2], a Narrated Action beat, which leads to [Nm3], a beat of Mixed NCE. In [Nm3] we get a mix of explicit reactions ("pleasantly," "savoring") and observations. The observation of the elegant blonde in [Nm3] triggers the Narrated Thought beat [Nt4]. In this short section, Barry has immediately set up an NCE-based writing style that reveals the narrator's presence in nearly every beat along with a focal character's individual perceptions and activities. Thus we get a sense that Barry's particular NCE-based writing style will probably fall somewhere in the middle of the intimacy scale.

[No5] Delilah smiled and asked me in French, "What are you thinking?"

Here [No5] is a typical initiating Narrated Observation beat.

[No6] She was wearing a simple, cream-colored silk wrap dress with tasteful but still tantalizing décolletage, and the candle on the table between us was casting distracting shadows. [Na7] I let my eyes linger where they wanted to linger, then smiled lasciviously and [Nv8] said, "About what I might want for dessert."

[No6] logically follows [No5]. It triggers [Na7] and [Nv8], which follow the natural response sequence. Notice the way [No6] and [Na7] are phrased. They, like the previous beats, have a subtle sense of narrative intrusion. Small little comments like "tasteful but still tantalizing" and "where they wanted to linger" give the reader the sense that the narrator (John Rain at the time he's telling the story) is commenting on the perceptions and activities that he (John Rain at the time the story was taking place) was experiencing.

> [No9] She smiled back. "Well, for that, you have to see the menu."
>
> [Nv10] "I'll have to take my time with that. If it all looks good enough, I might even order more than one."
>
> [No11] She raised an eyebrow. "You think you can handle that much?"
>
> [Na12] I looked into her blue eyes. [Nv13] "I don't know. I'll have to taste it and see."

Here we have a typical section of dialogue, rendered through the exchange of Narrated Vocalization and Narrated Observation beats (with a Narrated Action beat thrown in to keep things from getting monotonous). Notice each of these beats could stand as DCE. This is a pretty common technique. Often when authors portray conversations between characters, the prose is rendered in DCE, regardless of the intimacy of the NCE-based writing style in use.

> [Nm14] She gave me a challenging look, the kind that would make weak men wilt and strong men wild. [No15] "Then come back to my apartment. We'll see if your eyes are bigger than your stomach. But…"

[Nm14] is a beat of Mixed NCE that leads to [No15], a Narrated Observation beat. Note [Nm14]. Here we have an observation and a thought mixed together. Because of the way the observation and thought are phrased, I perceived this as a single beat of Mixed NCE. You might very well have notated these as separate beats.

[Nv16] "Yes?"

[No17] "You can't stay tonight. I have to leave early tomorrow."

[Nv18] "Where are you going?" I said, [Nm19] immediately irritated at myself for asking a question to which I already knew the answer. Or rather, the response.

[No20] "John. Why do you ask me that? You know I can't tell you."

[Nv21] "How long will you be gone?"

[No22] "And I can't tell you that, either. As you know."

[Nm23] I felt a stupid petulance taking hold of me and tried, without much success, to shrug it off. [Nt24] I shouldn't have pressed, but I said, [Nv25] "A day? A month? How long this time?"

[No26] She sighed. "Longer than a day, less than a month. I think."

Here we continue the dialogue with the exchange of Narrated Vocalization and Narrated Observation beats. Notice Barry consistently breaks up the Narrated Vocalization and Narrated Observation beats with short Narrated Thought beats and beats of Mixed NCE to help maintain a consistent writing style and to keep the dialogue exchange from getting monotonous.

[No29] An American in an expensive blazer and with perfectly groomed three-day facial stubble was blathering into his mobile phone at the table next to us. [Nt30] I hadn't noticed until just then, having been focused more on whether Delilah and I were speaking quietly enough not to be overheard than with whether anyone else was talking too loudly. [Na31] I looked over, [No32] and his girlfriend touched his arm to let him know his phone monologue was annoying someone. He glanced at me but didn't change his volume. [Nm33] My irritation with Delilah was looking for an outlet, and I considered snatching the phone out of his hand, breaking it in two, shoving one half down his throat...

Finally, [No29] is an initiating Narrated Observation beat. It triggers [Nt30] and [Na31]. [Na31], an "act of observing" Narrated Action beat, leads to [No32], which triggers [Nm33].

You should be getting the sense that notating NCE-based writing is not quite as easy as notating Narration- or DCE-based writing. There are many ways an author can create Direct, Mixed, and Consolidated NCE, and there are many ways to mix beats of Narration and DCE with NCE. What you are trying to do here is get the overall impression of how the writer is creating his or her particular writing style, how he or she is keeping it consistent, and how he or she is achieving certain effects.

And just as these prose samples were created from the writer's gut, your analyses will also originate somewhat from the gut. Let yourself feel how you perceive a particular work, determine the narrative schema, and notate accordingly. Even if your analyses don't match up precisely to mine, you should still find that each sample has an under-lying structure of basic beats (N, O, R, T, A, V), regardless of whether those beats are notated as DCE, NCE, or Narration.

PROSE SAMPLE: Michael Stackpole's *In Hero Years... I'm Dead*

For the last part of this assignment we'll work with the prose of best-selling author Michael Stackpole. Michael has been publishing fiction since 1994 and has had eight novels hit the New York Times best-seller list, including *Wedge's Gamble*, *Bacta War*, and *Isard's Revenge*. He is also the author of the Age of Discovery series and the novel *Conan the Barbarian*, based on the screenplay of the 2011 movie. The following prose sample is taken from Michael's superhero noir novel *In Hero Years... I'm Dead*. You can find more information about Michael and his work at `http://www.stormwolf.com/`.

This NCE-based writing sample contains a character narrator and a focal character, both of whom are "Mr. Smith."

> ...Why did I think the bank manager was a super-villain? He didn't particularly look like one. Then again, he wouldn't have been much of a super-villain if he had.

> Maybe it was his nervousness. He covered it, but he was trying too hard. I couldn't dial in just what he had to be nervous about.

> Then it dawned on me.

> Me.

> The cheap suit they'd given me hadn't stood up well against thirty-six hours of planes and airports. Neither had I. I wasn't quite coming apart at the seams like the suit, but my eyes burned. I was also drifting in and out— those little one second blank stares make most folks wary.

> Had I been him, with me standing there, I'd have speed-dialed Security and had them coming at a run.

> Then again, I might have been reading things completely wrong. I hadn't spoken to a bank manager in about two decades. I couldn't imagine they'd changed much over

time–machines need the same sort of cogs year in, year out. The last one I'd dealt with was probably the bank's chairman of the board.

My exhausted brain skipped back a step. I wondered what the manager had for a superpower. I looked for clues: the way he looked up from his desk, the quick smile, the casual tug at his cuff as he stood to offer me his hand; none of these were very helpful. I thought for a moment I'd lost it, then his powers came together with a name.

The Ingratiator.

He'd overplayed it with the smile. He'd added a hint of welcome surprise, but his office had a glass wall over-looking the bank's lobby. He couldn't have missed Invisible Lad coming for a visit, much less my approach. He probably figured me for Rumpled Man–able to wrinkle perma-press slacks in a single sit.

In his world, that would make me the villain.

Unaccustomed to his courtesy and temporarily mesmer-ized by it, I stared at his proffered hand. Too neat. Per-fect manicure. No scars. He wasn't a super-anything.

Check that. He could have been a mentalist. That smile, his manner; he definitely could have been a mind-reaper. I could see him in a hostage situation. He con-vinces the perps that all will be well; and will go better if they surrender. He'd never have to lay a glove on them.

I'd always had a problem with mentalists. Wasn't a day went by I didn't feel crowded in my own head. I really didn't need squatters.

The Ingratiator remained frozen with his hand out—waiting, wondering. His distress snapped me back into reality. Be good. I shook his hand heartily. No crushing on his part, just a firm grip, like he was pulling me from a collapsed skyscraper.

His smile brightened. He liked having folks see him as a savior.

"So pleased to finally meet you, Mister Smith." His smile hit the megawatt range. "Please be seated. May I get you coffee, tea, juice, water?"...

NORTAV ANALYSIS: Michael A. Stackpole's *In Hero Years... I'm Dead*

What follows is my NORTAV analysis of Michael's prose sample. Compare this to your analysis and note any differences.

{No1}[Nt2] Why did I think the bank manager was a super-villain? He didn't particularly look like one. Then again, he wouldn't have been much of a super-villain if he had.

Maybe it was his nervousness. He covered it, but he was trying too hard. I couldn't dial in just what he had to be nervous about.

Then it dawned on me.

Me.

Here we are immediately faced with an NCE-based writing style quite different than the previous ones we've seen. Michael opens with an implied Narrated Observation beat, {No1}, and a compound Narrated Thought beat [Nt2]. What's different here is that much of this Narrated

Thought beat is being used as a substitute for the implied Narrated Observation beat. And notice the way the beat is rendered. It's portrayed such that we get a sense that this is the character narrator, "Mr. Smith," telling us about his thoughts at the time the story took place. Thus, we are dealing with a beat of NCE. Interestingly, this particular use of an NCE beat and beat substitution gives us quite a distant feel, even though the beats are all DCE and Direct NCE.

> {No3}[Nt4] The cheap suit they'd given me hadn't stood up well against thirty-six hours of planes and airports. Neither had I. I wasn't quite coming apart at the seams like the suit, but my eyes burned. I was also drifting in and out—those little one second blank stares make most folks wary.
>
> Had I been him, with me standing there, I'd have speed-dialed Security and had them coming at a run.

[Nt2] leads to {No3} which leads to [Nt4], where we get more of the same beat substitution technique, except this time the narrator has switched the focus of the implied observation from the bank manager to himself. This is, again, the narrator "Mr. Smith" telling us about his thoughts at the time of the story, as he contemplated his own appearance and state of mind.

> [Nt5] Then again, I might have been reading things completely wrong. I hadn't spoken to a bank manager in about two decades. I couldn't imagine they'd changed much over time—machines need the same sort of cogs year in, year out. The last one I'd dealt with was probably the bank's chairman of the board.
>
> [Nt6] My exhausted brain skipped back a step. I wondered what the manager had for a superpower. [Na7] I looked for clues: {No8} [Nt9] the way he looked up from his desk, the quick smile, the casual tug at his cuff as he

stood to offer me his hand; none of these were very helpful. [Nt10] I thought for a moment I'd lost it, then his powers came together with a name.

The Ingratiator.

[Nt4] leads to [Nt5] where we get a more typical use of a Narrated Thought beat. [Nt5] leads to [Nt6], which leads to "act of observing" Narrated Action beat [Na7]. This leads to implied Narrated Observation beat {No8}, which leads to [Nt9], where we return to beat substitution. Here "Mr. Smith" starts analyzing what was observed in the implied Narrated Observation beat {No8}. Then [Nt9] leads us to another typical Narrated Thought beat, [Nt10].

[Nt11] He'd overplayed it with the smile. He'd added a hint of welcome surprise, but his office had a glass wall overlooking the bank's lobby. He couldn't have missed Invisible Lad coming for a visit, much less my approach. He probably figured me for Rumpled Man—able to wrinkle perma-press slacks in a single sit.

In his world, that would make me the villain.

Here [Nt10] leads to [Nt11], another Narrated Thought beat laden with beat substitution.

[Na12] Unaccustomed to his courtesy and temporarily mesmerized by it, I stared at his proffered hand. {No13} [Nt14] Too neat. Perfect manicure. No scars. He wasn't a super-anything.

[Nt11] then leads to [Na12], which is the first beat that ventures out of "Mr. Smith's" internal thoughts, though not much, as it is an internal action (an "act of observing"). [Na12] leads to implied Narrated Observation beat {No13} which triggers [Nt14], where "Mr. Smith" mulls over the implied beat.

[Nt15] Check that. He could have been a mentalist. That smile, his manner; he definitely could have been a mind-reaper. I could see him in a hostage situation. He convinces the perps that all will be well; and will go better if they surrender. He'd never have to lay a glove on them.

I'd always had a problem with mentalists. Wasn't a day went by I didn't feel crowded in my own head. I really didn't need squatters.

Here [Nt14] leads to [Nt15], another Narrated Thought beat with slight elements of beat substitution continued from [Nt14].

[No16] The Ingratiator remained frozen with his hand out—waiting, wondering. [Nt17] His distress snapped me back into reality. Be good. [Na18] I shook his hand heartily. {No19} [Nt20] No crushing on his part, just a firm grip, like he was pulling me from a collapsed skyscraper.

[Nt15] leads to [No16], our first un-implied Narrated Observation beat, which triggers [Nt17]. Notice what happens in this Narrated Thought beat. "Mr. Smith" has snapped back to reality. Meaning, the previous beats were "Mr. Smith" lost in thought. Michael portrays that "lost in thought" sensation expertly by keeping the reader entrenched within the focal character's mind with the use of implied Narrated Observation beats. We don't get any externally experienced beat until [No16] triggers [Na18]. And then we return to an implied Narrated Observation beat, followed by [Nt20], another Narrated Thought beat filled with beat substitution.

[No21] His smile brightened. [Nt22] He liked having folks see him as a savior.

[No23] "So pleased to finally meet you, Mister Smith." {No24} [Nt25] His smile hit the megawatt range. [No26]

"Please be seated. May I get you coffee, tea, juice, water?"

Finally, [Nt20] leads to [No21], where we get another typical Narrated Observation beat. This triggers [Nt22]. [No23] is an initiating Narrated Observation beat that leads to an implied beat and a triggered Narrated Thought beat [Nt25]. Again, here's another situation where an implied observation is substituted into a Narrated Thought beat. We end with [No26], another initiating Narrated Observation beat.

From analyzing the prose of just these four authors, we can see how there can be many different techniques for creating an NCE-based writing style. Here Michael uses no Narration beats and few, if any, Mixed or Consolidated NCE beats. You might suspect this would place his style somewhere in the middle range of intimacy, but by adding the technique of beat substitution in large quantities, Michael creates a more distant style than any of the other examples. And, of course, Michael uses his style consistently.

WRITING EXERCISE

For this exercise I want you to go back to your 50 DCE prose samples. Make a working copy to use for this exercise. In the working copy, create an NCE-based version of each of the 50 samples. Do this by mixing Narration into the existing DCE beats, or by merging the existing DCE beats together to form Mixed NCE beats, or by rolling up the existing DCE beats into Consolidated NCE beats. Change the phrasings or the order of the DCE beats to create NCE beats. Leave some beats as DCE if you wish. Add beats of Narration. Alternate and/or combine approaches. If you find that you simply can't come up with an appropriate NCE version of a beat, feel free to modify the beat or the prose chain if that helps.

Again, I will do two and notate them for clarity as an example:

(1)   DCE version:

[T1 (stimulus)] She was going to be late. [R2] A soft groan escaped her lips. [T3] Another interview blown! That was two in one week. [A4] She kicked off the covers.

[V5] "Damn it all to hell."

NCE version:

[Nm1] A groan escaped her lips when she realized she was going to be late. [Nt2] Another interview blown, and that was two in one week! [Na3] She kicked off the covers [Nv4] and cursed softly.

In the NCE-based version, I combined [T1] and [R2], added a narrative tag, and reversed the natural response sequence order to form [Nm1]. I combined the sentences in [T3] to form [Nt2], which would remain DCE. [A4] remained the same to form [Na4]. Remember, all DCE beats are notated as NCE in an NCE-based writing style. [V5] is rendered through a narrator (i.e. told) instead of experienced directly, to form [Nv4].

(2) DCE version:

[V1] "Shut up!" I shouted,

[R2] I slap a hand over my mouth. [T3] I have never blown up at anyone like this before, especially not a fellow teacher. [A4] I drop my hand back in my lap and pretend to smooth the wrinkles from my skirt.

[V5] "Melanie, I'm sorry. I shouldn't have said that."

NCE version:

[Nv1] I blow up at Melanie, and [Nc2] spend the next few seconds in a mixed state of shock, disbelief, and feigned avoidance. [Nc3] Finally, I work out a sullen apology, which sounds insincere even to my ears.

In the NCE-based version, [V1] is rendered through a narrator (i.e. told) instead of experienced directly, to form [Nv1]. The rest of the beats are consolidated together to form [Nc2] and [Nc3].

LET'S RECAP

By now you should understand that:

- Narrated Character Experience, or NCE, is one of three types of prose that a writer can use.

- NCE portrays the perceptions and activities of a focal character to the reader through a narrator.

- There are three categories of NCE beats: Direct NCE, Mixed NCE, and Consolidated NCE.

- Direct NCE are beats that represent an individual narrated character perception or activity. There are five types of Direct NCE beats: Narrated Observations, Narrated Reactions, Narrated Thoughts, Narrated Actions, and Narrated Vocalizations.

- Mixed NCE represents a mix of two or more narrated character perceptions or activities that cannot easily be broken into individual beats. There is only one type of beat, called a Mixed NCE beat.

- Consolidated NCE represents an abstraction or roll-up of two or more narrated character perceptions or activities, such that the individual perceptions or activities are sensed by the reader but not explicitly revealed in the prose. There is only one type of beat, called a Consolidated NCE beat.

- When performing a NORTAV analysis, always read the entire sample first to determine the narrative schema in use, then go back and notate individual beats accordingly.

- An NCE-based writing style can combine beats of DCE and/or Narration with the three categories of NCE beats to create many different styles whose intimacy falls somewhere between pure DCE-based and pure Narration-based styles.

We will build on the concepts I've just covered here. Make sure you understand everything in Chapter 5 before moving on to Chapter 6.

Remember: the NORTAV Method is not a silver bullet or a magic formula for crafting prose. It is a critical body of knowledge that every professional writer should understand. Your goal in this book is to learn that body of knowledge and apply it to your own unique writing process *in whatever way comes natural to you.*

Now let's move on to Chapter 6, where we will cover the Narrative Schema.

Chapter 6

THE NARRATIVE SCHEMA

Discovering the Narrative Schema

WHERE ARE WE IN THE BIG PICTURE?

Now that you understand what prose is and how it functions, and how the three types of prose are constructed, we will move on to the last part of learning how to construct a unit of rough prose: The Narrative Schema.

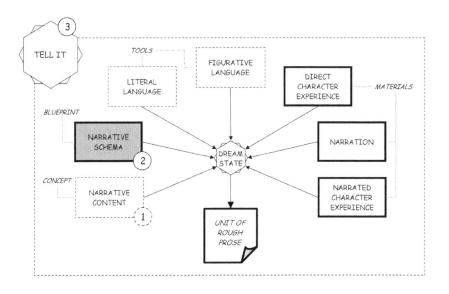

The Narrative Schema

THE NARRATIVE SCHEMA

What is a narrative schema?

We've talked generally about narrative schemas and writing styles from the start of this book. We know that a *narrative schema* is the narrative blueprint for creating a work of fiction. It describes one or more unique styles of writing based upon a specific use of narrators, narrative intrusion, points of view, narrative tense, prose types, and other storytelling factors, and the pattern for using those styles throughout the work of fiction. Each of these unique styles of writing is called a *narrative mode.*

> A ***Narrative Schema*** is a description of the narrative mode or modes in a work of fiction and the pattern of their use.

> A ***Narrative Mode*** is a specific set of narrative factors that describe one unique style of writing, or one unique way of creating and perceiving prose.

Thus, the narrative schema is made up of two parts. The first part defines the narrative mode or modes (unique writing styles) in use. The second part defines the pattern for using the narrative mode or modes across a work of fiction.

We know that a writer will work purposefully in one narrative mode at a time. We know that a narrative mode will set up a certain level of intimacy between the reader and the focal character. And we know that the reader will sense any change to the established narrative mode, so a writer must only change modes with intent. Indiscriminate changes in the narrative mode (by not using a mode consistently, for example) will cause the prose to become narratively confusing, amateurish, and difficult to read.

So how do we establish a narrative mode?

A narrative mode is a specific set of narrative factors that describe one unique writing style, or one unique way of creating and perceiving prose. There are six narrative factors a writer needs to consider and determine in order to establish a complete narrative mode. Each factor will impact the way prose is created by the writer and perceived by the reader, and a deviation or change in any factor could cause the reader to sense the narrative mode has changed.

The six factors of a narrative mode are:

(1) *Who is the narrator?*

A narrator is either omniscient, and therefore an all-knowing, god-like entity that can portray any aspect of the story world, story events, and story characters to the reader, or the narrator is a character narrator, in which case the character narrator can only reveal what he/she knows or knew about the story to the reader.

(2) *Will the narrator's presence be revealed to the reader?*

Here the writer must decide if the chosen narrator will reveal his or her presence to the reader. In other words, will the narrator's presence at the time the story is being told be evident to the reader, irrespective of the narrator's presence at the time of the actual story.

(3) *Who is the focal character?*

Here the writer decides if the narrative mode has a focal character and who that focal character will be. In other words, which character, if any, will have his or her perceptions and activities revealed by the narrator? (Note: Some modes can have more than one focal character.)

(4) *What prose type(s) and/or beat type(s) will be used?*

Here the writer decides which of the three prose types will be used in the narrative mode. The choice here is dependent on the previous factors. If the narrator will not be revealed, the only choice is DCE (thus establishing a DCE-based narrative mode). If the narrator will be revealed and there is a focal character, the choice is NCE, with or without DCE and Narration (establishing an NCE-based narrative mode). If there is no focal character (abstract or not), the only choice is Narration (establishing a Narration-based narrative mode). Additionally, this factor can also describe the ratio of the particular beats in use within the narrative mode.

(5) *What will be the narrative tense?*

Here the writer determines the tense used in the narrative mode.

(6) *What are the additional constraints?*

This factor is wide open to the writer and is where a writer can really get creative with her narrative modes. For instance, here she can choose to further limit in any respect the scope of knowledge revealed by a narrator. She can choose one or more specific and exclusive ways the narrator's presence might be revealed to the reader. She can restrict or tailor the use of a prose type or a beat. For instance, she may decide to not allow any ambiguous or non-conforming beats, or she may decide not to use any physical Reaction beats from a prose type. Anything goes here, and the writer is limited only by her imagination.

EXAMPLES OF NARRATIVE MODES

Now let's look at some examples of narrative modes. First, here is a list of the six narrative factors (we will call this list a template, even though you wingers out there will hate that term) that can be used to define a narrative mode at the start of every NORTAV analysis:

Narrator: *Identify the omniscient or character narrator.*

Narrative Intrusion: *Yes/No*

Focal Character(s): *Identify the focal character(s) if present.*

Prose Type(s) and/or Beat Types(s): *List the prose type(s)/beat(s) used and if possible the ratio of their use.*

Narrative Tense: *Past/Present/etc.*

Additional Constraints: *Describe any constraints, limits, or specific tailoring of any of above factors.*

Using this template, let's establish a specific narrative mode that we can use to tell a story (or portion of a story) about a character named Ben. For this example, the specific narrative mode should result in prose that conforms to the old "third-person omniscient point of view."

One way could be:

Narrator: *Omniscient*

Narrative Intrusion: *Yes*

Focal Character(s): *Ben*

Prose Type(s) and/or Beat Types(s): *NCE*

Narrative Tense: *Present*

Additional Constraints: *None*

In this NCE-based narrative mode, Ben's perceptions and activities would be portrayed in the present tense, with the presence of the narrator continuously detectable, using only beats of NCE.

Here's another example:

Narrator: *Omniscient*

Narrative Intrusion: *No*

Focal Character(s): *Ben*

Prose Type(s) and/or Beat Types(s): *DCE*

Narrative Tense: *Past*

Additional Constraints: *All dialogue tags to be embedded in Observation beats. No Reaction or Thought beats used.*

In this DCE-based narrative mode, Ben's perceptions and activities would be portrayed in the past tense, with no presence of the narrator detectable, with no Reaction or Thought beats used, and with any dialogue tags embedded into Ben's Observation beats.

Here's another example:

Narrator: *Omniscient*

Narrative Intrusion: *Yes*

Focal Character(s): *None*

Prose Type(s) and/or Beat Types(s): *Narration*

Narrative Tense: *Past*

Additional Constraints: *None*

In this Narration-based narrative mode we would get none of Ben's perceptions and activities. Rather, information about Ben would be portrayed in the past tense, with the presence of the narrator detectable throughout.

Examine each of these narrative modes carefully. Can you envision how you would construct prose using each one? Can you envision how you would perceive prose that was constructed from each one? Try creating a short sample of prose that conforms to each of these narrative modes. Can you see how drastically different the prose is for each? And yet all three samples would be considered "third-person omniscient point of view." By now you should fully understand why the old "point of view" labels are of little-to-no use to writers when trying to learn how to construct prose.

For practice, try creating different narrative modes that conform to some of the other old labels. Try first-person point of view. Try fly-on-the-wall (we did one of these already, remember?). Try third-person limited point of view. Try creating a few narrative modes that do not conform to any of the old labels.

We could create hundreds upon hundreds of unique narrative modes. I don't think we could ever create hundreds upon hundreds of unique old-style labels to uniquely describe each and every one.

THE NARRATIVE PATTERN

Often a writer will use one narrative mode throughout an entire work of fiction. There are many times, however, when a writer will use multiple narrative modes to portray a complete work of fiction. A story portrayed through the perspectives of several focal characters will use at least one narrative mode per focal character, as changing the focal character will usually change the narrative mode. A frame narrative, using another old term, will most likely use at least two different narrative modes, one for the outer story and one for the inner story.

If you've been keeping up so far, you can probably guess where this is heading. Old terms that deal with patterns like "frame narrative" are also inadequate. There are an infinite number of ways to assemble and use narrative modes in a work of fiction. If we can't define the use of narrative modes in a single work of fiction with old style labels like "frame narrative," what do we use?

> A **Narrative Pattern** describes how a narrative mode or modes are used throughout a work of fiction.

We use a narrative pattern. The *narrative pattern* is the second part of a narrative schema. It describes how a narrative mode or modes are used throughout a work of fiction. When there is more than one narrative mode in use, give each mode a unique name, such as NCE 1, Narration A, DCE 2, etc. and notate it in the template. Then after all narrative modes have been defined, describe exactly how the different narrative modes are used across the work of fiction at the end of the template.

Thus, a narrative template that defines a complete narrative schema would look as follows:

Narrative Mode: *Name of first mode.*

> **Narrator:** *Identify the omniscient or character narrator.*
>
> **Narrative Intrusion:** *Yes/No*
>
> **Focal Character(s):** *Identify the focal character(s) if present.*
>
> **Prose Type(s) and/or Beat Types(s):** *List the prose type(s) used and if possible the ratio of their use.*
>
> **Narrative Tense:** *Past/Present/etc.*
>
> **Additional Constraints:** *Describe any constraints, limits, or specific tailoring of any of above factors.*

Narrative Mode: *Name of second mode.*

> **Narrator:** *Identify the omniscient or character narrator.*
>
> **Narrative Intrusion:** *Yes/No*
>
> **Focal Character(s):** *Identify the focal character(s) if present.*
>
> **Prose Type(s) and/or Beat Types(s):** *List the prose type(s) used and if possible the ratio of their use.*
>
> **Narrative Tense:** *Past/Present/etc.*
>
> **Additional Constraints:** *Describe any constraints, limits, or specific tailoring of any of above factors.*

Narrative Pattern: *Describe the pattern for using the narrative modes throughout the work.*

Now, before you wingers think we're getting a little carried away with our use of these templates, I want you to consider a couple of things:

First, I am using these templates as a learning and analysis tool. Do I expect you to use them to define your narrative schemas for the rest of your writing career? Of course not! Some of you planners might do just that, though. Some of you wingers might never use one of these templates again. As always, what you take away from this book and how you apply it to your writing process depends on the kind of writer you are.

Second, most professional writers create and use narrative schemas subconsciously, or, at best, semi-consciously. In fact, often a writer will work at developing a specific narrative schema for years, perfecting it through endless trial-and-error practice and emulation. Some call this "finding your voice." And once "found," many professional writers will use the same "voice," the same narrative schema, in everything they produce. There's nothing wrong with that. If a writer can't somehow figure out how to create a narrative schema, be it consciously, semi-consciously, or subconsciously, she will have little hope of keeping her prose narratively consistent, accurate, and thus professional. You, however, can now accomplish this task consciously and expeditiously, by using these templates and your newly acquired knowledge of the three types of prose. And you can use these templates to create not only one voice, but many different voices!

AN EXAMPLE OF A NARRATIVE SCHEMA

Here's an example of a narrative schema. Take a close look at each mode and the narrative pattern. Try to understand exactly what the template is representing.

Narrative Mode: *Narration 1*

Narrator: *Omniscient*

Narrative Intrusion: *Yes*

Focal Character(s): *None*

Prose Type(s) and/or Beat Types(s): *Narration*

Narrative Tense: *Past*

Additional Constraints: *None*

Narrative Mode: *NCE 2*

Narrator: *Omniscient*

Narrative Intrusion: *Yes*

Focal Character(s): *Mayor Cornelius Smelting*

Prose Type(s) and/or Beat Types(s): *NCE*

Narrative Tense: *Past*

Additional Constraints: *None*

Narrative Mode: *DCE 3*

Narrator: *Omniscient*

Narrative Intrusion: *No*

Focal Character(s): *Mayor Cornelius Smelting*

Prose Type(s) and/or Beat Types(s): *DCE*

Narrative Tense: *Past*

Additional Constraints: *None*

Narrative Pattern: *Work of fiction opens with Narration 1, transitions to NCE 2 with the introduction of Mayor Cornelius Smelting, and then continues until the end using DCE 3.*

Here is a short example of prose that, silly as it is, conforms to this narrative schema. I will notate the sample with [Narration 1], [NCE 2], and [DCE 3] so you can see how I used the narrative modes according the narrative pattern. Read this sample and check it against the narrative schema. Make sure you can see exactly how the sample conforms to the narrative modes and the narrative pattern. Go ahead, I'll wait.

[Narration 1] Once upon a starlit summer evening in a little town in southeastern Connecticut, a town that's probably not too different from your own little town, a flying saucer set down smack dab in the middle of Main Street. It was a small thing, about the size of an old Volkswagen Beetle, all metal and rivets and glowing red thruster engines. As the engines whined down, a small hatch at the top of the craft popped open. Two tiny green men emerged, just as the townsfolk arrived.

The townsfolk, as you might imagine, were quite shocked to discover the source of all the commotion. A real, honest-to-goodness flying saucer had landed in their town! They gathered around the craft, jaws hanging open, eyes shot wide, mumbling in wonder. [NCE 2] The mayor of the little town, one Cornelius Smelting, was the first to recover. Being a man blessed with a big heart and an even bigger waist-line, he waddled up to the two tiny green men, his pudgy hand outstretched before him.

[DCE 3] "Greetings!" the mayor shouted. Could the creatures actually speak American? he wondered. The two tiny green men looked at each other in unison. Then one pulled a nasty-looking black object from a holster at its belt and pointed it straight at him.

The mayor gasped. They were going to shoot him! And with some alien pistol or ray gun! He would be vaporized in an instant!

The mayor squeezed his eyes shut...

Done? Great!

Now, a couple of things probably popped into your mind as you read and analyzed this sample.

First, it could very well be impossible to map out in great detail a complex narrative pattern used over a long work of fiction. The narrative pattern you define in your narrative schema should only be detailed enough to describe the basic use of narrative modes in a few sentences at most. Any more than that would be overkill, unless you happen to be the most left-brained planner on the planet!

Second, you may suspect that as I created this sample I had to go back and modify the narrative schema based on how the sample evolved.

This is true!

This is often how writing happens. As you work, your narrative schema (your specific "voice" for that work of fiction) may change and evolve. By the time you get to the end of your piece, though, you should have settled into a pretty precise narrative schema. Once you have, go back and revise your prose so the entire work conforms to the final version of your narrative schema.

And how would you do that?

You'd use a NORTAV analysis, of course!

MULTIPLE PROSE TYPES OR MULTIPLE NARRATIVE MODES?

You have now encountered two different situations where prose types can change within a work of fiction or even with a portion of a work.

In one case, prose types can change because the writer is using an NCE-based narrative mode which uses NCE along with DCE and/or Narration.

In the other case, prose types can change because the writer is alternating between different narrative modes that each use different prose types.

How can you tell which case you're dealing with when you encounter a change in prose types in a NORTAV analysis? For example, if you ran across a section of prose that opened with Narration, then transitioned to NCE, and then transitioned to DCE, how can you tell if you're dealing with one NCE-based narrative mode or with three separate narrative modes, one Narration-based, one NCE-based, and one DCE-based, and a narrative pattern? This can be difficult to determine, and it is often based simply on how you perceive the work. Here are five strategies, however, that can help you figure out which case you're dealing with:

(1) Pay attention to the overall feel of the narrative mode when the prose type changes. If the prose type changes and you sense a purposeful change in the writing style, (or if you can articulate a reason why the prose type changed) then you are likely dealing with a change in narrative modes. If the prose type changes and you do not sense a purposeful change in the writing style, then you are likely dealing with an NCE-based narrative mode.

(2) Try to notice if there's a distinct pattern in how the prose types are changing. If you find a distinct pattern, you're more likely to be dealing with multiple narrative modes.

(3) Try to notice if the different prose types are occurring in blocks or chunks. If they are, you're likely dealing with multiple narrative modes.

(4) Try to notice if the prose types are mixed together relatively consistently. If they are, then it's likely you're dealing with an NCE-based narrative mode.

(5) Finally, check all the narrative factors. If the prose type changes and there are changes in other narrative factors as well, then you are most likely dealing with a change in narrative modes.

Again, with shorter excerpts like the ones found in this book, it can sometimes be difficult to determine which of these cases you're dealing with. Do your best. When you move beyond this book and continue performing NORTAV analyses on your own (you are going to do that, right?), then you will have a much larger context in which to work, and can make a much more informed decision when determining the narrative schema of a work.

NORTAV ASSIGNMENT

For each of the following prose samples, perform a full NORTAV analysis. A "full" NORTAV analysis would include everything we have covered in this book, including identifying the narrative schema, all types of beats, all types of links, all focused beat use, all implied and initiating beats, all occurrences of beat ambiguity and non-conforming beats, all techniques such as beat substitution and beat reordering, all uses of the natural response sequence, and so forth.

Again, take your time to work through these analyses!

In the interest of space, I will keep my "full" NORTAV analyses limited to identifying the narrative schema, basic beat/link structure, and any notable, non-typical, or especially interesting aspects of the sample. For narrative patterns, you will obviously be restricted to notating only the patterns that occur within the sample.

You can do your work right in this book, or print/photocopy the sample and work with it separately. We will perform five analyses in this chapter. Compare your results with the NORTAV analyses I provide directly after each prose sample.

PROSE SAMPLE: Laurin Wittig's *Daring the Highlander*

For the first part of this assignment we'll work with the prose of award-winning author Laurin Wittig. Laurin is a two-time finalist in the Romance Writers of America Golden Heart contest and each of her books has landed on an Amazon Top 100 list. Laurin's first book, *The Devil of Kilmartin*, won a National Reader's Choice award. The following prose sample is taken from her novel *Daring the Highlander*, the second book of her MacLeod series. You can find more information about Laurin and her work at http://laurinwittig.com/.

... What did she know of love?

Nothing, it turned out.

She let the calm and quiet of the winter landscape seep into her, fortify her. She drew the sharp-edged air into her lungs. Sick of her own cowardice, she faced the castle only to find herself being watched.

Baltair, the clan's champion, stood between her and the castle. A slow smile spread across his ruddy face, pulling his narrow lips tight, and his crooked nose even further out of line than it usually was. The man really shouldn't smile. His eyes went to slits and he looked almost as if he were grimacing.

She'd like to grimace, too, but she managed to stop at a frown.

"Is there something you need?" she asked, clutching her bundle of plaid tightly to her like armor. The man was relentless and she was tired of it. He didn't seem to understand her when she told him she was not looking for a husband. Why couldn't anybody understand that? One thing she was beginning to understand was that when Baltair got it into his wee little mind that he wanted something...say, her...he was just as unyielding and just as hard of hearing as the stone wall his chest resembled.

"Why are you always in such a hurry to get away from

me, Morainn?" he asked, his voice low as if he spoke to a lover.

She clamped down on the urge to kick him in the shin...or maybe higher. She satisfied herself with the thought, not the action, and cocked her head at him. "I have much to do. Do you not as well?"

"Not so much that I cannot take time to woo my future bride." His nose shifted direction subtly with each word he spoke. His hair, so dark a brown 'twas almost black, writhed around his face in the breeze that was growing stronger, and colder, by the moment. "You used to have sweet words for Hamish. Do you not have a sweet word for me?"

Sweet words meant little and she certainly didn't have any for this big muttonhead. He was cut from the same rough cloth as the chief's offspring, wild, willful, and too sure the world should bow down at his feet – something she would never do.

"Hamish was my husband. You are not."

"Aye, but I will be." Baltair grinned at her.

"Only if I am dead and lying in my grave," she muttered, stepping around him. Unfortunately, he followed her, his long legs catching him up quickly.

"Was that an acceptance?" he asked.

She stopped in her tracks and glared at him. Irritation was an emotion she did not like and this man gave it to her in heaps.

"Baltair MacLeod, have you no ears? Can you not understand my words? I. Will. Never. Marry. Again. Not you, not anyone. Shall I repeat it again more slowly so you will understand it this time?"

The grin left his face and his eyes went black and stony...

NORTAV ANALYSIS: Laurin Wittig's *Daring the Highlander*

What follows is my NORTAV analysis of Laurin's prose sample. As always, compare this to your analysis and note any differences.

Narrative Mode: *NCE 1*

> **Narrator:** *Omniscient*
>
> **Narrative Intrusion:** *Yes*
>
> **Focal Character(s):** *Morainn MacRailt*
>
> **Prose Type(s) and/or Beat Types(s):** *NCE and DCE. Style uses mostly Direct NCE beats and DCE beats, with some limited use of Mixed NCE beats and Consolidated NCE beats.*
>
> **Narrative Tense:** *Past*
>
> **Additional Constraints:** *None*

Narrative Pattern: *NCE 1 used throughout.*

Analysis:

> [Nt1] What did she know of love?
>
> Nothing, it turned out.

Lauren opens the sample with [Nt1], a Narrated Thought beat. It is rendered with no sense of a narrator (i.e. it's DCE), but because Laurin will soon establish an NCE-based narrative mode, it is notated as Direct NCE. Again, read the entire sample and try to determine the narrative schema first, then go back and notate accordingly.

> [Nc2] She let the calm and quiet of the winter landscape

seep into her, fortify her. [Na3] She drew the sharp-edged air into her lungs. [Nm4] Sick of her own coward-ice, she faced the castle only to find herself being watched.

[Nt1] leads to [Nc2], a beat of Consolidated NCE. Here is where Laurin firmly establishes her NCE-based narrative mode. [Nc2] consolidates Morainn's observations and thoughts. She is observing the landscape, thinking about its tranquillity, and letting it calm and reassure her, all in the same beat. We aren't given these perceptions and activities individually or directly, yet we know they are occurring. They are rolled up into a higher concept and presented to us through the narrator.

[Nc2] leads to [Na3], a Narrated Action beat. [Na3] leads to [Nm4], a beat of Mixed NCE. Here Morainn goes from a thought to an action to a thought. They are so short, quick, and intertwined, they act (in my view) as a beat of Mixed NCE rather than as individual beats of Direct NCE.

[No5] Baltair, the clan's champion, stood between her and the castle. A slow smile spread across his ruddy face, pulling his narrow lips tight, and [Nt6] his crooked nose even further out of line than it usually was. The man really shouldn't smile. [No7] His eyes went to slits and he looked almost as if he were grimacing.

[Nm4] leads to [No5], a Narrated Observation beat. [No5] triggers [Nt6], a Narrated Thought beat. Note that the first part of this beat is a continuation of the previous Narrated Observation beat. [No5] begins as a standard Narrated Observation beat, but morphs into Morainn's conclusion of what it is she is seeing. This is common in NCE. Laurin is mixing together the character's thoughts and observations as they occur. In this case they are distinct enough to notate separately, however often you will have to make a gut call as to whether to notate them separately or combine them into a single beat of Mixed NCE.

> **A NORTAV Tip:**
> In a NORTAV analysis, when dealing with ambiguity between different NCE beat types, simply follow your gut, notate, and move on.

[No7] continues from [No5]. [No7] also mixes a slight sense of both observation and thought. As it is primarily an observation, I notated it as Direct NCE, but it could easily have been notated as Mixed NCE. Here we are dealing with an overlap between different categories of NCE beats. Ambiguity between different NCE beat types is far too detailed to worry about for this theory-lite book. When dealing with ambiguity between different NCE beats types, simply follow your gut, notate, and move on.

> [Nt8] She'd like to grimace, too, [Na9] but she managed to stop at a frown.

Here [Nt8], a Narrated Thought beat, is triggered by [No7]. It triggers [Na9], a Narrated Action beat. I notated these two beats separately because the individual perceptions and activities could be easily divided. Together, though, they do read more as Mixed NCE. Again, notate it depending on how you perceive it as a reader.

> [Nv10] "Is there something you need?" she asked, [Na11] clutching her bundle of plaid tightly to her like armor. [Nt12] The man was relentless and she was tired of it. He didn't seem to understand her when she told him she was not looking for a husband. Why couldn't anybody understand that? One thing she was beginning to understand was that when Baltair got it into his wee little mind that he wanted something...say, her...he was just as unyielding and just as hard of hearing as the stone wall his chest resembled.

[Nv10] is triggered by [No7]. Notice the natural response sequence in action here in the last few beats. [Nv10] leads to [Na11], a Narrated Action beat, which leads to [Nt12] a Narrated Thought beat. Also notice that all three beats here could be DCE.

Remember, DCE beats are perceived and notated as Direct NCE when working with an NCE-based narrative mode.

[No13] "Why are you always in such a hurry to get away from me, Morainn?" he asked, his voice low as if he spoke to a lover.

[Nm14] She clamped down on the urge to kick him in the shin...or maybe higher. [Nc15] She satisfied herself with the thought, not the action, [Na16] and cocked her head at him. [Nv17] "I have much to do. Do you not as well?"

[No13] is an initiating Narrated Observation beat (also DCE). It triggers [Nm14], a beat of Mixed NCE that combines Morainn's reaction and thought. [Nm14] leads to [Nc15], a beat of Consolidated NCE that rolls up her continued thought to a higher concept. That is, the reader isn't presented with Morainn's actual thoughts of satisfaction, but rather is told by the narrator that Morainn had gone through that internal experience. [Nc15] then triggers [Na16], a Narrated Action beat, and [Nv17], a Narrated Vocalization beat that could also stand as DCE.

[No18] "Not so much that I cannot take time to woo my future bride." His nose shifted direction subtly with each word he spoke. His hair, so dark a brown 'twas almost black, writhed around his face in the breeze that was growing stronger, and colder, by the moment. "You used to have sweet words for Hamish. Do you not have a sweet word for me?"

Here we have an initiating Narrated Observation beat, [No18].

[Nt19] Sweet words meant little and she certainly didn't have any for this big muttonhead. He was cut from the same rough cloth as the chief's offspring, wild, willful, and too sure the world should bow down at his feet—something she would never do.

[Nv20] "Hamish was my husband. You are not."

[No18] triggers [Nt19], a Narrated Thought beat, and [Nv20], a Narrated Vocalization beat.

[No21] "Aye, but I will be." Baltair grinned at her.

[Nv22] "Only if I am dead and lying in my grave," she muttered, [Na23] stepping around him. [No24] Unfortunately, he followed her, his long legs catching him up quickly.

[No21] is an initiating Narrated Observation beat. It triggers [Nv22], a Narrated Vocalization beat, and leads to [Na23], a Narrated Action beat. [No24] is another initiating Narrated Observation beat. The addition of "unfortunately" adds the sense of a narrator here.

[No25] "Was that an acceptance?" he asked.

[No25] is another initiating Narrated Observation beat.

[Nr26] She stopped in her tracks and glared at him. [Nt27] Irritation was an emotion she did not like and this man gave it to her in heaps.

[Nv28] "Baltair MacLeod, have you no ears? Can you not understand my words? I. Will. Never. Marry. Again. Not you, not anyone. Shall I repeat it again more slowly so you will understand it this time?"

[No25] triggers [Nr26], a Narrated Reaction beat, [Nt27], a Narrated

Thought beat, and [Nv28], a Narrated Vocalization beat.

[No29] The grin left his face and his eyes went black and stoney.

Finally, [No29] is an initiating Narrated Observation beat.

PROSE SAMPLE: A. J. Abbiati's *Death Comes on the Wind*

For the next part of the assignment we'll work with an excerpt from *Death Comes on the Wind*, the first episode from my fantasy novel *Fell's Hollow*. You can find more information about *Fell's Hollow* and my work at http://ajabbiati.com/.

> ... The *Destiny* sliced through the chop of the Sellum Sea, as stormwinds whipped from the west and stretched her sails taut. White-crested waves beat at her sides. Behind her, dark clouds smothered the horizon. Her masts creaked under the stress, and the sound of it joined the crashing of the surf and the squawking of the gulls that followed over her wake.
>
> She was an old ship, but she could still handle a rough sea. Originally a small Nyland frigate, she'd spent years running up and down the mainland coast chasing Ukrian pirates, spying on Kern, harassing Alar transports and warships with hit-and-run efficiency. But she was a private vessel now, refitted for fishnetting the deep gray waters of the Sellum, a mission less glorious, though hardly less dangerous.
>
> Her crew scurried about her hundred-foot deck as she ran before the wind. The evening before, they had finally finished their task. After a month at sea, the ship's hold held enough croll, haddock, and korshark to earn a hefty

sum on the docks at Fell's Hollow. The haul lent the ship ballast, yet not enough to prevent it from listing far to port as it slipped suddenly down the side of a ten-foot swell. The crew, seasoned as they were, scarcely noticed. They carried on with their work, tightening stays, battening hatches, securing topside barrels and equipment, while below deck a young fisherman new to the *Destiny*, and to life at sea, clutched the edges of a small table in a white-knuckled grip.

The ship leveled.

Chibb's ears burned with embarrassment. He was sitting down, for Ryke's sake, and still he'd almost toppled over. What would the old man think?

Across the table, Ossillard smiled warmly and the jagged scar that ran over one eye crinkled, a souvenir from a shipmate's poorly cast hook. He rubbed his well-weathered scalp, brown and hairless as a scrap of leather, but said nothing. On Chibb's first day at sea, Ossillard, an Alarman like himself, had taken to watching over Chibb like a kindly grandfather. He said he'd never met such a groundhugger before, and if he didn't take matters into his own gnarled hands, Chibb was bound to end up as croll chum by the end of the trip. Chibb was only nineteen. He'd grown up an orphan on the streets of Ithicar, begging and stealing his way through life. It had been a terrible existence. He knew there had to be something better out there for him, a life he could lead with his head held high, not bent in shame as he scoured the streets for scraps of food. When Chibb had signed on to the *Destiny*, he'd known nothing of a fisherman's life. He still knew nothing, or very little, anyway. So when Ossillard spoke, Chibb made it a point to listen...

NORTAV ANALYSIS: A. J. Abbiati's *Death Comes on the Wind*

What follows is my NORTAV analysis of the previous prose sample. As always, compare this to your analysis and note any differences.

Narrative Mode: *Narration 1*

    Narrator: *Omniscient*

    Narrative Intrusion: *Yes*

    Focal Character(s): *None*

    Prose Type(s) and/or Beat Types(s): *Narration*

    Narrative Tense: *Past*

    Additional Constraints: *None*

Narrative Mode: *NCE 2*

    Narrator: *Omniscient*

    Narrative Intrusion: *Yes*

    Focal Character(s): *Chibb*

    Prose Type(s) and/or Beat Types(s): *NCE and DCE*

    Narrative Tense: *Past*

    Additional Constraints: *None*

Narrative Mode: *DCE 3*

    Narrator: *Omniscient*

    Narrative Intrusion: *No*

    Focal Character(s): *Chibb*

    Prose Type(s) and/or Beat Types(s): *DCE*

    Narrative Tense: *Past*

    Additional Constraints: *None*

Narrative Pattern: *Sample opens in Narration 1, transitions to NCE 2* *with the introduction of the focal character Chibb, and then transitions to DCE 3 for the remainder of the sample.*

Analysis:

> [N1] The *Destiny* sliced through the chop of the Sellum Sea, as stormwinds whipped from the west and stretched her sails taut. White-crested waves beat at her sides. Behind her, dark clouds smothered the horizon. Her masts creaked under the stress, and the sound of it joined the crashing of the surf and the squawking of the gulls that followed over her wake.

The excerpt begins with [N1], where an omniscient narrator sets up the current topic at hand: There is no focal character here. The narrator reveals to the reader that the *Destiny* is in the midst of trying to outrun an approaching storm.

> [N2] She was an old ship, but she could still handle a rough sea. Originally a small Nyland frigate, she'd spent years running up and down the mainland coast chasing Ukrian pirates, spying on Kern, harassing Alar transports and warships with hit-and-run efficiency. But she was a private vessel now, refitted for fishnetting the deep gray waters of the Sellum, a mission less glorious, though hardly less dangerous.

In [N2], the narrator expands on the topic set in [N1] by providing the reader with some background information on the ship that reveals how and why the ship can handle the rough seas.

> [N3] Her crew scurried about her hundred-foot deck as she ran before the wind.

[N3] is another Narration beat that takes us back to the visual image established in [N1]. Here the narrator returns to describing the ship in its current state, adding the details of the crew at work.

[N4] The evening before, they had finally finished their task. After a month at sea, the ship's hold held enough croll, haddock, and korshark to earn a hefty sum on the docks at Fell's Hollow. The haul lent the ship ballast, yet not enough to prevent it from listing far to port as it slipped suddenly down the side of a ten-foot swell. The crew, seasoned as they were, scarcely noticed. They carried on with their work, tightening stays, battening hatches, securing topside barrels and equipment,

Here the narrator gives us another Narration beat, [N4]. The narrator adds on more information, building the scene. This beat links back to the crew that was introduced in the previous beat and to the ship.

[Na5] while below deck a young fisherman new to the *Destiny*, and to life at sea, clutched the edges of a small table in a white-knuckled grip.

How did you notate this beat? Here the narrator has moved the reader inside the ship, introduces a specific crewman, and gives the reader some background information on the young sailor. The last part of the line is the first occurrence of a focal character's perceptions and activities. Thus, this is a beat of Direct NCE. It describes the activity of a focal character, Chibb, rendered to the reader through the narrator. Hence, we have purposefully transitioned from a Narration-based narrative mode to an NCE-based narrative mode.

[No6] The ship leveled.

Here the narrator begins to vanish. Though this beat is DCE, we notate it as Direct NCE because the current narrative mode is NCE-based.

[Nr7] Chibb's ears burned with embarrassment.

[Nr7] is a typical Narrated Reaction beat. This is Chibb's reaction, but it is being told to us by the narrator. The addition of "with embarrassment" is the narrator's intrusion.

[T8] He was sitting down, for Ryke's sake, and still he'd almost toppled over. What would the old man think?

Here the writer purposefully transitions from an NCE-based narrative mode to a DCE-based narrative mode. The narrator's presence has now vanished. This is a typical DCE Thought beat.

We begin to see that the writer (me in this case) has started the reader at a "wide-angle," distanced view of the scene with the use of an omniscient narrator and Narration, then moved the reader closer to the perceptions and activities of the focal character by slipping into NCE, and finally zoomed right into the character's perceptions and activities by transitioning to DCE. If this "zooming in" feeling isn't obvious to you, go back and reread the un-notated version of the sample. Pay close attention to how you perceive the prose as the narrative mode purposefully transitions from Narration-based to NCE-based to DCE-based. Also, go back and reread the five strategies for determining if multiple prose types are the result of one NCE-based narrative mode or multiple narrative modes. Try to see how the strategies apply here.

[O9] Across the table, Ossillard smiled warmly and the jagged scar that ran over one eye crinkled, a souvenir from a shipmate's poorly cast hook. He rubbed his well-weathered scalp, brown and hairless as a scrap of leather, but said nothing.

Here we have a typical Observation beat.

[T10] On Chibb's first day at sea, Ossillard, an Alarman like himself, had taken to watching over Chibb like a kindly grandfather. He said he'd never met such a groundhugger before, and if he didn't take matters into his own gnarled hands, Chibb was bound to end up as croll chum by the end of the trip. Chibb was only nineteen. He'd grown up an orphan on the streets of Ithicar, begging and stealing his way through life. It had been a terrible existence. He knew there had to be something better out there for him, a life he could lead with his head held high, not bent in shame as he scoured the streets for scraps of food. When Chibb had signed on to the *Destiny*, he'd known nothing of a fisherman's life. He still knew nothing, or very little, anyway. So when Ossillard spoke, Chibb made it a point to listen.

Finally we have a typical compound Thought beat.

Notice two things here. First, again, this is a compound beat. I easily could have broken this into several Thought beats, but as they are working as a single unit in the prose chain (i.e. one hunk of thought brought on by the sight of Ossillard), I combined them. Second, this is tied back to [010] through a stimulus/response link.

PROSE SAMPLE: Lexi Revellian's *Remix*

For the next part of this assignment we'll work with the prose of best-selling author Lexi Revellian. Lexi has written several novels, including *Remix* and *Replica*. Noted for selling over 45,000 books in her first year of publishing, Lexi's novel *Remix* spent eight months on the UK Kindle Top 100 List. The following prose sample is taken from *Remix*. You can find out more information about Lexi and her work at her website: http://www.lexirevellian.com/.

... I didn't see the man straight away.

The sun was shining, so I'd taken my breakfast toast and coffee out on the terrace. I strolled to the far corner to admire a view I never tire of: a London roofscape, a glimpse of trees in Hoxton Square two streets away, and the distant Gherkin gleaming in the early morning sun. Already the faint hum of traffic competed with the coo of a courting pigeon. My blackbird hopped towards me, bright eye cocked, waiting for his ration of sultanas. I put them in the dish, turned, and stopped dead.

There was a stranger asleep on my outdoor sofa – my new expensive sofa that I can't really afford and shouldn't have bought – a scruffy mongrel curled up beside him. The man wore jeans and a sweatshirt; below the old jacket draped over him, grubby fraying trainers stuck out, incongruous against the cream cushions.

My first impulse was to shake him awake, and tell him to get off my property, now. How the hell had he got up here? With a dog? My flat is on top of the building, immune to burglars, or so I'd thought. But on reflection, he might be dangerous...a schizophrenic, a drug addict – though a pretty fit one if he climbed up here – a psychopath... His face reminded me of someone I knew, but I couldn't think who. It would come back to me. Older than I was, I'd say, probably late twenties; dark hair, eyebrows and eyelashes, unshaven, regular features smoothed in the innocence of sleep. Good cheekbones and jawline. The sort of face I might find interesting attached to someone who wasn't a vagrant trespassing on my rooftop.

I backed away. My mobile was recharging by my bed. I would tiptoe across the terrace and through the French windows, slide them gently shut and ring the police.

The dog's head lifted, bright brown eyes shining through fur sticking up in all directions. He hopped off the sofa, and trotted over, claws clicking on the tiled surface. He looked at the plate in my hand, then back at me, triangular ears pricked, expression optimistic; his tail wagged, and he made a small hopeful sound.

Hastily I crouched and handed him a piece of toast to silence him.

Too late. The man's eyes opened. Sitting up, he ran a hand through hair as rough as the dog's, and swung his worn trainers to the floor. He was nearer the door than I was. He looked at me. I was quite decent in my towelling robe, but I'd have felt happier dressed. I edged towards the safety of my flat. The man got lithely to his feet. He was six foot tall, lean and muscular under his shabby clothes, and a seedling of panic unfurled below my diaphragm. If we both went for the door, he'd get there first.

"I'd like you to leave. Now. Or I'm calling the police." There was a noticeable tremor in my voice. Damn...

NORTAV ANALYSIS: Lexi Revellian's *Remix*

What follows is my NORTAV analysis of Lexi's prose sample. As always, compare this to your analysis and note any differences.

Narrative Mode: *NCE 1*

> **Narrator:** *Caz Tallis*
>
> **Narrative Intrusion:** *Yes*
>
> **Focal Character(s):** *Caz Tallis*
>
> **Prose Type(s) and/or Beat Types(s):** *NCE and DCE. Style uses mostly DCE and Direct NCE.*
>
> **Narrative Tense:** *Past*
>
> **Additional Constraints:** *None*

Narrative Pattern: *Sample uses NCE 1 throughout.*

Analysis:

> [No1] I didn't see the man straight away.

[No2] The sun was shining, so [Na3] I'd taken my breakfast toast and coffee out on the terrace. [Na4] I strolled
to the far corner to admire a view I never tire of: [No5] a
London roofscape, a glimpse of trees in Hoxton Square
two streets away, and the distant Gherkin gleaming in
the early morning sun. Already the faint hum of traffic
competed with the coo of a courting pigeon. My blackbird hopped towards me, bright eye cocked, waiting for
his ration of sultanas. [Na6] I put them in the dish,
turned, and [Na7] stopped dead.

From a NORTAV analysis perspective, this is a very interesting start.
Lexi begins with a mini-flashback. We don't get to the current time of
the story until [Na6], but this is all notated as one level. Remember we
talked about notating some flashbacks in levels, such as [T-A6]? We
did that because the presentation of the prose changed when the focal
character went from "recalling" the memories in the current time of
the story to "reliving" them in a past time of the story. That is, the
perception of the current story time beat was lost or "hidden" from the
reader. In this case, even though the verb tenses used here sets up the
same sort of situation, I notated this as a single level because this is not
coming directly from Caz the focal character. This is all being told to us
by Caz the narrator, and as such we don't get a sense that we are losing
the perception of any beats at the current time of the story. Again, pay
very close attention to how flashbacks are being rendered by the
author and notate accordingly, using levels if there's a need to keep
track of current time beats and past time beats.

That said, we begin with [No1], a Narrated Observation beat, which is
actually the narrator telling the reader what the focal character did not
observe. That leads to [No2], another Narrated Observation beat,
which leads to Narrated Action beat [Na3]. [Na3] leads to Narrated
Action beat [Na4], which leads to Narrated Observation beat [No5].
[No5] leads to Narrated Action beat [Na6], which leads to Narrated
Action beat [Na7]. [Na7] is not combined with [Na6] because it's used
specifically in the prose chain, as we're about to see.

[No8] There was a stranger asleep on my outdoor sofa – my new expensive sofa that I can't really afford and shouldn't have bought – a scruffy mongrel curled up beside him. The man wore jeans and a sweatshirt; below the old jacket draped over him, grubby fraying trainers stuck out, incongruous against the cream cushions.

Here, Narrated Observation beat [No8] follows [Na7] out of the normal natural response sequence. Note that Lexi is using the same technique we discussed earlier: she reorders her beats to manufacture a certain sense of suspense. It works well in this situation because this is the opening of the book. The suspense works to immediately hook the reader. Also note the use of the present tense in "...I can't really afford..." Is this Caz the character thinking this as the events were happening? Is this Caz the narrator telling the reader she still can't afford the sofa, thus implying Caz is still not financially stable at the time the story is being told? As of yet, we don't know enough to tell. The point is, knowing how to perform a NORTAV analysis gives you the tools to recognize these interesting areas in the prose and ask appropriate questions. The NORTAV analysis is more than just a tool for learning how authors craft their prose. It is also a tool for becoming a much more observant, much more critical reader.

[Nt9] My first impulse was to shake him awake, and tell him to get off my property, now. How the hell had he got up here? With a dog? My flat is on top of the building, immune to burglars, or so I'd thought. But on reflection, he might be dangerous...a schizophrenic, a drug addict – though a pretty fit one if he climbed up here – a psychopath... His face reminded me of someone I knew, but I couldn't think who. It would come back to me. Older than I was, I'd say, probably late twenties; dark hair, eyebrows and eyelashes, unshaven, regular features smoothed in the innocence of sleep. Good cheekbones and jawline. The sort of face I might find interesting attached to someone who wasn't a vagrant trespassing on my rooftop.

Here [No8] triggers this long compound Narrated Thought beat [Nt9]. It begins as a typical beat of NCE, but slowly becomes more and more like DCE.

[Na10] I backed away. [Nt11] My mobile was recharging by my bed. I would tiptoe across the terrace and through the French windows, slide them gently shut and ring the police.

[No8] also triggers Narrated Action beat [Na10], which then leads to Narrated Thought beat [Nt11].

[No12] The dog's head lifted, bright brown eyes shining through fur sticking up in all directions. He hopped off the sofa, and trotted over, claws clicking on the tiled surface. He looked at the plate in my hand, then back at me, triangular ears pricked, expression optimistic; his tail wagged, and he made a small hopeful sound.

Here [No12] is an initiating Narrated Observation beat.

[Na13] Hastily I crouched and handed him a piece of toast to silence him.

[No12] triggers this Narrated Action beat [Na13]. Notice here the narrator begins to make her presence known again. "Hastily..." and "to silence him" are both narrative intrusions that explain the character's actions to the reader.

[Nt14] Too late. [No15] The man's eyes opened. Sitting up, he ran a hand through hair as rough as the dog's, and swung his worn trainers to the floor. [Nt16] He was nearer the door than I was. [No17] He looked at me.

[Nt18] I was quite decent in my towelling robe, but I'd have felt happier dressed. [Na19] I edged towards the safety of my flat. [No20] The man got lithely to his feet. He was six foot tall, lean and muscular under his shabby clothes, and [Nr21] a seedling of panic unfurled below my diaphragm. [Nt22] If we both went for the door, he'd get there first.

Here we have a series of events that begin with [Nt14], which is out of normal order. [No15] is an initiating Narrated Observation beat that triggers [Nt14], but because we are being told about these perceptions and activities from a narrator, the narrator can choose to change the normal order to create suspense, as we've already seen. Remember, the fact that the beats are being reordered at all is an indicator of the narrator's presence. In fact, it's the only indicator in this entire passage. The rest of the beats are really DCE and follow a couple of iterations of the natural response sequence. That is, [No15] triggers [Nt18] and [Na19], then [No20] triggers [Nr21] and [Nt22].

[Nv23] "I'd like you to leave. Now. Or I'm calling the police." [No24] There was a noticeable tremor in my voice. [Nt25] Damn.

[No19] also triggers Narrated Vocalization beat [Nv23]. Finally, [Nv23] leads to Narrated Observation beat [No24], which triggers Narrated Thought beat [Nt25]. All these beats are DCE.

PROSE SAMPLE: Miguel de Cervante's *Don Quixote*

For the next part of this assignment we'll work with a sample of prose taken from Miguel de Cervante's classic novel *Don Quixote*. For more information about Cervante and his work, you can visit Project Gutenberg at http://www.gutenberg.org/.

... Cide Hamete Benengeli, the Arab and Manchegan author, relates in this most grave, high-sounding,

minute, delightful, and original history that after the discussion between the famous Don Quixote of La Mancha
and his squire Sancho Panza which is set down at the
end of chapter twenty-one, Don Quixote raised his eyes
and saw coming along the road he was following some
dozen men on foot strung together by the neck, like
beads, on a great iron chain, and all with manacles on
their hands. With them there came also two men on
horseback and two on foot; those on horseback with
wheel-lock muskets, those on foot with javelins and
swords, and as soon as Sancho saw them he said:

"That is a chain of galley slaves, on the way to the galleys
by force of the king's orders."

"How by force?" asked Don Quixote; "is it possible that
the king uses force against anyone?"

"I do not say that," answered Sancho, "but that these are
people condemned for their crimes to serve by force in
the king's galleys."

"In fact," replied Don Quixote, "however it may be, these
people are going where they are taking them by force,
and not of their own will."

"Just so," said Sancho.

"Then if so," said Don Quixote, "here is a case for the
exercise of my office, to put down force and to succour
and help the wretched."

"Recollect, your worship," said Sancho, "Justice, which is
the king himself, is not using force or doing wrong to
such persons, but punishing them for their crimes."

The chain of galley slaves had by this time come up, and

Don Quixote in very courteous language asked those who were in custody of it to be good enough to tell him the reason or reasons for which they were conducting these people in this manner. One of the guards on horseback answered that they were galley slaves belonging to his majesty, that they were going to the galleys, and that was all that was to be said and all he had any business to know.

"Nevertheless," replied Don Quixote, "I should like to know from each of them separately the reason of his misfortune;" to this he added more to the same effect to induce them to tell him what he wanted so civilly that the other mounted guard said to him:

"Though we have here the register and certificate of the sentence of every one of these wretches, this is no time to take them out or read them; come and ask themselves; they can tell if they choose, and they will, for these fellows take a pleasure in doing and talking about rascalities."

With this permission, which Don Quixote would have taken even had they not granted it, he approached the chain and asked the first for what offences he was now in such a sorry case.

He made answer that it was for being a lover...

NORTAV ANALYSIS: Miguel de Cervante's *Don Quixote*

What follows is my NORTAV analysis of Cervante's prose sample. As always, compare this to your analysis and note any differences.

Narrative Mode: *Narration 1*

   Narrator: *Omniscient*

Narrative Intrusion: *Yes*

Focal Character(s): *None*

Prose Type(s) and/or Beat Types(s): *Narration*

Narrative Tense: *Past*

Additional Constraints: *None*

Narrative Mode: *NCE 2*

Narrator: *Omniscient*

Narrative Intrusion: *Yes*

Focal Character(s): *Don Quixote*

Prose Type(s) and/or Beat Types(s): *NCE. Style uses mostly Direct NCE and summarized Direct NCE.*

Narrative Tense: *Past*

Additional Constraints: *None*

Narrative Pattern: *Sample opens with Narration 1 and transitions to NCE 2.*

Analysis:

[N1] Cide Hamete Benengeli, the Arab and Manchegan author, relates in this most grave, high-sounding, minute, delightful, and original history that after the discussion between the famous Don Quixote of La Mancha and his squire Sancho Panza which is set down at the end of chapter twenty-one, [Na2] Don Quixote raised his eyes and saw [No3] coming along the road he was following some dozen men on foot strung together by the neck, like beads, on a great iron chain, and all with manacles on their hands. With them there came also two men on horseback and two on foot; those on horseback with wheel-lock muskets, those on foot with javelins and swords, and as soon as [No4] Sancho saw them he said:

"That is a chain of galley slaves, on the way to the galleys by force of the king's orders."

[Nv5] "How by force?" asked Don Quixote; "is it possible that the king uses force against anyone?"

Here the excerpt begins with a beat of Narration, [N1], where the narrator is addressing the reader directly, providing the reader with a bit of story background. [N1] leads to Narrated Action beat [Na2], where the narrator zooms into the story and begins to describe an activity of focal character Don Quixote.

Because we sense this purposeful zooming in or change in the writing style, and because other factors of the narrative mode have changed (adding a focal character), the narrative mode has changed. [Na2] leads to Narrated Observation beat [No3], which leads to Narrated Observation beat [No4]. [No4] is not part of [No3], for it is acting as an initiating beat that triggers Narrated Vocalization beat [Nv5].

[No6] "I do not say that," answered Sancho, "but that these are people condemned for their crimes to serve by force in the king's galleys."

[Nv7] "In fact," replied Don Quixote, "however it may be, these people are going where they are taking them by force, and not of their own will."

[No8] "Just so," said Sancho.

[Nv5] "Then if so," said Don Quixote, "here is a case for the exercise of my office, to put down force and to succour and help the wretched."

[No10] "Recollect, your worship," said Sancho, "Justice, which is the king himself, is not using force or doing wrong to such persons, but punishing them for their crimes."

Here we have several Narrated Observation beats and several Narrated Vocalization beats that make up an exchange of dialogue.

> [No11] The chain of galley slaves had by this time come up, and [Nv12] Don Quixote in very courteous language asked those who were in custody of it to be good enough to tell him the reason or reasons for which they were conducting these people in this manner. [No13] One of the guards on horseback answered that they were galley slaves belonging to his majesty, that they were going to the galleys, and that was all that was to be said and all he had any business to know.

[No11] is an initiating Narrated Observation beat that triggers Narrated Vocalization beat [Nv12]. [Nv12] is followed by initiating Narrated Observation beat [No13]. Note that [Nv12] and [No13] are both summarized beats. Because each represents a summary of a single perception or activity, they are notated as Direct NCE, not mixed or Consolidated NCE.

> [Nv14] "Nevertheless," replied Don Quixote, "I should like to know from each of them separately the reason of his misfortune;" [Nm15] to this he added more to the same effect to induce them to tell him what he wanted so civilly that [No16] the other mounted guard said to him:
>
> "Though we have here the register and certificate of the sentence of every one of these wretches, this is no time to take them out or read them; come and ask themselves; they can tell if they choose, and they will, for these fellows take a pleasure in doing and talking about rascalities."

Here, [No13] triggers Narrated Vocalization beat [Nv14], which leads to Mixed NCE beat [Nm15]. [Nm15] is a mix of vocalization and thought. [No16] is an initiating Narrated Observation beat.

[Nc17] With this permission, which Don Quixote would have taken even had they not granted it, [Na18] he approached the chain and [Nv19] asked the first for what offences he was now in such a sorry case.

[No20] He made answer that it was for being a lover.

[No16] leads to Consolidated NCE beat [Nc17]. [Nc17] is a roll up of Quixote's thoughts and assumptions that occur as a result of [No16]. [Nc17] triggers Narrated Action beat [Na18] and Narrated Vocalization beat [Na19].

Finally, [No20] is an initiating Narrated Observation beat.

PROSE SAMPLE: Victorine Lieske's *Not What She Seems*

For the last part of this assignment we'll work with the prose of author Victorine Lieske. A recently published author, Victorine has written various short stories and two novels: *The Overtaking* and *Not What She Seems*, the latter of which became a New Your Times best-seller. The following prose sample is taken from *Not What She Seems*. You can find more information about Victorine and her work at her website: http://www.victorinelieske.com/.

… Steven stalked down the hotel hallway toward his room, gripping his briefcase, glad that no one was around. He needed to get out of his Armani suit before someone recognized him. Not that anyone staying in this run-down hotel would be hanging around his social circles. But someone might recognize him from the news.

Excitement shot through him. He almost felt like a little kid. If he could get away with it, he would be just another regular person by tomorrow.

He heard footsteps coming up the stairs. A young tow-headed boy appeared, followed by his mother. The child ran down the hall sideswiping him, knocking his brief-case out of his hand. Files and papers spilled out onto the floor.

The boy turned around. "Oh, sorry." He bent down and scooped up some files, while his mother rushed to help as well.

"No problem, I need to sort through these anyway."

The young woman flashed a smile at him, and then turned to her son. "Connor, you need to be more care-ful," she said, getting down on her hands and knees. Her hair was piled on top of her head in a loose bun, with several curly blond strands hanging down. She was quite attractive, despite her frumpy sweat pants and t-shirt. Steven found himself checking out her left hand. No ring. Then he mentally smacked himself. What was he doing? He needed to get away, and have some time for himself. Forget about women. They all wanted the same thing from him. He had six point four billion reasons why any woman would want to be with him. Unfor-tunately, none of them had anything to do with his per-sonality.

Oh, he was good looking enough. He knew that. His jet black hair and bright blue eyes turned plenty of heads. But he could always tell the moment they recognized him, and the mild interest would be replaced with strong attraction.

The woman handed him a pile of papers, with an apolo-getic look on her face. "Sorry about that. He's just been cooped up in the car too long I think." She stood and brushed some hair from her face.

"It's no big deal." He adjusted his overnight bag on his shoulder. "Thank you," he said, searching her face for any sign of recognition.

"You're welcome." She shied away from his blatant staring, looking to the floor, then to her son. "Come on, Connor, we need to get going."

Steven turned around. She hadn't recognized him. That was a good thing. His plan might work. Pulling out his key card, he walked to his door while they disappeared into their own room. He made a mental note of the woman's room number. Maybe he would pay for her bill as well. Her tattered clothes gave him the impression the seventy five dollars a night might be a bit steep for her…

NORTAV ANALYSIS: Victorine Lieske's *Not What She Seems*

What follows is my NORTAV analysis of Victorine's prose sample. As always, compare this to your analysis and note any differences.

Narrative Mode: *DCE 1*

> **Narrator:** *Omniscient*
>
> **Narrative Intrusion:** *No*
>
> **Focal Character(s):** *Steven*
>
> **Prose Type(s) and/or Beat Types(s):** *DCE. Style uses DCE and minor uses of ambiguous and/or non-conforming NCE.*
>
> **Narrative Tense:** *Past*
>
> **Additional Constraints:** *None*

Narrative Pattern: *Sample uses DCE 1 throughout.*

Analysis:

[A1] Steven stalked down the hotel hallway toward his room, gripping his briefcase, [T2] glad that no one was around. [T3] He needed to get out of his Armani suit before someone recognized him. Not that anyone staying in this run-down hotel would be hanging around his social circles. But someone might recognize him from the news.

We open with Action beat [A1], which leads to Thought beat [T2]. [T2] leads to Thought beat [T3]. There is no sense of a narrator here at all.

[R4] Excitement shot through him. [T5] He almost felt like a little kid. If he could get away with it, he would be just another regular person by tomorrow.

[T3] triggers Reaction beat [R4] and Thought beat [T5]. Remember when I said most but not all Reaction beats are triggered by Observation beats? This is a great example of how a Thought beat can act as a stimulus. Here it triggers a Reaction beat and another subsequent Thought beat, which follow the natural response sequence perfectly.

[O6] He heard footsteps coming up the stairs. A young tow-headed boy appeared, followed by his mother. The child ran down the hall sideswiping him, knocking his briefcase out of his hand. Files and papers spilled out onto the floor.

[O7] The boy turned around. "Oh, sorry." He bent down and scooped up some files, while his mother rushed to help as well.

[V8] "No problem, I need to sort through these anyway."

[O6] is an initiating Observation beat. This leads to Observation beat [O7], which triggers Vocalization beat [V8]. Note the slight narrative intrusion in [O6], with the use of the tag "he heard." This casts [O6] as a bit of non-conforming NCE.

[O9] The young woman flashed a smile at him, and then turned to her son. "Connor, you need to be more careful," she said, getting down on her hands and knees. Her hair was piled on top of her head in a loose bun, with several curly blond strands hanging down. [T10] She was quite attractive, despite her frumpy sweat pants and t-shirt. Steven found himself checking out her left hand. No ring. Then he mentally smacked himself. What was he doing? He needed to get away, and have some time for himself. Forget about women. They all wanted the same thing from him. He had six point four billion reasons why any woman would want to be with him. Unfortunately, none of them had anything to do with his personality.

[O9] is an initiating Observation beat. This triggers Thought beat [T10]. Notice a couple of things about [T10]. First, it's a compound beat. This could have been broken into several smaller Thought beats. Second, notice the slight narrative intrusions that render this beat somewhat non-conforming. Can you find them? They are "Steven found himself..." and "he mentally smacked himself..." Again, because a consistent DCE-based narrative mode has been established, we gloss over slight, infrequent narrative intrusions.

[T11] Oh, he was good looking enough. He knew that. His jet black hair and bright blue eyes turned plenty of heads. But he could always tell the moment they recognized him, and the mild interest would be replaced with strong attraction.

[T10] triggers Thought beat [T11].

[O12] The woman handed him a pile of papers, with an apologetic look on her face. "Sorry about that. He's just been cooped up in the car too long I think." She stood and brushed some hair from her face.

[V13] "It's no big deal." [A14] He adjusted his overnight bag on his shoulder. [V15] "Thank you," he said, [A16] searching her face for any sign of recognition.

Here [O12] is an initiating Observation beat that triggers Vocalization beat [V13]. [O12] also leads to Action beat [A14], Vocalization beat [V15], and Action beat [A16].

[O17] "You're welcome." She shied away from his blatant staring, looking to the floor, then to her son. "Come on, Connor, we need to get going."

[A18] Steven turned around. [T19] She hadn't recognized him. That was a good thing. His plan might work. [A20] Pulling out his key card, he walked to his door [O21] while they disappeared into their own room. [T22] He made a mental note of the woman's room number. Maybe he would pay for her bill as well. Her tattered clothes gave him the impression the seventy five dollars a night might be a bit steep for her.

Finally, [O17] is an initiating Observation beat that leads to [A18]. [T19] is a Thought beat. What beat does [T19] link back to? Correct. There is no beat that leads to or triggers [T19]. [T19] is an initiating Thought beat. As we've seen so far, most initiating beats come in the form of Observation beats, when something outside the focal character interrupts into the prose chain and captures the focal character's attention. Here it is the focal character's own sudden realization that interrupts into the prose chain.

[A18] then leads to [A20], as it continues the series of events the focal character is performing. [O21] is an Observation beat that occurs at the same time as [A20]. Last, [O21] triggers Thought beat [T22].

WRITING EXERCISE

There are two parts to this exercise. For the first part I want you to invent five different narrative modes of your own. Mix up the factors. Find different and interesting ways to modify the factors and notate them as additional constraints. Then, for each narrative mode, construct at least ten beats of prose that conform to it. Try to reflect each factor of the narrative mode at least once. When you're creating the prose, write whatever comes to mind. The narrative content is not important. What is important is that you attempt to do this exercise by constructing your prose *as consciously as possible*, through the use of beats and links that conform to each specific narrative mode. Try not to fall into your dreamstate. Again, *this is an exercise*. It is not meant to replace your actual writing process.

I will do one and notate it for clarity:

Narrative Mode: *NCE 1*

  Narrator: *Paul*

  Narrative Intrusion: *Yes*

  Focal Character(s): *Paul*

  Prose Type(s) and/or Beat Types(s): *NCE and DCE. Style uses only Direct NCE and DCE beats.*

  Narrative Tense: *Past*

  Additional Constraints: *All Reactions beats are reflected in physical or vocal form only.*

Narrative Pattern: *Sample uses NCE 1 throughout.*

Prose Sample:

  [No] I saw Barkles scoot after his rubber bone, slide across the slick wooden floor, and collide into his water dish. He looked up at me, puppy eyes questioning, droplets dripping off his droopy ears.

  [Nr] I snorted. [Nt] Barkles was my new black lab. My new, very uncoordinated black lab. The last black lab, the last pet, I would ever own.

[Na] I bent over, scratched his chin, [Nr] and yanked my hand back when [No] Barkles flopped over onto his side and nipped me a good one.

[Nt] The boy could bite! I knew I would have to do something about that before Rachel, my pet-unfriendly girlfriend, returned from Barchmount Heights. [Nt] That little excursion of hers was a point of contention between us. Had been since she had first suggested it back in September. I figured five girls alone on a ski trip could only mean trouble. I was about to find out just how right I was.

[Na] As I lay there playing with Barkles, [No] my proof came knocking at my front door.

For part two of this exercise, choose any two of your narrative modes and come up with a narrative pattern to combine their use. Next, create a short sample of prose that conforms to the two narrative modes and the narrative pattern (i.e. to the complete narrative schema).

LET'S RECAP

By now you should understand that:

- A narrative schema describes the narrative mode or modes used in a work of fiction, and the pattern of their use.

- A narrative mode is a unique style of writing.

- A narrative mode can be defined by six narrative factors.

- The number of unique narrative modes that can be created is limitless.

- A narrative pattern identifies how a narrative mode or modes are used throughout a work of fiction.

- The number of unique narrative patterns that can be created is limitless.

- In a NORTAV analysis, when dealing with ambiguity between different NCE beat types, simply follow your gut, notate, and move on.

We have now finished covering the NORTAV Method. If you made it this far...

Congratulations!

You are now well on your way to learning how to construct professional quality prose. Now that you have an understanding of this new and exciting body of knowledge, we will move on to Chapter 7, where I will give you some tips and suggestions on how to incorporate it into your own unique writing process.

Chapter 7

*INCORPORATING THE NORTAV METHOD
INTO YOUR WRITING PROCESS*

Making Use of the NORTAV Method

WHERE ARE WE IN THE BIG PICTURE?

Now that you understand the NORTAV Method, it's time to talk a little about how to incorporate this new body of knowledge into your own writing process. This is a short chapter because, in truth, only you can determine how best to work the NORTAV Method into your own personal, unique way of constructing prose. Every writer is different. Every writer will want to use the NORTAV Method differently. In fact, by now I'm sure you've already come up with a few ideas for doing just that. I do, however, have five suggestions you might want to consider.

Let's look at each in turn.

USE THE NORTAV METHOD AS A LEARNING TOOL

Whether or not you decide to incorporate the NORTAV Method into some phase of your writing process, I hope you've realized just how powerful a resource it can be for discovering how professional authors are constructing their prose.

Throughout the course of this book you have analyzed prose samples from over a dozen award-winning and best-selling authors. You have used the NORTAV analysis to break apart and examine those prose samples in order to understand how each author is employing the same basic set of tools (beats, links, prose types, narrative modes, narrative patterns, etc.) to construct their prose. You have seen how each author has his or her own voice and how each uses these tools differently to achieve certain effects. With the NORTAV Method, you now have the means to continue your journey of discovery.

Therefore, my first suggestion is, even if you don't incorporate it into your writing process, *never* stop using the NORTAV Method as a learning tool.

DO NOTHING AT ALL

Do nothing at all? Really? That's correct. My second suggestion is for those extreme wingers out there who couldn't imagine a time when they would ever change their muse-driven writing process. If you're one of these right-brained writers, don't try to incorporate the NOR-TAV Method into your process at all. Do nothing. If you have taken the time to learn the NORTAV Method, and especially if you continue to use the NORTAV Method as a tool for discovering how your favorite authors are constructing their prose, then slowly but surely the concepts of the NORTAV Method will work their way into your writing process on their own.

Think back to that Language Arts class with Mrs. Rice. When she taught you about simple, compound, complex, and compound-complex sentences, did you run off and try to consciously incorporate them into your writing? Probably not. But those concepts got in there just the same. The simple fact that your subconscious mind now understands the NORTAV Method is enough. So, again, to you extreme wingers out there: Leave it to your subconscious. It will eventually incorporate the NORTAV Method for you.

USE THE NORTAV METHOD TO PERFECT YOUR CURRENT WORK-IN-PROGRESS

My third suggestion is to start by analyzing your own writing. Perform a NORTAV analysis on your latest work-in-progress. Try to discover the narrative modes and narrative patterns you have been using semi-consciously or subconsciously up to this point. Document your current narrative mode(s) and narrative pattern in a narrative schema. Once you have done that, go back and revise your work-in-progress accordingly. Then, each time you revise your work-in-progress, bounce it against your narrative schema. Correct any place where the prose doesn't conform, or tweak any place where the prose could better conform. As you continue to cycle between writing and revision, you should start to naturally construct prose that better conforms to your narrative schema right from the start, and you should require less and less revision as you go.

USE THE NORTAV METHOD TO CREATE A NEW NARRATIVE SCHEMA FOR YOUR NEXT WORK

My fourth suggestion is to create a brand new narrative schema, then use it to guide your next work. Start with one DCE-based narrative mode. This will tend to keep things simple. Choose the past tense and an omniscient narrator. Choose a single focal character. Use this narrative mode throughout the entire work-in-progress. This is probably the easiest narrative schema to work with at first. Master this style of writing and then start introducing more complex narrative schemas as you move on to other projects.

USE THE NORTAV METHOD AS A REVISION TOOL

My fifth and final suggestion is for every writer to use the NORTAV Method as a mandatory revision tool. I'll cover this suggestion a bit further in the next chapter.

LET'S RECAP

At this point you should have a few ideas on how to incorporate the NORTAV Method into your own learning and writing process. Now we will move on to Chapter 8, where I will give you some tips and suggestions for putting a professional shine on your prose.

Chapter 8

ADDING THE FINAL POLISH TO YOUR PROSE

Revision Strategies

WHERE ARE WE IN THE BIG PICTURE?

Now that you understand the NORTAV Method and perhaps have a few ideas as to how to incorporate it into your learning and writing process, there is still one topic left to cover. Look again at this diagram from Chapter 1:

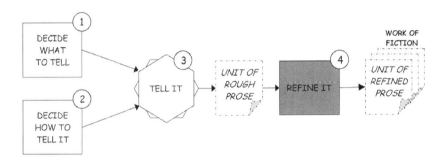

Step 4 of the Basic Four-Step Prose Construction Process

Remember, this diagram represents the basic four-step prose construction process. In Step 1 you decide what you want to tell. That is, you determine the narrative content. In Step 2 you decide how to tell it. That is, you determine the narrative schema. In Step 3 you fall into your dreamstate and merge information from the narrative content and the narrative schema with your knowledge of literal and figurative language and the three types of prose to form units of rough prose. Now we need to cover what happens in Step 4. We need to look at the different ways to refine rough prose into professional quality prose.

THE FOUR Cs OF REVISION

No professional's prose is perfect. Every published work will include some irregularities, mistakes, or rough areas that simply never get smoothed or corrected. It is up to each writer to determine how much revision should be performed on her rough prose. If you're an experienced writer who cranks out near-perfect quality prose in the first draft, you may not spend much time in revision at all, beyond a simple typo check. Those writers who do not produce near-perfect quality prose in their first draft, however, should spend some time and energy revising their work. Additionally, the style or genre of the work will impact how much time and energy should be spent in revision. Prose that's meant for light reading will not require as much revision as prose that's meant to be literary. In general, each writer needs to determine how much energy to spend in revision, but every writer should spend some amount of time revising their work.

What should a writer look for in the revision phase? Four things: All professional quality prose is *consistent, correct, concise,* and *clear.* If you remember our definition of prose from Chapter 2, we said that prose was a distilled set of writing that portrays a story or story segment through a narrator and/or through a character's senses. When you distill your prose, you are making sure your prose is consistent, correct, concise, and clear. Each of these aspects implies a different set of revision techniques, so let's look at each in turn.

BEING CONSISTENT

Professional quality prose will conform consistently and accurately to a narrative schema. Readers will intuitively understand a work of fiction's narrative modes and narrative pattern and will know, either consciously, semi-consciously, or subconsciously, when a writer deviates from the established mode or pattern. When there is a deviation, the reader may become confused, or simply feel the writing is somehow "off." Either way, you've lost a reader.

As a first step in your revision process, perform a NORTAV analysis on your prose. If you haven't done so already, determine the narrative mode(s) and the narrative pattern of your work-in-progress and then check each and every beat. Does each beat conform to all aspects of the narrative schema? Does your use of narrative modes conform to the narrative pattern? If you are transitioning from one narrative mode to the next, is your transition implemented smoothly, purposefully, and clearly? Are you changing narrative modes for a valid reason? Are there any beats that are unintentionally ambiguous or non-conforming that could be rephrased or recast such that they conform to the narrative schema? If you're working in an NCE-based narrative mode, are your narrative intrusions handled similarly and consistently throughout the work-in-progress?

Have you...?

I could list a hundred things to check in this step of the revision process. In short, it is up to you as the writer to fully understand each factor of your narrative schema. Once you do, make sure you are implementing the narrative schema consistently and accurately throughout your work-in-progress.

BEING CORRECT

Professional quality prose is free of errors. In this step of the revision process, go through and make sure every bit of your prose is grammatically correct. Check your spelling throughout the work-in-progress. Make sure you have knot misused any homophones, like I just did here. Make sure you you haven't duplicated any words, like I just did here. Make sure you haven't improperly punctuated your prose; like I just did here. If you have used improper grammar, like sentence fragments, make sure you've done so for a good reason. Like here.

Bottom line: Get yourself a dictionary and a grammar textbook. Take an advanced class in English grammar and syntax. Do everything in your power to learn how to properly use the tools in your literal and figurative language toolboxes. Nothing will make your prose seem less professional than an incorrect use of language.

BEING CONCISE

Professional quality prose is free of superfluous and extraneous words and phrases. For this step of the revision process, grab a copy of Strunk and White's *The Elements of Style*. Find the section on omitting needless words. Read it, study it, and apply its principles throughout your work-in-progress. This wonderful textbook will teach you everything you need to keep your writing as concise as possible. It takes a lot of mental energy to write fiction, but it also takes a lot of mental energy to read it. When a reader wades through fifteen words of prose to absorb something that could have been said in five, the reader will find your prose verbose, amateurish, and tiring. Like good chocolate fudge, professional quality prose is dense.

BEING CLEAR

Professional quality prose is always clear and easy to parse in a single pass. Meaning, the reader should never have to struggle to read a passage of prose in order to render the images or ideas across her mind's eye. That's not to say that every reader will understand every concept a writer deals with, or recognize every word a writer uses. But, given that the concepts and vocabulary are within a reader's grasp, the reader should never have to work hard at envisioning the story or following the narrator's train of thought. Professional quality prose is constructed such that the story or ideas flow smoothly and effortlessly across the reader's mind's eye.

Now, looking back at the last three Cs of revision you'll notice that each can be handled with one or two good reference tools. You can use the NORTAV Method to keep your prose consistent. You can use a dictionary and a good grammar textbook to keep your prose correct. You can use *The Elements of Style* to keep your prose concise. But, unfortunately, there are few single books or resources out there that will help you construct prose that is stylistically clear and easy to parse. There is certainly a wealth of good advice on the subject, but that advice seems to be scattered about, buried like little golden nuggets within many different resources. What follows are the top ten golden nuggets I've dug up over the years. Keep this list handy and use it as a resource for keeping your prose clear.

(1) *Maintain accuracy.*

Prose is created from your dreamstate. It's dredged up from the creative side of your brain. This side of the brain is notoriously sloppy. Inaccuracy can rear its ugly head in your prose in all sorts of ways: a wrong use of a word or phrase, an improperly structured metaphor, a poorly positioned modifier, etc. Go through your prose line by line and ask yourself if it is portraying (or saying) precisely what you meant it to portray (or say). Ask yourself if the line could somehow be misread or misinterpreted. This can be difficult to do because a) you're not an un-biased reader of your own work; you know what it is the prose is supposed to portray, and b) reading with an eye toward accuracy is an acquired skill. Do your best, or hire a sharp-eyed copyeditor to do it for you. Here's just one example of inaccurately rendered prose:

> I raked my hands through my hair like a baboon picking bugs from its fur.

Unclear or inaccurate metaphors abound in unprofessional writing. Both sides of a metaphor must somehow match. The closer the match, the more accurate the metaphor. The more accurate the metaphor, the clearer the prose. Here the raking motion in the first half of this metaphor clashes with the picking motion in the second half. Poor metaphors are only one of many, many ways prose can be rendered inaccurately.

(2) *Avoid simultaneity.*

It is always easier for a reader to parse through prose that portrays events one at a time. When events happen simultaneously, it forces the reader to parse each event separately and then stop to re-envision them as they happen together.

Go through your prose and look for any use of "-ing" or "as" or "while" or any other construct that indicates two or more events are occurring simultaneously. If you can make them occur serially, do so.

Simultaneous events are also famous for creating inaccuracies. For instance:

> Running to the door, I peered out the peep-hole.

Technically, this implies that the character is peering out the peep-hole while he or she is running to the door. Impossible at best, an embarrassment to the writer at worst. So, in general, remove any simultaneous events from your writing that you can. Only use simultaneous events when absolutely necessary, and when you do use them, make sure you check them for accuracy.

(3) *Don't over modify clauses.*

When a reader parses prose, she will imagine one piece of the story at a time. If she has to backtrack and re-imagine anything, the writing becomes less clear. We saw this with simultaneity. Over modifying your clauses will also cause the reader to backtrack. Look at this example:

> The boy gave the girl a kiss.

Here is an independent clause consisting of four parts: the boy, gave, the girl, and a kiss (i.e. subject, verb, indirect object, direct object). We can read this unmodified clause and parse it easily across the mind's eye in a single pass. Now let's start adding modifiers one at a time and see what happens.

> The blue-eyed boy gave the girl a kiss.

> The blue-eyed boy quickly gave the girl a kiss.

> The blue-eyed boy quickly gave the little red-headed girl a kiss.

The blue-eyed boy quickly gave the little red-headed girl a sloppy kiss on the cheek.

The blue-eyed, burly boy quickly and shyly gave the little red-headed girl a sloppy kiss on the cheek.

At some point, these examples will have gone from being clear and easy to parse to being muddy and difficult to parse. Which one did it for you? There is no definitive answer here. Every reader will parse prose differently. Every clause will consist of different parts and a different number of parts. Every modifier is different. Some modifiers are short, and some are long and more complex. It's up to the writer to decide how and how much to modify the parts of her clauses. The rule of thumb here is to modify the parts of a clause only up to a point where you can assure most readers will be able to parse through it in a single pass. This is a gut call. Read each of your clauses and pay attention to how easily the image or concept appears across your mind's eye. If you struggle in the least, you can bet the farm your reader will struggle as well. And doubly so.

(4) *Maintain symmetry.*

Readers are intensely sensitive to patterns and symmetry in writing. When writing is symmetric, the reader is eased through the parsing process. When writing is asymmetric or disjointed, that is, when the writer establishes a pattern and then does not adhere to that pattern, the reader has to frequently stop to reorganize images or thoughts in her mind's eye. Thus, symmetric writing is clear writing. Asymmetric or disjointed writing is unclear writing.

Writers create patterns in their writing all the time. Sometimes it is done purposefully, sometimes not. Search your prose for any patterns you may have established and make sure your prose is following those patterns consistently. Patterns can be established in a multitude of ways, far too many to ever put in a checklist. Discovering patterns in your writing is an acquired skill. The more you practice finding them, the more you will be aware of them as you create them, and the more you will adhere to them. Let's look at an example:

> Dale selected three tubes of paint, brush, and a canvas. He set the brush in an empty jar, placed the canvas on an easel, and the paint he squeezed onto a palette.

Looking closely at this example, we see a few patterns have been established and then, for lack of a nicer word, violated. First, the series of items in the first sentence all appear with some type of leading modifier ("three tubes of," "a") except "brush." Next, the items appear in a certain order, and then in the following sentence the items appear again in a different order. Finally, the phrasing of the first two actions (verbs) in the second sentence set a pattern, which is then violated in the third action. Cleaning up this example so that the patterns are constructed symmetrically will make it clearer and easier to parse:

> Dale selected a brush, a canvas, and three tubes of paint. He set the brush in an empty jar, placed the canvas on an easel, and squeezed the paint onto a palette.

Notice here we have reordered the first sentence so that the items appear in the same order as they do in the second sentence. Notice we have added an "a" before "brush" in the first sentence so that the three listed items read similarly. Notice in the second sentence we put the verb "squeezed" at the start of the final phrase so that it is structured similarly to the first two phrases.

As I've said and as you can probably imagine, patterns can be established in a multitude of ways. Learn to recognize when you have created any kind of pattern in your prose, and make sure that the pattern is adhered to. The more symmetric your use of patterns, the clearer the prose will become.

Should all prose follow every pattern it establishes?

Of course not!

Simply be aware that the more noticeable the pattern is to the reader, the more any reoccurrence of that pattern should remain symmetric.

(5) *Don't unnecessarily repeat words or concepts.*

We know that readers are intensely sensitive to patterns. The use of individual words or concepts can also cause patterns. When a writer needlessly repeats the same word in close proximity, the reader, consciously, semi-consciously, or subconsciously, will pause to try to understand the pattern the writer is implying. When the writer repeats words purposefully, and does it symmetrically, the reader is presented with clear, pleasing, easy-to-parse prose, like this example:

> He gave her the knife, the knife he had kept hidden for years, the knife he had used to murder BlackJack Johnson.

Here the word (or phrase, actually) "the knife" is repeated three times in proximity. It is repeated purposefully and symmetrically and reinforces the importance of the knife to the situation at hand. The reader parses through the clause easily and only once. Now look at this example:

> Larry was expecting to have the nightmare again. He had been suffering from a recurring nightmare filled with snakes and spiders. He'd been having the nightmare on and off for months, but when his stress level rose, the nightmare was there waiting for him as soon as he closed his eyes.

Here the word "nightmare" repeats several times within three sentences. Because there is no symmetry or pattern in use here, the recurring word jars the reader and slows down the parsing process. It makes the prose less clear because the reader, most likely subconsciously, will slow down and try to uncover a reason for the repetition. In this example, the writer should revise this so that either the word is used in a purposeful, repeating pattern, or the word is only used once.

What, then, constitutes close proximity? How close can two words be without jarring the reader?

Again, this is a gut call. The more unique the word, the greater the distance. The less unique, the less the distance. But even a word like "from" or "or" can jar the reader if it is repeated within a matter of a few words. Notice this last sentence. The word "or" repeats within the span of two words. Did you detect the repetition? Notice the word "a" repeats at the end of the sentence within a span of four words. Did you detect that repetition? If you notice an unintentional repetition of a word in the slightest, you should recast your prose so it's only used once.

A last note on repeating words: When you catch one and want to correct the repetition, don't simply replace a reoccurrence with a synonym or a pronoun. In doing so you have only traded one problem for another. Instead of having a repeating word, you have a repeating reference. Use synonyms only as a last resort and pronouns as a second-to-last resort. More often than not, repeating words can be eliminated by making the prose more concise and/or by rephrasing.

Repeating concepts will also jar the reader and make the writing less clear. If you have told (or shown) the reader that a certain sofa is bright red, you don't need to mention it again unless you have a very good reason. If you have told (or shown) a reader that a character is angry, then you don't need to do so again until you are ready to remind the reader of that fact. If you have told (or shown) the reader a character has stepped out of the house, you don't have to remind the reader that the character is outdoors. The art of not repeating words or concepts is just that... an art. Review your prose with an eye for repeating words and concepts and then follow your instinct when revising.

(6) *Avoid awkward constructs.*

Simply the way certain words or phrases come together can cause readers to stumble as they parse through prose. Sometimes it's an unfortunate pairing of two words in proximity that might spark a different image in the reader's mind than was intended by the writer. Sometimes it's a poor arrangement of clauses. Sometimes it's a choice or arrangement of words or phrases that would be difficult to pronounce if the words were read aloud, as most readers will "hear" themselves speak the prose in their mind's eye/ear. Sometimes it's a strange or jarring combination of stresses and syllables that causes the rhythm of the writing to stagger and skip.

Unfortunately, there are hundreds of ways a writer can create awkward prose. Amateur writers are experts at it. Here's one way:

> I walked down the street and then ran into Tom Thomson.

While otherwise perfectly correct, the use of "walked" and "ran" in this close context could cause the reader to imagine the focal character was walking down the street and then suddenly broke out into a run. It isn't until we get to "Tom Thomson" that we realize the focal character didn't break out into a run after all, but rather "met" someone. The duel meaning of the work "ran" could cause the sentence to read awkwardly for some readers, which would cause those readers to have to go back and re-imagine this event again.

To avoid awkwardness in your writing, read the work-in-progress aloud. Several times. Reading aloud will bring to light most places where your prose remains clunky, misleading, or generally awkward and hard to parse.

(7) *Avoid vague, abstract constructs.*

Concrete writing is clear. Vague or abstract writing is less clear. Look at these two examples:

> Scratching at trembling arms, I walked down to the dock.

> Sometimes when he touched the hardened surface, he thought it was a sort of cocoon with life transforming underneath.

Where is the article or modifier before "trembling arms" in the first example? Where is the article or modifier before "life transforming" in the second example? They are missing, as the writer is trying to use these phrases abstractly rather than concretely, which makes the writing less clear. Now look at these modified versions:

> Scratching at my trembling arms, I walked down to the dock.

> Sometimes when he touched the hardened surface, he thought it was a sort of cocoon with some unborn life transforming underneath.

While the writing here is still not great, at least the writing is clearer after having the abstractions corrected. Go through your prose and make sure each beat is rendered as concretely as possible. Abstractions are harder to envision within a reader's mind's eye than concrete images. Keep your prose concrete whenever possible.

(8) *Avoid stringing together too many phrases.*

Avoid the temptation to add detail to your writing by tacking on a litany of phrases to main clauses, especially when those phrases begin with "that" or "which." For example:

> I went down to the grocery store that had been there for over fifty years, which some might think was a terribly long time for a grocery store to exist in St. Kelvin, since so many terrible things had happened there in the early 30s, which of course was when the Depression was in full swing.

Stringing together too many phrases will cause the reader to have to pause and reread phrases over and over in order to envision the entire sentence as a conceptual whole.

(9) *Avoid the passive voice.*

Never use the passive voice when you can use the active voice. If you don't understand what that means, read the section on passive voice in *The Elements of Style* and follow Strunk's advice.

In short, never write:

The pistol was given to me by Pete.

Instead, write:

Pete gave me the pistol.

(10) *Minimize adjectives and adverbs by using strong nouns and verbs.*

This one is straight forward. Each time you run across an adverb or an adjective in your prose, try to eliminate it by using a better choice of noun or verb that encapsulates the intent of the adverb or adjective.

For example:

The strange creature ran quickly down the street.

Could become:

The beast bolted down the street.

LET'S RECAP

By now you should understand that:

- Professional prose is consistent, correct, concise, and clear, i.e. it is distilled.

- Consistent prose is prose that conforms consistently and accurately to a narrative schema.

- Correct prose is prose that contains no typos and no unintentional grammatical, punctuation, or spelling errors.

- Concise prose is prose that is free of superfluous or extraneous words and phrases.

- Clear prose is prose that can be parsed easily in a single pass.

And now we've reached the end of this book. If you have taken the time and put in the effort to study the concepts I've covered here, and if you have worked through all the assignments and exercises, you should now know everything you need to know in order to create professional quality prose. All that's left is *conscious* practice, practice, practice!

My advice to you now is, *don't stop here*! I have included an appendix containing fifteen more NORTAV analyses. Go through them and perform your own analyses. Compare yours to mine. Learn from the examples of these professional authors. Then move on and perform your own NORTAV analyses on the prose of your favorite authors. Continue to learn from them. Now and forever.

Finally, I encourage you to visit http://thenortavmethod.com/, where I will post more NORTAV analyses, writing tips, information on upcoming workshops, and other fun and interesting stuff.

I hope you've enjoyed learning about the NORTAV Method as much as I've enjoyed developing and teaching it!

So, until next time...

Keep creatin'!

Appendix

FIFTEEN ADDITIONAL NORTAV ANALYSES

NORTAV Analysis #1: Barry Eisler's *The Lost Coast*

PROSE SAMPLE

For this analysis we will look at an excerpt from *The Lost Coast*, a short story by Barry Eisler. For more information about Barry and his work, you can visit http://www.barryeisler.com/.

... The sun was setting on the redwoods and Larison thought it was time to find a place to stop. He'd been driving north from Los Angeles for ten days, sometimes moving continuously during the daylight hours, other times going not very far at all, never more than one night in the same place. He knew the people looking for him had no way to track him, but even if they did, there would inevitably be some lag between the moment they could find and fix him and the deployment of actual forces. The more he kept moving, the more any information his pursuers managed to develop would be useless by the time they could do anything to act on it.

He'd been traveling the coastal highway, but north of Westport it had turned inland, the terrain apparently too rugged for the road to continue along the Pacific, and not long after it had died without fanfare, collapsing into Route 101. He knew from the map on the passenger seat that 101, also called the Redwood Highway, would meander northwest along the King mountain range before reuniting with the Pacific somewhere north of Ferndale. The area in between, cut off from coastal access, was known colloquially as the Lost Coast, a name Larison had found strangely alluring when he'd first heard it years before. He imagined black sand beaches, prehistoric redwood forests, towns as remote and strange as creatures from the Galapagos. Maybe he would spend a few days in the area, passing through disconnected burgs like Petrolia and Honeydew and Shelter Cove, dots on the map next to him. He felt secretly pleased at the notion of a man like himself disappearing in a place that by its name declared it couldn't be found.

A road sign told him he was thirty miles from Arcata. He'd never been there, but he knew of it. An old mining and then timber nexus on Arcata Bay, now mostly a college town. He'd find a hotel that would take cash and not demand ID. If that didn't pan out, he'd keep going and find something else. There was always another town.

It was nearly dark as he left the highway, the sliver of a crescent moon hanging low in the sky. He didn't have a car navigation system or even a cell phone, either of which could be tracked, but he didn't really need the technology, either. There was usually a logic in the layout of small towns, with independent restaurants and retail establishments in the center, gas stations, supermarkets, and other chains farther out, and the more sprawling single family dwellings on the periphery. Some were easier to navigate than others, but it didn't matter one way or the other. He was rarely in a hurry.

He found his way by the usual signs to the center of Arcata, which, as it happened, was impossible to miss: a large square plaza surrounded by bars, restaurants, and small shops...

NORTAV ANALYSIS

Narrative Mode: *NCE 1*

Narrator: *Omniscient*

Narrative Intrusion: *Yes*

Focal Character(s): *Larison*

Prose Type(s) and/or Beat Types(s): *NCE and DCE. Style uses mostly DCE and little-to-no Direct NCE beats.*

Narrative Tense: *Past*

Additional Constraints: *None*

Narrative Pattern: *NCE 1 throughout.*

Analysis:

[No1] The sun was setting on the redwoods and [Nt2] Larison thought it was time to find a place to stop. [Nt3] He'd been driving north from Los Angeles for ten days, sometimes moving continuously during the daylight hours, other times going not very far at all, never more than one night in the same place. He knew the people looking for him had no way to track him, but even if they did, there would inevitably be some lag between the moment they could find and fix him and the deployment of actual forces. The more he kept moving, the more any information his pursuers managed to develop would be useless by the time they could do anything to act on it.

Barry opens with Narrated Observation beat [No1] that triggers Narrated Thought beat [Nt2]. [Nt2] triggers compound Narrated Thought beat [Nt3]. This is another great example of how a writer will use a triggered thought to provide the reader with background information. Here [Nt3] is perceived as Larison mulling over what's been happening, and his thought process reveals background information, catching the reader up on Larison's recent activities in a sort of mini-flashback.

[Nt4] He'd been traveling the coastal highway, but north

of Westport it had turned inland, the terrain apparently too rugged for the road to continue along the Pacific, and not long after it had died without fanfare, collapsing into Route 101. He knew from the map on the passenger seat that 101, also called the Redwood Highway, would meander northwest along the King mountain range before reuniting with the Pacific somewhere north of Ferndale. The area in between, cut off from coastal access, was known colloquially as the Lost Coast, a name Larison had found strangely alluring when he'd first heard it years before. He imagined black sand beaches, prehistoric redwood forests, towns as remote and strange as creatures from the Galapagos. Maybe he would spend a few days in the area, passing through disconnected burgs like Petrolia and Honeydew and Shelter Cove, dots on the map next to him. [Nm5] He felt secretly pleased at the notion of a man like himself disappearing in a place that by its name declared it couldn't be found.

Here [Nt3] triggers more musings in compound Narrated Thought beat [Nt4]. [Nt4] reveals even more background information. [Nt4] leads/triggers [Nm5]. [Nm5] is a Mixed NCE beat that includes a reaction and a thought. Technically, [Nt4] leads to the thought portion of [Nm5], which triggers the reaction portion of [Nm5]. Barry is most likely doing this subconsciously, but notice how tight and well-linked the prose is. Barry leads the reader from one beat to the next so the prose is easy to read and follow. Also notice [Nm5] firmly establishes the narrative mode as NCE-based.

[Nm6] A road sign told him he was thirty miles from Arcata. [Nt7] He'd never been there, but he knew of it. An old mining and then timber nexus on Arcata Bay, now mostly a college town. He'd find a hotel that would take cash and not demand ID. If that didn't pan out, he'd keep going and find something else. There was always another town.

Here [Nm6] is an initiating Mixed NCE beat. It combines an observation and a thought. The observation portion interrupts into the prose chain. [Nm6] triggers the train of thought in [Nt7]. Notice the style Barry is using is very intimate, formed by combining lots of DCE with just enough NCE beats to keep the reader reminded of the narrator's presence.

> [Nm8] It was nearly dark as he left the highway, the sliver of a crescent moon hanging low in the sky. [Nt9] He didn't have a car navigation system or even a cell phone, either of which could be tracked, but he didn't really need the technology, either. There was usually a logic in the layout of small towns, with independent restaurants and retail establishments in the center, gas stations, supermarkets, and other chains farther out, and the more sprawling single family dwellings on the periphery. Some were easier to navigate than others, but it didn't matter one way or the other. He was rarely in a hurry.

[Nm8] is a Mixed NCE beat that contains bits of observations and action. It links logically back to [Nm6] as it continues the description of Larison's travel. [Nt9] is an initiating compound Narrated Thought beat.

> [Nc10] He found his way by the usual signs to the center of Arcata, which, as it happened, was impossible to miss: a large square plaza surrounded by bars, restaurants, and small shop.

Finally, [Nc10] is an initiating Consolidated NCE beat linked logically back to [Nm8]. It rolls up Larison's actions, thoughts, and observations into a higher level concept that includes Larison's unmentioned perceptions and activities.

NORTAV Analysis #2: Blake Crouch's *Desert Places*

PROSE SAMPLE

For this analysis we will look at an excerpt from *Desert Places*, a novel by Blake Crouch. For more information about Blake and his work, you can visit his website at http://www.blakecrouch.com/.

> ... On a lovely May evening, I sat on my deck, watching the sun descend upon Lake Norman. So far, it had been a perfect day. I'd risen at 5:00 A. M. as I always do, put on a pot of French roast, and prepared my usual breakfast of scrambled eggs and a bowl of fresh pineapple. By six o'clock, I was writing, and I didn't stop until noon. I fried two white crappies I'd caught the night before, and the moment I sat down for lunch, my agent called. Cynthia fields my messages when I'm close to finishing a book, and she had several for me, the only one of real importance being that the movie deal for my latest novel, Blue Murder, had closed. It was good news of course, but two other movies had been made from my books, so I was used to it by now.
>
> I worked in my study for the remainder of the afternoon and quit at 6:30. My final edits of the new as yet untitled manuscript would be finished tomorrow. I was tired, but my thriller, The Scorcher, would be on bookshelves within the week. I savored the exhaustion that followed a full day of work. My hands sore from typing, eyes dry and strained, I shut down the computer and rolled back from the desk in my swivel chair.
>
> I went outside and walked up the long gravel drive toward the mailbox. It was the first time I'd been out all

day, and the sharp sunlight burned my eyes as it squeezed through the tall rows of loblollies that bordered both sides of the drive. It was so quiet here. Fifteen miles south, Charlotte was still gridlocked in rush-hour traffic, and I was grateful not to be a part of that madness. As the tiny rocks crunched beneath my feet, I pictured my best friend, Walter Lancing, fuming in his Cadillac. He'd be cursing the drone of horns and the profusion of taillights as he inched away from his suite in uptown Charlotte, leaving the quarterly nature magazine Hiker to return home to his wife and children. Not me, I thought, the solitary one.

For once, my mailbox wasn't overflowing. Two envelopes lay inside, one a bill, the other blank except for my address typed on the outside. Fan mail.

Back inside, I mixed myself a Jack Daniel's and Sun-Drop and took my mail and a book on criminal pathology out onto the deck. Settling into a rocking chair, I set everything but my drink on a small glass table and gazed down to the water. My backyard is narrow, and the woods flourish a quarter mile on either side, keeping my home of ten years in isolation from my closest neighbors. Spring had not come this year until mid-April, so the last of the pink and white dogwood blossoms still specked the variably green interior of the surrounding forest...

NORTAV ANALYSIS

Narrative Mode: *NCE 1*

    Narrator: *Andrew Z. Thomas*

    Narrative Intrusion: *Yes*

    Focal Character(s): *Andrew Z. Thomas*

Prose Type(s) and/or Beat Types(s): *NCE and DCE. Style uses mostly NCE with a few instances of DCE.*

Narrative Tense: *Past*

Additional Constraints: *None*

Narrative Pattern: *NCE 1 throughout.*

Analysis:

[Nm1] On a lovely May evening, I sat on my deck, watching the sun descend upon Lake Norman. [Nt2] So far, it had been a perfect day. I'd risen at 5:00 A. M. as I always do, put on a pot of French roast, and prepared my usual breakfast of scrambled eggs and a bowl of fresh pineapple. By six o'clock, I was writing, and I didn't stop until noon. I fried two white crappies I'd caught the night before, and the moment I sat down for lunch, my agent called. Cynthia fields my messages when I'm close to finishing a book, and she had several for me, the only one of real importance being that the movie deal for my latest novel, Blue Murder, had closed. It was good news of course, but two other movies had been made from my books, so I was used to it by now.

Blake opens with [Nm1], a beat of Mixed NCE which immediately establishes the NCE-based narrative mode. [Nm1] combines bits of narrative information, action, and observation. [Nm1] leads to [Nt2], a compound Narrated Thought beat. In [Nt2] Andrew is reflecting back on his day in the form of a mini-flashback, which provides the reader with necessary background information. Again, a favorite technique of professional writers.

[Na3] I worked in my study for the remainder of the afternoon and quit at 6:30. [Nt4] My final edits of the new as yet untitled manuscript would be finished tomorrow. [Nm5] I was tired, but my thriller, The Scorcher, would be on bookshelves within the week. [Nm6] I savored the exhaustion that followed a full day of work. My hands sore from typing, eyes dry and strained, [Na7] I shut down the computer and rolled back from the desk in my swivel chair.

[Nt2] leads to [Na3], a Narrated Action beat where the reader returns from the mini-flashback to the current time established in [Nm1]. [Na3] leads to [Nt4], a Narrated Thought beat, which leads to [Nm5], a beat of Mixed NCE that includes an observation and a thought. [Nm5] leads to Mixed NCE beat [Nm6], which includes bits of observations and thought. [Nm6] leads to [Na7], a Narrated Action beat.

[Na8] I went outside and walked up the long gravel drive toward the mailbox. [Nt9] It was the first time I'd been out all day, and [No10] the sharp sunlight burned my eyes as it squeezed through the tall rows of loblollies that bordered both sides of the drive. [Nt11] It was so quiet here. Fifteen miles south, Charlotte was still grid-locked in rush-hour traffic, and [Nm12] I was grateful not to be a part of that madness. [No13] As the tiny rocks crunched beneath my feet, [Nt14] I pictured my best friend, Walter Lancing, fuming in his Cadillac. He'd be cursing the drone of horns and the profusion of taillights as he inched away from his suite in uptown Charlotte, leaving the quarterly nature magazine Hiker to return home to his wife and children. Not me, I thought, the solitary one.

[Na7] leads to [Na8], a Narrated Action beat. [Na8] leads to [Nt9], a Narrated Thought beat. [Nt9] leads to [No10], a Narrated Observation beat. [No10] leads to [Nt11], a Narrated Thought beat. [Nt11] triggers [Nm12], a beat of Mixed NCE that includes bits of reaction and thought. Narrated Observation beat [No13] continues where [Na8] left off. Compound Narrated Thought beat [Nt14] continues where [Nt11] left off.

{No15} [Nt16] For once, my mailbox wasn't overflowing. [No17] Two envelopes lay inside, one a bill, the other blank except for my address typed on the outside. [Nt18] Fan mail.

Here, implied initiating Narrated Observation beat {Nt15} leads to [Nt16], a Narrated Thought beat. Narrated Observation beat [No17] continues from the implied Narrated Observation beat. One could have dropped the implied Narrated Observation beat and assumed that these beats were out of normal order, but for me it felt more like a continuation that followed the normal order of events. In other words, Andrew sees something in his mailbox (implied), realizes it's not overflowing, and then takes a closer look at what's inside.

Finally, [No17] triggers Narrated Thought beat [Nt18].

[Na19] Back inside, I mixed myself a Jack Daniel's and Sun-Drop and took my mail and a book on criminal pathology out onto the deck. Settling into a rocking chair, I set everything but my drink on a small glass table and [Na20] gazed down to the water. [Nm21] My backyard is narrow, and the woods flourish a quarter mile on either side, keeping my home of ten years in isolation from my closest neighbors. Spring had not come this year until mid-April, so the last of the pink and white dogwood blossoms still specked the variably green interior of the surrounding forest.

Here [Na19] is an initiating compound Narrated Action beat that restarts the story at some point in time after [Nt18]. [Na19] leads to Narrated Action beat [Na20]. [Na20] is not combined with [Na19] because it has a specific role in the prose chain. It triggers [Nm21], a compound beat of Mixed NCE. [Nm21] includes several observations and thoughts.

NORTAV Analysis #3: Bob Mayer's Duty, Honor, Country – A Novel of West Point and the Civil War

PROSE SAMPLE

For this analysis we will look at an excerpt from *Duty, Honor, Country: A Novel of West Point and the Civil War*, by Bob Mayer. For more information about Bob and his work, you can visit his website at http://www.bobmayer.org/.

… "To, duty, honor, and country," William Tecumseh Sherman proposed, raising his mug of ale.

He shoved his chair back, along with his classmate who sat at the same table. The mugs were clunked together, whereupon the two turned their backs to each other and imbibed. Done, they turned to the table and reclaimed their seats inside the tavern on the west bank of the Hudson River, just outside of the Military Academy post limits.

"Tell me, Mister Sherman," a young cadet leaning against the bar asked, "why do you say honor in the center as the linchpin between duty and country, and not loyalty?"

Before Sherman could respond, his classmate, a lean young man with a hatchet face under short, thick black hair, drawled in a low, southern voice. "Why, honor is all a man has, Mister Cord."

Cord laughed. "Where I come from, we couldn't afford honor, Mister King."

The three cadets were the only customers left in the

dimly lit tavern, with dawn less than an hour off. A rough wooden plank bar stretched across one side of the room. Behind it, head slumped onto the scarred surface, was the proprietor, Benny Havens. His loud snoring sawed through the room. Clanking noises came through the curtain behind him, where his daughter, Lidia, was cleaning up the remains of the party that had covered most of the night as many members of the class of 1840 had celebrated their pending graduation. Cord was not a member of '40, but finishing his plebe year, class of '43.

King shook his head, but didn't immediately pursue Cord's observation. "A toast without a fine cigar is practically wasted."

He unbuttoned his dress grey tunic and withdrew a pair of cigars. "Direct from my home in Charleston, where they came straight from Havana." He extended one to Sherman.

The two Firsties went through the lighting ritual, to add to the lingering cloud from the night's revelries.

King blew a puff of smoke Cord's way. "With your grades and conduct record, Mister Cord, one could not expect any different."

"Here, here." Sherman slapped a hand on the scarred wooden table. "None of that. It's not fair." He had fiery red hair and thick sideburns that tapered toward the point of his chin, not quite meeting.

"Cord is the Immortal in every section, Cump," King said. "Last in every one! An honorable man would not hold such a record. He should have more pride. He should have the decency to study."

"Mister Cord studies," Sherman said. He turned to Cord with a grin. "You do, don't you?"

Benny Havens lifted his head off the bar and blearily gazed about, like an old hound dog sensing trouble at a distance.

Cord was of average size and tightly built. His face was pleasant, made more so by a wide mouth that was most amendable to a cheerful expression...

NORTAV ANALYSIS

Narrative Mode: *DCE 1*

    Narrator: *Omniscient*

    Narrative Intrusion: *No*

    Focal Character(s): *Abstract*

    Prose Type(s) and/or Beat Types(s): *DCE*

    Narrative Tense: *Past*

    Additional Constraints: *None*

Narrative Pattern: *DCE 1 throughout*

Analysis:

[O1] "To, duty, honor, and country," William Tecumseh Sherman proposed, raising his mug of ale.

Bob opens with a bit of Sherman's speech. Without knowing who the focal character is, we don't know if this is Sherman's Vocalization beat (making Sherman the focal character) or an Observation beat from another character (making the other character the focal character). In actuality, it's neither. By the end of this sample we realize we are dealing with an abstract focal character (at least as far as this excerpt goes). Thus, we perceive each of these DCE beats as sight, sound, and smell observations coming from an invisible, non-commenting entity on the scene. If we read beyond this excerpt, we may discover the narrative mode to be different. That's fine. As always, in a NORTAV analysis we're limited to describing the sample at hand.

> [O2] He shoved his chair back, along with his classmate who sat at the same table. The mugs were clunked together, whereupon the two turned their backs to each other and imbibed. Done, they turned to the table and reclaimed their seats inside the tavern on the west bank of the Hudson River, just outside of the Military Academy post limits.

[O1] leads to [O2]. Notice in addition to getting sight and sound information, we're also getting some additional incidental narrative information. The abstract focal character reveals that the two men are classmates. And that they are on the west bank of the Hudson. Slipping in incidental narrative information like this when using an abstract focal character is fine, as the reader will still perceives this as "fly on the wall," provided the information does not include comments or opinions or conclusions, as that would cause the reader to feel the narrator is a specific personality in the story and not just an abstract, observing entity.

> [O3] "Tell me, Mister Sherman," a young cadet leaning against the bar asked, "why do you say honor in the center as the linchpin between duty and country, and not loyalty?"

[O2] leads to [O3]. Again, sight and sound observations only.

> [O4] Before Sherman could respond, his classmate, a lean young man with a hatchet face under short, thick black hair, drawled in a low, southern voice. "Why, honor is all a man has, Mister Cord."

Next, [O3] leads to [O4].

[O5] Cord laughed. "Where I come from, we couldn't afford honor, Mister King."

[O4] leads to [O5]. More sights and sounds.

[O6] The three cadets were the only customers left in the dimly lit tavern, with dawn less than an hour off. A rough wooden plank bar stretched across one side of the room. Behind it, head slumped onto the scarred surface, was the proprietor, Benny Havens. His loud snoring sawed through the room. Clanking noises came through the curtain behind him, where his daughter, Lidia, was cleaning up the remains of the party that had covered most of the night as many members of the class of 1840 had celebrated their pending graduation. Cord was not a member of '40, but finishing his plebe year, class of '43.

[O5] leads to [O6]. More sights, sounds, and small bits of objective incidental narrative information.

[O7] King shook his head, but didn't immediately pursue Cord's observation. "A toast without a fine cigar is practically wasted." He unbuttoned his dress grey tunic and withdrew a pair of cigars. "Direct from my home in Charleston, where they came straight from Havana." He extended one to Sherman.

[O8] The two Firsties went through the lighting ritual, to add to the lingering cloud from the night's revelries.

[O9] King blew a puff of smoke Cord's way. "With your grades and conduct record, Mister Cord, one could not expect any different."

[O6] leads to [O7], which leads to [O8], which leads to [O9]. More sights, sounds, and bits of objective incidental narrative information.

[010] "Here, here." Sherman slapped a hand on the scarred wooden table. "None of that. It's not fair." He had fiery red hair and thick sideburns that tapered toward the point of his chin, not quite meeting.

[09] leads to [010]. Up until now one could have made an argument that Sherman is acting as the focal character, with an additional constraint that excludes his internal thoughts or reactions from the narrative mode. But here we get an external observation of Sherman's appearance, which could not be coming from Sherman himself. This beat is where, for me, the mode was solidified as DCE-based with an abstract focal character. Again, this determination is based solely on the prose presented in the excerpt. The narrative mode might actually be something completely different. Only with the complete context could we be sure.

[011] "Cord is the Immortal in every section, Cump," King said. "Last in every one! An honorable man would not hold such a record. He should have more pride. He should have the decency to study."

[012] "Mister Cord studies," Sherman said. He turned to Cord with a grin. "You do, don't you?"

[013] Benny Havens lifted his head off the bar and blearily gazed about, like an old hound dog sensing trouble at a distance.

[014] Cord was of average size and tightly built. His face was pleasant, made more so by a wide mouth that was most amendable to a cheerful expression.

[010] leads to [011], which leads to [012], which leads to [013], which leads to [014]. Again, more sight and sound observations.

With no discernible focal character, this was a tricky excerpt to analyze. Is this really a DCE-based narrative mode with an abstract focal character? Pick up Bob's novel and find out for yourself. Remember, context is king. When continuing on with your learning process, you will have access to the complete context of a work of fiction. Use every bit of it.

NORTAV Analysis #4: Charles Dicken's The Mystery of *Edwin Drood*

PROSE SAMPLE

For this analysis we will look at an excerpt from *The Mystery of Edwin Drood*, a classic novel by Charles Dickens. For more information about Charles Dickens and his work, you can visit Project Gutenberg at `http://www.gutenberg.org/`.

... An ancient English Cathedral Tower? How can the ancient English Cathedral tower be here! The well-known massive gray square tower of its old Cathedral? How can that be here! There is no spike of rusty iron in the air, between the eye and it, from any point of the real prospect. What is the spike that intervenes, and who has set it up? Maybe it is set up by the Sultan's orders for the impaling of a horde of Turkish robbers, one by one. It is so, for cymbals clash, and the Sultan goes by to his palace in long procession. Ten thousand scimitars flash in the sunlight, and thrice ten thousand dancing-girls strew flowers. Then, follow white elephants caparisoned in countless gorgeous colours, and infinite in number and attendants. Still the Cathedral Tower rises in the background, where it cannot be, and still no writhing figure is on the grim spike. Stay! Is the spike so low a thing as the rusty spike on the top of a post of an old bedstead that has tumbled all awry? Some vague period of drowsy laughter must be devoted to the consideration of this possibility.

Shaking from head to foot, the man whose scattered consciousness has thus fantastically pieced itself together, at length rises, supports his trembling frame upon his arms, and looks around. He is in the meanest and closest of small rooms. Through the ragged window-curtain, the light of early day steals in from a miserable court. He lies, dressed, across a large unseemly bed, upon a bedstead that has indeed given way under the weight upon it. Lying, also dressed and also across the bed, not longwise, are a Chinaman, a Lascar, and a haggard woman. The two first are in a sleep or stupor; the last is blowing at a kind of pipe, to kindle it. And as she blows, and shading it with her lean hand, concentrates its red spark of light, it serves in the dim morning as a lamp to show him what he sees of her.

'Another?' says this woman, in a querulous, rattling whisper. 'Have another?'

He looks about him, with his hand to his forehead.

'Ye've smoked as many as five since ye come in at midnight,' the woman goes on, as she chronically complains. 'Poor me, poor me, my head is so bad. Them two come in after ye. Ah, poor me, the business is slack, is slack! Few Chinamen about the Docks, and fewer Lascars, and no ships coming in, these say! Here's another ready for ye, deary. Ye'll remember like a good soul, won't ye, that the market price is dreffle high just now? More nor three shillings and sixpence for a thimbleful! And ye'll remember that nobody but me (and Jack Chinaman t'other side the court; but he can't do it as well as me) has the true secret of mixing it? Ye'll pay up accordingly, deary, won't ye?'...

NORTAV ANALYSIS

Narrative Mode: *NCE 1*

Narrator: *Omniscient*

Narrative Intrusion: *Yes*

Focal Character(s): *"The man whose scattered consciousness..."*

Prose Type(s) and/or Beat Types(s): *NCE and DCE*

Narrative Tense: *Present*

Additional Constraints: *None*

Narrative Pattern: *NCE 1 throughout.*

Analysis:

{No1}[Nt2] An ancient English Cathedral Tower? How can the ancient English Cathedral tower be here! The well-known massive gray square tower of its old Cathedral? How can that be here! There is no spike of rusty iron in the air, between the eye and it, from any point of the real prospect. What is the spike that intervenes, and who has set it up? Maybe it is set up by the Sultan's orders for the impaling of a horde of Turkish robbers, one by one. It is so, for cymbals clash, and the Sultan goes by to his palace in long procession. Ten thousand scimitars flash in the sunlight, and thrice ten thousand dancing-girls strew flowers. Then, follow white elephants caparisoned in countless gorgeous colours, and infinite in number and attendants. Still the Cathedral Tower rises in the background, where it cannot be, and still no writhing figure is on the grim spike. Stay! Is the spike so low a thing as the rusty spike on the top of a post of an old bedstead that has tumbled all awry? Some vague period of drowsy laughter must be devoted to the consideration of this possibility.

Dickens opens with {No1}, an implied Narrated Observation beat that leads to [Nt2], a compound Narrated Thought beat. Nearly all of [Nt2] is acting as a substitute for the focal character's implied observation.

{No3}[Nr4] Shaking from head to foot, [Na5] the man

whose scattered consciousness has thus fantastically pieced itself together, at length rises, supports his trembling frame upon his arms, and looks around. [No6] He is in the meanest and closest of small rooms. Through the ragged window-curtain, the light of early day steals in from a miserable court. [No7] He lies, dressed, across a large unseemly bed, upon a bedstead that has indeed given way under the weight upon it. Lying, also dressed and also across the bed, not longwise, are a Chinaman, a Lascar, and a haggard woman. The two first are in a sleep or stupor; the last is blowing at a kind of pipe, to kindle it. [No8] And as she blows, and shading it with her lean hand, concentrates its red spark of light, [Nt9] it serves in the dim morning as a lamp to show him what he sees of her.

{No3} is an initiating implied Narrated Observation beat. Here something (waking up) causes the focal character to shake in Narrated Reaction beat [Nr4]. [Nr4] leads to [Na5], a Narrated Action beat. [Na5] leads to [No6], a Narrated Observation beat. This leads to the next Narrated Observation beat [No7], which leads to [No8]. [No8] leads to Narrated Thought beat [Nt9].

[No10] 'Another?' says this woman, in a querulous, rattling whisper. 'Have another?'

[No10] is an initiating Narrated Observation beat.

[Na11] He looks about him, with his hand to his forehead.

[No10] triggers [No11], a Narrated Action beat.

[No12] 'Ye've smoked as many as five since ye come in at midnight,' the woman goes on, as she chronically complains. 'Poor me, poor me, my head is so bad. Them two come in after ye. Ah, poor me, the business is slack, is slack! Few Chinamen about the Docks, and fewer Lascars, and no ships coming in, these say! Here's another ready for ye, deary. Ye'll remember like a good soul, won't ye, that the market price is dreffle high just now? More nor three shillings and sixpence for a thimbleful! And ye'll remember that nobody but me (and Jack Chinaman t'other side the court; but he can't do it as well as me) has the true secret of mixing it? Ye'll pay up accordingly, deary, won't ye?'

Finally, [No12] is another initiating Narrated Observation beat.

NORTAV Analysis #5: Dean Wesley Smith's *The Old Girlfriend of Doom*

PROSE SAMPLE

For this analysis we will look at an excerpt from *The Old Girlfriend of Doom*, a short story by Dean Wesley Smith. For more information about Dean and his work, you can visit his website at `http://www.deanwesleysmith.com/`.

> ... Sometimes even superheroes can't save the day, or the girl, or the dog, and that fact is even sadder when the girl is one of the superhero's old girlfriends.
>
> Honest, Poker Boy, and just about every superhero, once had a childhood, a life as a young adult, without powers. I only discovered my Poker Boy super abilities later in life, after I had lived a fairly regular life until the age of twenty-nine. Little did I know that someday I would put on the black leather jacket and the fedora-like hat and become Poker Boy, savior of blind women, lost husbands, and dogs.
>
> It was Christmas Eve, a holiday for me just about like every other one. I was home, alone, in my double-wide mobile home that I had bought twenty years ago with the money from my winnings in a poker tournament. The green couch and chairs had come with it, and so far I had seen no reason to replace the perfectly good, but dog-ugly furniture. As a national-level poker player, I had more than enough money in a dozen accounts to buy a nice home, and nice furniture, but since I was in poker rooms and hotels more than I was here, what was the point?
>
> Besides I spent most of my time with Patty Ledgerwood,

aka Front Desk Girl, in her apartment in Las Vegas. She was working tonight, pulling a double shift, so we had no plans until later in the week.

I was watching some lame Christmas program on television and eating a television dinner with fried chicken and the really good cherry desert. I had about two hours to get to the casino to sign up for the poker tournament, and I was enjoying the quiet, to be honest.

Then there was knock on my door.

As Poker Boy, I very seldom have the people who need help come to me, but there have been exceptions. And since I wasn't expecting any company, I figured right off this was one of those exceptions.

I opened the front door of my double-wide mobile home and saw my old girlfriend, Julie Down, standing there on the other side of the screen door. Of course, right at that moment I didn't know It was Julie. All I could see was that it was some woman about my age with a nice smile and an over-built chest.

"Hi," Julie said, smiling at me as I stood there, hand on the wooden door, staring at her though the screen.

Now I have a great memory for faces across poker tables. I can tell you the moment a person sits down if I have played with them before, the style of their play, and their poker tells. I won't remember their names, but I know the important stuff and how to take their money...

NORTAV ANALYSIS

Narrative Mode: *NCE 1*

    Narrator: *Poker Boy*

Narrative Intrusion: *Yes*

Focal Character(s): *Poker Boy*

Prose Type(s) and/or Beat Types(s): *NCE and Narration. Style includes NCE beats with a heavy mix of Narration.*

Narrative Tense: *Past*

Additional Constraints: *None*

Narrative Pattern: *NCE 1 throughout.*

Analysis:

> [N1] Sometimes even superheroes can't save the day, or the girl, or the dog, and that fact is even sadder when the girl is one of the superhero's old girlfriends.

Dean opens with [N1], a Narration beat. This is Poker Boy, in his role as the narrator, talking directly to the reader.

> [N2] Honest, Poker Boy, and just about every superhero, once had a childhood, a life as a young adult, without powers. I only discovered my Poker Boy super abilities later in life, after I had lived a fairly regular life until the age of twenty-nine. Little did I know that someday I would put on the black leather jacket and the fedora-like hat and become Poker Boy, savior of blind women, lost husbands, and dogs.

[N1] leads to [N2], a compound Narration beat. Here Poker Boy continues to tell his background story to the reader, adding more general information about himself and superheroes.

> [N3] It was Christmas Eve, a holiday for me just about like every other one. I was home, alone, in my double-wide mobile home that I had bought twenty years ago with the money from my winnings in a poker tour-nament. The green couch and chairs had come with it,

and so far I had seen no reason to replace the perfectly good, but dog-ugly furniture. As a national-level poker player, I had more than enough money in a dozen accounts to buy a nice home, and nice furniture, but since I was in poker rooms and hotels more than I was here, what was the point?

[N2] leads to [N3], a compound Narration beat. Notice here that we begin to get a sense of Poker Boy as a character at the time of the story. We get the story's time (Christmas Eve) and place (Poker Boy's double-wide). But as of yet we aren't getting Poker Boy's perceptions and activities at the time of the story. This is still Poker Boy, the narrator, telling us about story information, and thus this is still Narration.

[N4] Besides I spent most of my time with Patty Ledgerwood, aka Front Desk Girl, in her apartment in Las Vegas. She was working tonight, pulling a double shift, so we had no plans until later in the week.

[N3] leads to [N4], a compound Narration beat, which portrays more story information. We are not yet experiencing Poker Boy's perceptions and activities from the time of the story, but we get the sense that we're about to.

[Na5] I was watching some lame Christmas program on television and eating a television dinner with fried chicken and the really good cherry desert. [Nm6] I had about two hours to get to the casino to sign up for the poker tournament, and I was enjoying the quiet, to be honest.

[N4] leads to [Na5], a Narrated Action beat. Here is the first time we get Poker Boy's perceptions or activities at the time of the story. So, if we've transitioned from Narration to NCE, why doesn't our template have two narrative modes and a narrative pattern that describes the pattern? Again, it's a gut call. For me, the writing style through the entire piece feels the same. It's a very un-intimate style of NCE, and the reader gets a strong sense of Poker Boy the narrator throughout the entire sample. When the Narrated Action beat occurred, I didn't sense the narrative mode change. Thus, in my view there is only one narrative mode in use here, and it's NCE-based with a heavy mix of Narration throughout.

Finally, [Na5] leads to [Nm6], a beat of Mixed NCE. This beat mixes a thought, a reaction, and narrative information. Now we're starting to perceive the beats a little more from within Poker Boy the focal character at the time of the story, and a little less from Poker Boy the narrator at the time he's telling the story.

> [No7] Then there was knock on my door.

[No7] is a typical initiating Narrated Observation beat.

> [Nt8] As Poker Boy, I very seldom have the people who need help come to me, but there have been exceptions. And since I wasn't expecting any company, I figured right off this was one of those exceptions.

[No7] triggers [Nt8], a Narrated Thought beat.

> [Na9] I opened the front door of my double-wide mobile home and [No10] saw my old girlfriend, Julie Down, standing there on the other side of the screen door. [Nt11] Of course, right at that moment I didn't know it was Julie. [No12] All I could see was that it was some woman about my age with a nice smile and an over-built chest.

[No7] leads to/triggers [Na9], a Narrated Action beat, which leads to [No10], a Narrated Observation beat. [No10] leads to [Nt11], a Narrated Thought beat, which leads to [No12], a Narrated Observation beat. Notice the ordering of these beats. They don't follow the natural response sequence too closely, nor do they have to. These beats are narrated to the reader after the character has experienced them, and thus they can come in any order the narrator chooses. In fact, by not following the natural response sequence too closely, Dean maintains the un-intimate, Narration-heavy feel of the writing style.

> [No13] "Hi," Julie said, smiling at me as [Na13] I stood there, hand on the wooden door, staring at her though the screen.

[No13] is an initiating Narrated Observation beat. [Na13] is a Narrated Action beat which continues the action started in [Na9].

> [N14] Now I have a great memory for faces across poker tables. I can tell you the moment a person sits down if I have played with them before, the style of their play, and their poker tells. I won't remember their names, but I know the important stuff and how to take their money.

Finally, [Na13] leads to [N14], a Narration beat.

NORTAV Analysis #6: Edgar Allan Poe's *The Murders in the Rue Morgue*

PROSE SAMPLE

For this analysis we will look at an excerpt from *The Murders in the Rue Morgue*, a classic short story by Edgar Allan Poe. For more information about Poe and his work, you can visit Project Gutenberg at http://www.gutenberg.org/.

> ... The analytical power should not be confounded with ample ingenuity; for while the analyst is necessarily ingenious, the ingenious man is often remarkably incapable of analysis. The constructive or combining power, by which ingenuity is usually manifested, and to which the phrenologists (I believe erroneously) have assigned a separate organ, supposing it a primitive faculty, has been so frequently seen in those whose intellect bordered otherwise upon idiocy, as to have attracted general observation among writers on morals. Between ingenuity and the analytic ability there exists a difference far greater, indeed, than that between the fancy and the imagination, but of a character very strictly analogous. It will be found, in fact, that the ingenious are always fanciful, and the truly imaginative never otherwise than analytic.

> The narrative which follows will appear to the reader somewhat in the light of a commentary upon the propositions just advanced.

> Residing in Paris during the spring and part of the summer of 18—, I there became acquainted with a Monsieur C. Auguste Dupin. This young gentleman was of an excellent—indeed of an illustrious family, but, by a variety of

untoward events, had been reduced to such poverty that the energy of his character succumbed beneath it, and he ceased to bestir himself in the world, or to care for the retrieval of his fortunes. By courtesy of his creditors, there still remained in his possession a small remnant of his patrimony; and, upon the income arising from this, he managed, by means of a rigorous economy, to procure the necessaries of life, without troubling himself about its superfluities. Books, indeed, were his sole luxuries, and in Paris these are easily obtained.

Our first meeting was at an obscure library in the Rue Montmartre, where the accident of our both being in search of the same very rare and very remarkable volume, brought us into closer communion. We saw each other again and again. I was deeply interested in the little family history which he detailed to me with all that candor which a Frenchman indulges whenever mere self is his theme. I was astonished, too, at the vast extent of his reading; and, above all, I felt my soul enkindled within me by the wild fervor, and the vivid freshness of his imagination. Seeking in Paris the objects I then sought, I felt that the society of such a man would be to me a treasure beyond price; and this feeling I frankly confided to him. It was at length arranged that we should live together during my stay in the city; and as my worldly circumstances were somewhat less embarrassed than his own, I was permitted to be at the expense of renting, and furnishing in a style which suited the rather fantastic gloom of our common temper, a time-eaten and grotesque mansion, long deserted through superstitions into which we did not inquire, and tottering to its fall in a retired and desolate portion of the Faubourg St. Germain...

NORTAV ANALYSIS

Narrative Mode: *Narration 1*

Narrator: *"I"*

Narrative Intrusion: *Yes*

Focal Character(s): *None*

Prose Type(s) and/or Beat Types(s): *Narration*

Narrative Tense: *Past*

Additional Constraints: *None*

Narrative Mode: *NCE 2*

Narrator: *"I"*

Narrative Intrusion: *Yes*

Focal Character(s): *"I"*

Prose Type(s) and/or Beat Types(s): *NCE and Narration. Style uses mostly beats of Consolidated NCE.*

Narrative Tense: *Past*

Additional Constraints: *None*

Narrative Pattern: *Narration 1 transitions to NCE 2, which is then used from that point forward.*

[N1] The analytical power should not be confounded with ample ingenuity; for while the analyst is necessarily ingenious, the ingenious man is often remarkably incapable of analysis. The constructive or combining power, by which ingenuity is usually manifested, and to which the phrenologists (I believe erroneously) have assigned a separate organ, supposing it a primitive faculty, has been so frequently seen in those whose intellect bordered otherwise upon idiocy, as to have attracted general observation among writers on morals. Between ingenuity and the analytic ability there exists a difference far greater, indeed, than that between the fancy and the imagination, but of a character very strictly analogous. It will be found, in fact, that the ingenious are always fanciful, and the truly imaginative never otherwise than analytic.

Poe opens with [N1], a compound Narration beat. Here the narrator begins philosophizing directly to the reader, revealing his opinion that analytical ability does not necessarily equate to ingenuity.

[N2] The narrative which follows will appear to the reader somewhat in the light of a commentary upon the propositions just advanced.

[N1] leads to [N2], a Narration beat that ties the previous philosophizing to what is about to come.

[N3] Residing in Paris during the spring and part of the summer of 18—, I there became acquainted with a Monsieur C. Auguste Dupin. This young gentleman was of an excellent—indeed of an illustrious family, but, by a variety of untoward events, had been reduced to such poverty that the energy of his character succumbed beneath it, and he ceased to bestir himself in the world, or to care for the retrieval of his fortunes. By courtesy of his creditors, there still remained in his possession a small remnant of his patrimony; and, upon the income arising from this, he managed, by means of a rigorous economy, to procure the necessaries of life, without troubling himself about its superfluities. Books, indeed, were his sole luxuries, and in Paris these are easily obtained.

Here we sense a change in narrative modes. That is, this is where we change from the first mode (Narration 1) to the second mode (NCE 2). The piece opened with straight Narration, a discussion between the narrator and the reader. [N3], another compound Narration beat, begins the actual story itself. Even though the type of beat is the same as the previous beat, the storyteller has changed gears and begins relating his tale with much less sense that he's addressing the reader directly. In this beat the reader is introduced to a character, Dupin, and is given some information about him.

> [Nc4] Our first meeting was at an obscure library in the Rue Montmartre, where the accident of our both being in search of the same very rare and very remarkable volume, brought us into closer communion.

[N3] leads to [Nc4], a Consolidated Narration beat. This beat is a touch ambiguous. Are we still dealing with story information, or are we now beginning to get a sense of the narrator's perceptions and activities as the focal character, albeit rolled up and consolidated? To me there is an underlying sense of the narrator's actions, observations, and thoughts as they occurred at the time of the story. And also, since we are in an NCE-based narrative mode, any ambiguous NCE/Narration beats are notated as NCE.

> [Nc5] We saw each other again and again. [Nc6] I was deeply interested in the little family history which he detailed to me with all that candor which a Frenchman indulges whenever mere self is his theme. [Nc7] I was astonished, too, at the vast extent of his reading; and, above all, I felt my soul enkindled within me by the wild fervor, and the vivid freshness of his imagination. [Nc8] Seeking in Paris the objects I then sought, I felt that the society of such a man would be to me a treasure beyond price; and this feeling I frankly confided to him. [Nc9] It was at length arranged that we should live together during my stay in the city; and as my worldly circumstances were somewhat less embarrassed than his own, I was permitted to be at the expense of renting, and furnishing

> in a style which suited the rather fantastic gloom of our common temper, a time-eaten and grotesque mansion, long deserted through superstitions into which we did not inquire, and tottering to its fall in a retired and desolate portion of the Faubourg St. Germain.

Finally [Nc4] leads to a series of Consolidated Narration beats [Nc5] through [Nc9], one leading to the next, to the next, etc. Like [Nc4], these all have an underlying sense of the narrator's perceptions and activities at the time the story occurred, but they are abstracted to a much higher level.

One could have set up a narrative schema for this analysis that contained a single NCE-based narrative mode if you sensed that the opening Narration felt like the same writing style or gave you the same narrative feel as the rest of the piece. If you notated this excerpt that way, that's fine.

NORTAV Analysis #7: Gemma Halliday's *A High Heels Haunting*

PROSE SAMPLE

For this analysis we will look at an excerpt from *A High Heels Haunting*, a novella by Gemma Halliday. For more information about Gemma, you can visit her website at http://www.gemmahalliday.com/.

... They were beautiful.

I stared down at the box in my hands, recently delivered via one UPS guy whose name I could never remember. My fingers had trembled as I'd opened it up. I never did things like this. Bought such extravagant, silly things for myself. But these – these I hadn't been able to resist. The second I'd seen them on the website, I'd known I had to have them.

The site had featured a woman in a short, black cocktail dress, about fifteen vavavoom points higher than anything I'd dare to wear, standing in the middle of a crowded room. All eyes were on her, every woman wanting to be her, every man wanting to own her. But I could tell by the look in her eyes that no one owned her. Not a manager breathing down her neck from nine to five, not an ex-boyfriend who couldn't tell her from a doormat, not a mother relentlessly pointing out a multitude of shortcomings. No, she was a woman unto herself, and she answered to no one.

On her arm was a man who made my mouth water. He personified the tall, dark and handsome look – square jaw, rich, chocolate colored eyes, broad shoulders beneath a blazer that was airbrushed onto a gym-made frame. He was like an orgasm on screen.

Yep, the woman in the ad had everything. Everything I never would. I just wasn't destined for that kind of life. Me? I had a real person life. A cat. A cubicle. A hatchback that was nearing the hundred thousand mile mark and had certain parts held together with duct tape. But, for the most part, I was okay with that. My life wasn't the worst, right? I mean, who really has a supermodel's life anyway?

But as I stared at the website, somehow it was like I was five years old again watching Disney's version of Cinderella on TV and wishing I was the princess. Somehow, despite my thirty years experience telling me differently, I once again believed in fairy tales – that me, plain-Jane Kya Bader, web designer, Silicon Valley single, and Match.com subscriber, could be that woman.

Even after I got home from work, changed into my favorite pair of drawstring flannels with the little Corona bottles on them and a faded UCSC sweatshirt, ate my Lean Cuisine in front of a rerun of Seinfeld, and checked my email while Tabby the Cat tried to molest my laptop screen, I couldn't stop thinking about the website. And somehow, the page popped up on my screen again. That woman. That man.

That life.

The site sold shoes. I know, not unique items. Hundreds of websites did. But, these were different. On Supermodel's feet sat a pair of insanely high, red stilettos. Ankle straps embedded with tiny, sparkling rhinestones, toes pointy in a way real feet never were, heels ending in a dangerous silver tip. Totally impractical. Totally beautiful...

NORTAV ANALYSIS

Narrative Mode: *NCE 1*

Narrator: *Kya Bader*

Narrative Intrusion: *Yes*

Focal Character(s): *Kya Bader*

Prose Type(s) and/or Beat Types(s): *NCE and DCE. Style uses mostly NCE.*

Narrative Tense: *Past*

Additional Constraints: *None*

Narrative Pattern: *NCE 1 throughout.*

Analysis:

[Nt1] They were beautiful.

Gemma opens with [Nt1], a Narrated Thought beat. While this is DCE, we will soon find the narrative mode in use is NCE-based.

[Nm2] I stared down at the box in my hands, [Nt3] recently delivered via one UPS guy whose name I could never remember. [Nm4] My fingers had trembled as I'd opened it up. [Nt5] I never did things like this. Bought such extravagant, silly things for myself. But these – these I hadn't been able to resist. The second I'd seen them on the website, I'd known I had to have them.

[Nt1] leads to [Nm2], a beat of Mixed NCE that includes an "act of observing" action and an observation. [Nm2] triggers [Nt3], a Narrated Thought beat, which leads to [Nm4]. [Nm4] is a beat of Mixed NCE that combines a reaction and an action. Notice that there is a flashback happening here. In this case we don't really get a sense that there is an embedded level here. This comes across not so much as the focal character thinking back on these events as much as the narrator telling us of events, both current and past. Thus, I did not use a leveled notation here.

Next, [Nm4] leads to [Nt5], a compound Narrated Thought beat which continues the flashback.

> [No6] The site had featured a woman in a short, black cocktail dress, about fifteen vavavoom points higher than anything I'd dare to wear, standing in the middle of a crowded room. [Nt7] All eyes were on her, every woman wanting to be her, every man wanting to own her. But I could tell by the look in her eyes that no one owned her. Not a manager breathing down her neck from nine to five, not an ex-boyfriend who couldn't tell her from a doormat, not a mother relentlessly pointing out a multitude of shortcomings. No, she was a woman unto herself, and she answered to no one.

Here [Nt5] leads to [No6], a Narrated Observation beat which continues the flashback. Note the phrase "about fifteen vavavoom points higher than anything I'd date to wear." Is this Kya's thought at the time she saw the woman? Is this Kya's commentary at the time she's telling us the story? If the former, this would be a beat of Mixed NCE (an observation and a thought mixed together). I perceive it as the latter, so I notated it as a Narrated Observation beat.

Making these kinds of detailed determinations can be difficult. Is it important that we get each one correct? No! Remember, prose is created subconsciously and then we analyze it subjectively (for the most part). The point of the NORTAV Method is to add some method to the madness that is prose construction. Just enough so that you can start noticing (and learning from) the patterns in the Matrix.

[No6] leads to [Nt7], a compound Narrated Thought beat that continues the flashback and includes some beat substitution.

[Nm8] On her arm was a man who made my mouth water. He personified the tall, dark and handsome look – square jaw, rich, chocolate colored eyes, broad shoulders beneath a blazer that was airbrushed onto a gym-made frame. He was like an orgasm on screen.

[Nt7] leads to [Nm8], a compound beat of Mixed NCE that continues the flashback. It contains several mixed observations, thoughts, and reactions.

[Nt9] Yep, the woman in the ad had everything. Everything I never would. I just wasn't destined for that kind of life. Me? I had a real person life. A cat. A cubicle. A hatchback that was nearing the hundred thousand mile mark and had certain parts held together with duct tape. But, for the most part, I was okay with that. My life wasn't the worst, right? I mean, who really has a supermodel's life anyway?

[Nm8] triggers to [Nt9], a compound Narrated Thought beat that continues the flashback. Here Kya is musing over the sight of the woman, comparing the woman's life to her own.

[Nm10] But as I stared at the website, somehow it was like I was five years old again watching Disney's version of Cinderella on TV and wishing I was the princess. [Nt11] Somehow, despite my thirty years experience telling me differently, I once again believed in fairy tales – that me, plain-Jane Kya Bader, web designer, Silicon Valley single, and Match.com subscriber, could be that woman.

Next, [Nt9] leads to [Nm10], a beat of Mixed NCE that combines an action and thought and continues the flashback. [Nm10] leads to [Nt11], a Narrated Thought beat that continues the flashback.

[Nm12] Even after I got home from work, changed into my favorite pair of drawstring flannels with the little Corona bottles on them and a faded UCSC sweatshirt, ate my Lean Cuisine in front of a rerun of Seinfeld, and checked my email while Tabby the Cat tried to molest my laptop screen, I couldn't stop thinking about the website. [No13] And somehow, the page popped up on my screen again. [Nt14] That woman. That man.

That life.

Here [Nt11] leads to [Nm12], a beat of Mixed NCE that combines a summary of actions and thought and continues the flashback. [Nm12] leads to [No13], a Narrated Observation beat that continues the flashback. [No13] triggers [Nt14], a Narrated Thought beat that continues the flashback.

[N15] The site sold shoes. I know, not unique items. Hundreds of websites did. But, these were different. [Nm16] On Supermodel's feet sat a pair of insanely high, red stilettos. Ankle straps embedded with tiny, sparkling rhinestones, toes pointy in a way real feet never were, heels ending in a dangerous silver tip. [Nt17] Totally impractical. Totally beautiful.

Finally, [N15] is an initiating Narration beat. [Nm16], a beat of Mixed NCE (observations and thought) that is logically linked back to [No13] and which continues the flashback, leads to [Nt17], a Narrated Thought beat that signals the end of the flashback, as it puts us back to the current story time established in [Nt1] and [Nm2].

This was not an easy sample to notate. Dealing with a narrator and a character simultaneously often creates difficulties when trying to decide if a particular beat is originating from the character at the time of the story, or if it's originating from the narrator at the time the story is being told. Adding a flashback to the mix makes this even harder to notate. If you made it through this analysis, give yourself a hand! From a NORTAV analysis standpoint, this is about as complex as it gets.

NORTAV Analysis #8: Guido Henkel's *Demon's Night*

PROSE SAMPLE

For this analysis we will look at an excerpt from *Demon's Night*, a novel by Guido Henkel. For more information about Guido and his work, you can visit his website at http://guidohenkel.com/.

> … The London fog had eyes tonight. Ugly, yellow eyes with slits for pupils. Eyes that seemed to hover without body, suspended in the mist. Watchman Edward Norrington knew nothing about them as he slowly made his usual rounds under the gaslight lamps in the yard of St. Katherine's Dock, but he would see them soon. All too soon.
>
> Light fog had settled over the city earlier in the evening, creating tepid halos around the lamps that lined the cobblestone streets. Despite the fog, the air was crisp and cold but clean and free of the usual smells of the city because of the wind that had prevailed during the day. It was late October and, clearly, it would be snowing soon.
>
> The eyes in the fog did not blink. They seemed to hide in the mist with their translucent stare, but their gaze was firmly trained upon the night watchman.
>
> For fifteen years, Norrington had been walking this part of the gates, and as he did every night, he slowly came down the rough stairs that connected the gate with the other side of the building. The stocky man looked over the city as he descended, noticing the lights being dimmed by the mist and losing themselves in the darkness of the night.

"Always with the bloody knees," he cursed under his breath as he labored down the stairs. His arthritis always gave him trouble with the onset of the cold season.

Norrington's breath came in short bursts and to slow his racing heart he directed his eyes towards the Thames, towards the looming dark shape of a tall ship tied up along the pier, lightly swaying in the water.

He shivered for a moment, unaware of the greedy eyes on his back and the strange mist that began to form around them. It might have been but a swirl of fog consolidating in the air, except for its odd green tint.

Barely visible in the lazy fog, Norrington thought the river looked surprisingly dull on this day, with only occasional speckles of light reflecting on the water. He ran his eyes over the outline of the dark ship, and as so many times before, he wondered what it would be like to set sail and see the world. He had never left England; barely ever set foot outside of London, in fact. The thought of visiting foreign countries unsettled his senses as much as it fascinated him. Norrington rubbed his hands together for warmth and pulled his earlobes, deep in thought.

Behind him, the mist in the doorway had begun to grow steadily, its color becoming more vibrant in a noxious green. The cloud grew and, for a moment, it seemed as if a claw had appeared out of the undulating mist, reaching for the old man. But the talons were gone in a flash when the distant cracking of a whip cut sharply through the silent air…

NORTAV ANALYSIS

Narrative Mode: *NCE 1*

Narrator: *Omniscient*

Narrative Intrusion: *Yes*

Focal Character(s): *Norrington*

Prose Type(s) and/or Beat Types(s): *NCE and Narration. Style uses straight Narration beats and NCE beats that has had incidental narrative information tacked on.*

Narrative Tense: *Past*

Additional Constraints: *None*

Narrative Pattern: *NCE 1 throughout.*

Analysis:

[N1] The London fog had eyes tonight. Ugly, yellow eyes with slits for pupils. Eyes that seemed to hover without body, suspended in the mist. [Nc2] Watchman Edward Norrington knew nothing about them as he slowly made his usual rounds under the gaslight lamps in the yard of St. Katherine's Dock, but he would see them soon. All too soon.

Guido opens with [N1], a Narration beat that begins to describe a strange creature to the reader. This description comes from the narrator himself. It does not come from a focal character. [N1] leads to [Nc2], a beat of Consolidated NCE. This Consolidated NCE beat is a roll up of the focal character's action along with added incidental narrative information. That is, we get Norrington's rolled up action ("made his usual rounds") plus incidental information that could only come from the narrator.

[No3] Light fog had settled over the city earlier in the evening, creating tepid halos around the lamps that lined the cobblestone streets. Despite the fog, the air was crisp and cold but clean and free of the usual smells of the city because of the wind that had prevailed during the day. It was late October and, clearly, it would be snowing soon.

Here [Nc2] leads to [No3], a compound Narrated Observation beat with incidental narrative information tacked on to add detail.

[N4] The eyes in the fog did not blink. They seemed to hide in the mist with their translucent stare, but their gaze was firmly trained upon the night watchman.

Here [No3] leads to [N4], a Narration beat that continues the description of the unseen creature.

[Na5] For fifteen years, Norrington had been walking this part of the gates, and as he did every night, he slowly came down the rough stairs that connected the gate with the other side of the building. The stocky man looked over the city as he descended, [No6] noticing the lights being dimmed by the mist and losing themselves in the darkness of the night.

Next, [Na4] leads to [Na5], a compound Narrated Action beat with more incidental narrative information tacked on. [Na5] leads to [No6], a Narrated Observation beat.

{No7}[Nv8] "Always with the bloody knees," he cursed under his breath [Na9] as he labored down the stairs. [Nt10] His arthritis always gave him trouble with the onset of the cold season.

[Na6] leads to {No7}, an implied initiating Narrated Observation beat in which Norrington feels pain and discomfort. {Na7} triggers [Nv8], a Narrated Vocalization beat. [Na9], a Narrated Action beat, continues on from [Na5]. [Nt10], a Narrated Thought beat, is triggered from {No7}. Now, [Nt10] could also be a beat of Narration. It depends on if you think this is Norrington's thought or the narrator's added detail. I believe it feels like the former.

[Nr11] Norrington's breath came in short bursts and [Nm12] to slow his racing heart he directed his eyes towards the Thames, towards the looming dark shape of a tall ship tied up along the pier, lightly swaying in the water.

Here, [Nr11] is a direct response to the strain of [Na9], which leads to [Nm12]. [Nm12], a beat of Mixed NCE, mixes thought, observation, and action.

{No13} [Nr14] He shivered for a moment, [N15] unaware of the greedy eyes on his back and the strange mist that began to form around them. It might have been but a swirl of fog consolidating in the air, except for its odd green tint.

{No13} is an implied initiating Narrated Observation beat. Norrington feels the cold in his bones. This triggers [Nr14], a Narrated Reaction beat, which leads to [N15], a beat of Narration where the narrator continues his description of the strange creature.

{No16} [Nt17] Barely visible in the lazy fog, Norrington thought the river looked surprisingly dull on this day, with only occasional speckles of light reflecting on the water. [Na18] He ran his eyes over the outline of the dark ship, and as so many times before, [Nt19] he wondered what it would be like to set sail and see the world. He had never left England; barely ever set foot outside of London, in fact. The thought of visiting foreign countries unsettled his senses as much as it fascinated him. [Nm20] Norrington rubbed his hands together for warmth and pulled his earlobes, deep in thought.

Here we get the same set up as before. {No16} is an implied initiating Narrated Observation beat. Norrington looks at the river. This leads to [Nt17], a Narrated Thought beat that includes beat substitution (we get some of the sense of the implied observation embedded in here). This leads to [Na18], a Narrated Action beat, which leads to [Nt19], a compound Narrated Thought beat. [Nt19] leads to [Nm20], a beat of Mixed NCE that mixes action and thought.

> [N21] Behind him, the mist in the doorway had begun to grow steadily, its color becoming more vibrant in a noxious green. The cloud grew and, for a moment, it seemed as if a claw had appeared out of the undulating mist, reaching for the old man. But the talons were gone in a flash when the distant cracking of a whip cut sharply through the silent air.

Finally, we end with [N21], a beat of Narration where the narrator continues on with his description of the strange creature.

NORTAV Analysis #9: John Locke's *Lethal People*

PROSE SAMPLE

For this analysis we will look at an excerpt from *Lethal People*, a novel by John Locke. For more information about John and his work, you can visit his website at http://donovancreed.com/.

> ... The fire started in Greg and Melanie's basement just after midnight and crept upward through the stairwell silently, like a predator tracking food.
>
> Greg had never read the stats or he'd have known that home fires can turn deadly in just two minutes and that his odds of waking up were three to one.
>
> Against.
>
> And yet both he and Melanie had managed it. Was it because she'd screamed? He wasn't sure. But she was screaming now. Groggy, disoriented, coughing, Greg stumbled to the door. Like millions of others, he'd seen the movie Backdraft, and although the proper term for the event depicted in the film was a "flashover" and not a "backdraft," he'd learned enough to touch the back of his hand to the top of the door, the doorknob, and the crack between the door and door frame before flinging it open.
>
> As he did that, Melanie rolled to the edge of the bed and grabbed her cell phone from the charging cradle on the nightstand. She pressed 911 and cupped her hand around the speaker. Now that Greg was in motion, she felt better, like part of a team instead of an army of one. Only moments ago, Melanie had taken her panic out on

Greg's comatose body by kicking, punching, and scream-
ing him awake. When he finally began to stir, she'd
slapped him hard across the face several times.

Now they were working together. They'd silently assessed
the situation and assigned each other specific roles in an
unspoken plan. He'd get the kids; she'd get the firemen.

Melanie couldn't hear anything coming from the phone
and wondered if she'd misdialed. She terminated the call
and started over. A sudden blast of heat told her Greg
had gotten the door open. Melanie looked up at him,
and their eyes met. She held his gaze a moment and
time seemed to stop while something special passed
between them. It was just a split second, but they managed to get eight years of marriage into it.

Greg set his jaw and gave her a nod of reassurance, as if
to say he'd seen what lay beyond the door and that
everything was going to be all right.

Melanie wasn't buying. She'd known this man since the
first week of college, knew all his looks. What she'd seen
in his eyes was helplessness. And fear.

Greg turned away from her, shielded his face, and hurled
himself into the rising flames. She couldn't hear the 911
operator over the roaring noise, but she heard Greg bar-
reling up the stairs yelling to the children.

She yelled, "I love you!" but her words were swallowed
up in the blaze. The searing heat scorched her blistered
throat. Melanie clamped her mouth shut and turned her
attention back to the phone. Was someone on the other
end? She dropped to her hands and knees, cupped her
fingers around the mouthpiece, and shouted her mes-

sage as clearly as possible to the dispatcher she hoped was listening...

NORTAV ANALYSIS

Narrative Mode: *NCE 1*

Narrator: *Omniscient*

Narrative Intrusion: *Yes*

Focal Character(s): *Greg, Melanie*

Prose Type(s) and/or Beat Types(s): *NCE, DCE, and Narration. Style uses mostly NCE and Narration beats.*

Narrative Tense: *Past*

Additional Constraints: *None*

Narrative Pattern: *NCE 1 throughout.*

Analysis:

[N1] The fire started in Greg and Melanie's basement just after midnight and crept upward through the stairwell silently, like a predator tracking food.

Greg had never read the stats or he'd have known that home fires can turn deadly in just two minutes and that his odds of waking up were three to one.

Against.

And yet both he and Melanie had managed it.

John opens with a compound Narration beat [N1]. Here the narrator opens the scene by providing a bit of background information and introducing two characters, Greg and Melanie.

[Nt2] Was it because she'd screamed? He wasn't sure.

> But she was screaming now. [Nm3] Groggy, disoriented, coughing, [Na4] Greg stumbled to the door. [Na5] Like millions of others, he'd seen the movie Backdraft, and although the proper term for the event depicted in the film was a "flashover" and not a "backdraft," he'd learned enough to touch the back of his hand to the top of the door, the doorknob, and the crack between the door and door frame before flinging it open.

[N1] leads to [Nt2], a Narrated Thought beat. Here we begin to get a sense of the focal character Greg's perceptions and activities. [Nt2] leads to [Nm3], a beat of Mixed NCE that includes observations and a reaction. Here is where we definitely know we have slipped into the perceptions and activities of Greg. [Nm3] leads to [Na4], a Narrated Action beat (DCE), which leads to [Na5], a compound Narrated Action beat that has either incidental thoughts or incidental narrative information tacked on, depending on how you perceive the beat.

> [Na6] As he did that, Melanie rolled to the edge of the bed and grabbed her cell phone from the charging cradle on the nightstand. She pressed 911 and cupped her hand around the speaker. [Nt7] Now that Greg was in motion, she felt better, like part of a team instead of an army of one. Only moments ago, Melanie had taken her panic out on Greg's comatose body by kicking, punching, and screaming him awake. When he finally began to stir, she'd slapped him hard across the face several times.

[Na5] leads to [Na6], a Narrated Action beat. What do you notice here? The prose slips out of Greg's perceptions and activities, gives a bit of short narrative direction ("As he did that…") and then slips into Melanie's perceptions and activities. Now, with a change in focal characters, wouldn't the narrative mode change? Normally it would, but a writer can create a single narrative mode with multiple focal characters if the "feel" of the writing doesn't change when bouncing back and forth between focal characters. This is tricky to do. Here John's narrator is so apparent that he can seamlessly move from one character to the next because the overall "feel" of the style is that the narrator is up front, telling us the story. Since that feel continues, the mode doesn't seem to shift when the focal character changes.

Moving on, [Na6] leads to compound Narrated Thought beat [Nt7], which provides the reader with a little bit of background information in the form of a mini-flashback.

> [Nt8] Now they were working together. They'd silently assessed the situation and assigned each other specific roles in an unspoken plan. He'd get the kids; she'd get the firemen.

[Nt7] leads to compound Narrated Thought beat [Nt8], which continues the mini-flashback.

> [No9] Melanie couldn't hear anything coming from the phone [Nt10] and wondered if she'd misdialed. [Nc11] She terminated the call and started over. [Nm12] A sudden blast of heat told her Greg had gotten the door open. [Na13] Melanie looked up at him, and [No14] their eyes met. [Na15] She held his gaze a moment and [Nt16] time seemed to stop while something special passed between them. It was just a split second, but they managed to get eight years of marriage into it.

[Nt8] leads to [No9], a Narrated Observation beat that brings us back to the current story time. [No9] triggers [No10], which triggers [Nc11], a Condensed NCE beat that rolls up Melanie's action to a higher level concept. [Nm12] is an initiating beat of Mixed NCE that includes observation and thought. It leads to [Na13], a Narrated Action beat that leads to Narrated Observation beat [No14]. [No14] leads to [Na15], a Narrated Action beat, which leads to [Nt16], a Narrated Thought beat. In [Nt16] there is a little sense of ambiguity, as it isn't precisely clear if this is coming from the narrator or if this is Melanie's thoughts. In an NCE-based narrative mode, tie goes to NCE and we notate accordingly.

> [Nm17] Greg set his jaw and gave her a nod of reassurance, as if to say he'd seen what lay beyond the door and that everything was going to be all right.

[Nt16] leads to [Nm17], a beat of Mixed NCE that includes observation and thought.

> [Nt18] Melanie wasn't buying. She'd known this man since the first week of college, knew all his looks. What she'd seen in his eyes was helplessness. And fear.

[Nm17] leads to [Nt18], a compound Narrated Thought beat.

> [No19] Greg turned away from her, shielded his face, and hurled himself into the rising flames. {No20} [Nt21] She couldn't hear the 911 operator over the roaring noise, but she heard Greg barreling up the stairs yelling to the children.

[Nt18] leads to [No19], a Narrated Observation beat. {No20} is an implied initiating Narrated Observation beat, which triggers [Nt21], a Narrated Thought beat that includes beat substitution.

> [Nv22] She yelled, "I love you!" [No23] but her words were swallowed up in the blaze. The searing heat scorched her blistered throat. [Nr24] Melanie clamped her mouth shut and [Na25] turned her attention back to the phone. [Nt26] Was someone on the other end? [Na27] She dropped to her hands and knees, cupped her fingers around the mouthpiece, and [Nm28] shouted her message as clearly as possible to the dispatcher she hoped was listening.

Finally, [Nt21] triggers [Nv22], a Narrated Vocalization beat, which leads to [No23], a compound Narrated Observation beat. [No23] triggers [Nr24], a Narrated Reaction beat. [Nr24] leads to [Na25], a Narrated Action beat. [Na25] leads to [Nt26], a Narrated Thought beat. [Nt26] triggers Narrated Action beat [Na27] and [Nm27], a beat of Mixed NCE that includes a vocalization and thought.

NORTAV Analysis #10: Laurin Wittig's *Charming the Shrew*

PROSE SAMPLE

For this analysis we will look at an excerpt from *Charming the Shrew*, a novel by Laurin Wittig. For more information about Laurin and her work, you can visit her website at `http://laurinwittig.com/`.

... Robert the Bruce, king of Scotland, shouldn't be dying.

Tayg Munro tried to understand this strange twist of fate as he huddled near a stingy fire, wrapped tightly in his plaid against the bone-chilling cold of the Scottish winter. Smoke from the army's cookfires drifted, leaving a faint gray haze both within and without the palisaded walls of the nearby fort. He could just make out the rise of the motte, a huge earthen hill clad in dirty drifts of snow, upon which sat the timbered tower where the king languished, growing ever weaker.

Despite the death of Longshanks, Edward I of England, in midsummer, and despite the relief afforded by Edward II's disinterest in war, Scotland's fate had not yet been determined. All seemed now to hang on the vagaries of a stubborn wasting disease.

The irony that all that the Scots had endured and overcome at Longshanks's hand might now be lost to a wasting illness was not missed by Tayg. He did not think there was another leader who could unite the varied peoples of Scotland. The loss of Sir William Wallace had been a terrible blow to their fight to rid themselves of England's grasp but the Bruce had stepped in and raised Sir William's banner of freedom with admirable strength and passion.

Now, though, 'twas rumored that the king would not last the night. Gillies had been sent hither and yon in search of a cure. Healers had come from as far away as the Kilmartin glen in the far west. But hope blew away on the sharp winter wind.

Tayg stirred the fire and glanced across its feeble flames at his companions in this endeavor: red-haired Duncan MacCulloch, his best friend and cousin; auld Gair of MacTavish, whom he'd met when first he joined the Bruce's band; quiet young Tearlach Munro, another cousin; and Tayg's older brother, Robbie the Braw, revered by all who knew him. Only the king was a better leader of men as far as Tayg was concerned.

But even Robbie wore the expression so common among their company: fatigue edged by despair. Indeed, each of his companions wore it as they sat hunched near the fire. All were good men who had lost someone or something to this constant battle against both the English and their own countrymen. Each had his own reason for being here, not the least of which was an abiding belief that King Robert was the last hope for Scotland's future. 'Twas a heavy mantle for such a young monarch.

The Scottish Earls had not been quick to rally to the cause. The Munros' own neighbor and ally, the Earl of Ross, was none too pleased that the sons of Munro were following the king, for Ross was on the side of whoever won this fight for Scotland and he had not yet firmly laid his sword at anyone's feet. Yet Tayg's brother Robbie had decided to support the Bruce and their father had agreed...

NORTAV ANALYSIS

Narrative Mode: *NCE 1*

Narrator: *Omniscient*

Narrative Intrusion: *Yes*

Focal Character(s): *Tayg Munro*

Prose Type(s) and/or Beat Types(s): *NCE and DCE. Style uses mostly DCE and Direct NCE which reveals a recurring-yet-subtle presence of the narrator.*

Narrative Tense: *Past*

Additional Constraints: *None*

Narrative Pattern: *NCE 1 throughout.*

Analysis:

[Nt1] Robert the Bruce, king of Scotland, shouldn't be dying.

Laurin opens with [Nt1], a Narrated Thought beat. While this is DCE, we will soon find the narrative mode in use is NCE-based.

[Nt2] Tayg Munro tried to understand this strange twist of fate as [Na3] he huddled near a stingy fire, wrapped tightly in his plaid against the bone-chilling cold of the Scottish winter. [No4] Smoke from the army's cookfires drifted, leaving a faint gray haze both within and without the palisaded walls of the nearby fort. He could just make out the rise of the motte, a huge earthen hill clad in dirty drifts of snow, upon which sat the timbered tower where the king languished, growing ever weaker.

[Nt1] leads to [Nt2], a Narrated Thought beat. Here the narrator's presence is noticed by the phrasing only. The narrator is telling us what Tayg is thinking, though she's not commenting on the thought herself. [Nt2] leads to [Na3], a Narrated Action beat with some incidental observation tacked on. [Na3] leads to [No4], a compound Narrated Observation beat. Here the narrator is only noticed through the use of a tag.

> [Nt5] Despite the death of Longshanks, Edward I of England, in midsummer, and despite the relief afforded by Edward II's disinterest in war, Scotland's fate had not yet been determined. All seemed now to hang on the vagaries of a stubborn wasting disease.

[No4] leads to/triggers [Nt5], a compound Narrated Thought beat that provides the reader with some background information. This could all be DCE, as there is no sense of a narrator here.

> [Nt6] The irony that all that the Scots had endured and overcome at Longshanks's hand might now be lost to a wasting illness was not missed by Tayg. He did not think there was another leader who could unite the varied peoples of Scotland. The loss of Sir William Wallace had been a terrible blow to their fight to rid themselves of England's grasp but the Bruce had stepped in and raised Sir William's banner of freedom with admirable strength and passion.

[Nt5] leads to/triggers [Nt6], another compound Narrated Thought beat that provides the reader with more background information. This could all be DCE, but there is a tag embedded in here, revealing the very subtle narrator.

> [Nt7] Now, though, 'twas rumored that the king would not last the night. Gillies had been sent hither and yon in search of a cure. Healers had come from as far away as the Kilmartin glen in the far west. But hope blew away on the sharp winter wind.

[Nt6] leads to/triggers [Nt7], yet another compound Narrated Thought beat that provides the reader with more background information. This could all be DCE. There are no tags here. Notice the dialect of the focal character slips in as well, making the NCE-based mode even more intimate than it already was.

> [Na8] Tayg stirred the fire and glanced across its feeble flames at his companions in this endeavor: {No9}[Nt10] red-haired Duncan MacCulloch, his best friend and cousin; auld Gair of MacTavish, whom he'd met when first he joined the Bruce's band; quiet young Tearlach Munro, another cousin; and Tayg's older brother, Robbie the Braw, revered by all who knew him. Only the king was a better leader of men as far as Tayg was concerned.

[Nt7] leads to [Na8], a Narrated Action beat. [Na8] leads to {No9}, an implied Narrated Observation beat, which leads to compound Narrated Thought beat [Nt10] that includes a lot of beat substitution. These last two beats could easily have been notated as a beat of Mixed NCE, where we are getting observations and thoughts mixed together. Because Laurin's NCE-based style is so intimate, I chose to notate as Direct NCE, which is a more intimate choice than Mixed NCE.

> {No11} [Nt12] But even Robbie wore the expression so common among their company: fatigue edged by despair. Indeed, each of his companions wore it as they sat hunched near the fire. [Nt13] All were good men who had lost someone or something to this constant battle against both the English and their own countrymen. Each had his own reason for being here, not the least of which was an abiding belief that King Robert was the last hope for Scotland's future. 'Twas a heavy mantle for such a young monarch.

[Nt10] leads to {No11}, an implied Narrated Observation beat, which leads to [Nt12], another compound Narrated Thought beat that continues the implied beat/beat substitution style in use. [Nt12] leads to [Nt13], a compound Narrated Thought beat that moves Tayg's thought process forward.

> [Nt14] The Scottish Earls had not been quick to rally to the cause. The Munros' own neighbor and ally, the Earl of Ross, was none too pleased that the sons of Munro were following the king, for Ross was on the side of whoever won this fight for Scotland and he had not yet firmly laid his sword at anyone's feet. Yet Tayg's brother Robbie had decided to support the Bruce and their father had agreed.

Finally, [Nt13] leads to [Nt14], another compound Narrated Thought beat that continues Tayg's thought process.

NORTAV Analysis #11: Lawrence Block's *The Sins of the Fathers*

PROSE SAMPLE

For this analysis we will look at an excerpt from *The Sins of the Fathers*, a novel by Lawrence Block. For more information about Lawrence and his work, you can visit `http://www.lawrenceblock.com/`.

> ... He was a big man, about my height with a little more flesh on his heavy frame. His eyebrows, arched and prominent, were still black. The hair on his head was iron gray, combed straight back, giving his massive head a leonine appearance. He had been wearing glasses but had placed them on the oak table between us. His dark brown eyes kept searching my face for secrets messages. If he found any, his eyes didn't reflect them. His features were sharply chiseled—a hawk-bill nose, a full mouth, a craggy jawline—but the full effect of his face was as a blank stone tablet waiting for someone to scratch commandments on it.
>
> He said, "I don't know very much about you, Scudder."
>
> I knew a little about him. His name was Cale Hanniford. He was around fifty-five years old. He lived upstate in Utica, where he had a wholesale drug business and some real estate holdings. He had last year's Cadillac parked outside at the curb. He had a wife waiting for him in his room at the Carlyle.
>
> He had a daughter in a cold steel drawer at the city mortuary.
>
> "There's not much to know," I said. "I used to be a cop."

"An excellent one, according to Lieutenant Koehler."

I shrugged.

"And now you're a private detective."

"No."

"I thought—"

"Private detectives are licensed. They tap telephones and follow people. They fill out forms, they keep records, all of that. I don't do those things. Sometimes I do favors for people. They give me gifts."

"I see."

I took a sip of coffee. I was drinking coffee spiked with bourbon. Hanniford had a Dewar's and water in front of him but wasn't taking much interest in it. We were in Armstrong's, a good sound saloon with dark wood walls and a stamped tin ceiling. It was two in the afternoon on the second Tuesday in January, and we had the place pretty much to ourselves. A couple of nurses from Roosevelt Hospital were nursing beers at the far end of the bar, and a kid with a tentative beard was eating a hamburger at one of the window tables.

He said, "It's difficult for me to explain what I want you to do for me, Scudder."

"I'm not sure if there's anything I can do for you. Your daughter is dead. I can't change that. The boy who killed her was picked up on the spot. From what I read in the papers, it couldn't be more open-and-shut if they had the homicide on film." His face darkened; he was seeing that film now, the knife slashing. I went on quickly. "They picked him up and booked him and slapped him in the Tombs. That was Thursday?" He nodded. "And Saturday morning they found him hanging in his cell. Case closed."

"Is that your view? That the case is closed?"

"From a law enforcement standpoint."

"That's not what I meant..."

NORTAV ANALYSIS

Narrative Mode: *NCE 1*

Narrator: *Scudder*

Narrative Intrusion: *Yes*

Focal Character(s): *Scudder*

Prose Type(s) and/or Beat Types(s): *NCE, DCE, and Narration. Style uses mostly DCE with infrequent occurrences of NCE and Narration.*

Narrative Tense: *Past*

Additional Constraints: *None*

Narrative Pattern: *NCE 1 throughout.*

Analysis:

[No1] He was a big man, about my height with a little more flesh on his heavy frame. His eyebrows, arched and prominent, were still black. The hair on his head was iron gray, combed straight back, giving his massive head a leonine appearance. {No2}[Nt3] He had been wearing glasses but had placed them on the oak table between us. His dark brown eyes kept searching my face for secrets messages. If he found any, his eyes didn't reflect them.

[No4] His features were sharply chiseled—a hawk-bill nose, a full mouth, a craggy jawline—but the full effect of his face was as a blank stone tablet waiting for someone to scratch commandments on it.

Lawrence opens with [No1], a compound Narrated Observation beat. This is DCE, with little-to-no sense of a narrator. We perceive this beat along with Scudder. [No1] leads to {No2}, where we get the sense that Scudder notices the other man's eyes. {No2} leads to [Nt3], a Narrated Thought beat which describes Scudder's thoughts about the implied observation. [Nt3] leads to [No4], a Narrated Observation beat that borders on Mixed NCE (seems to include slight bits of thought as well).

[No5] He said, "I don't know very much about you, Scudder."

[No4] leads to initiating Narrated Observation beat [No5], which is DCE.

[Nt6] I knew a little about him. His name was Cale Hanniford. He was around fifty-five years old. He lived upstate in Utica, where he had a wholesale drug business and some real estate holdings. He had last year's Cadillac parked outside at the curb. He had a wife waiting for him in his room at the Carlyle.

He had a daughter in a cold steel drawer at the city mortuary.

[No5] triggers [Nt6], a compound Narrated Thought beat that also has little-to-no sense of a narrator. We are starting to see how Lawrence's style is very intimate. Scudder the narrator is providing us with his perceptions and activities at the time of the story will little intrusion.

[Nv7] "There's not much to know," I said. "I used to be a cop."

[No8] "An excellent one, according to Lieutenant Koeh-ler."

[Na9] I shrugged.

[No10] "And now you're a private detective."

[Nv11] "No."

[No12] "I thought—"

[Nv13] "Private detectives are licensed. They tap tele-phones and follow people. They fill out forms, they keep records, all of that. I don't do those things. Sometimes I do favors for people. They give me gifts."

[No14] "I see."

Here [Nt6] leads to an exchange of dialogue in beats [Nv7] through [No14]. This is all DCE, one beat leading or triggering the next, notated as Direct NCE.

[Na15] I took a sip of coffee. [N16] I was drinking coffee spiked with bourbon. Hanniford had a Dewar's and wa-ter in front of him but wasn't taking much interest in it. We were in Armstrong's, a good sound saloon with dark wood walls and a stamped tin ceiling. It was two in the afternoon on the second Tuesday in January, and we had the place pretty much to ourselves. [No17] A couple of nurses from Roosevelt Hospital were nursing beers at the far end of the bar, and a kid with a tentative beard was eating a hamburger at one of the window tables.

[No14] leads to [Na15], a Narrated Action beat. [N16] is an initiating Narration beat. Look at this beat closely. Here Scudder the narrator interrupts into the prose chain to provide the reader with a little set up information. None of this reflects Scudder's actual perceptions and activities at the time of the story. Though there is a subtle sense of Scudder the narrator throughout most of this prose, it is this beat that finally confirms the narrative mode is NCE-based.

[N16] leads to Narrated Observation beat [No17]. Even though [No17] is a continuation of the Narration started in [N16], in this beat we start to fall back into Scudder's actual perceptions and activities at the time of the story.

> [No18] He said, "It's difficult for me to explain what I want you to do for me, Scudder."

Here Narrated Observation beat [No18] continues on from [No14].

> [Nv19] "I'm not sure if there's anything I can do for you. Your daughter is dead. I can't change that. The boy who killed her was picked up on the spot. From what I read in the papers, it couldn't be more open-and-shut if they had the homicide on film." [No20] His face darkened; [Nt21] he was seeing that film now, the knife slashing. [Nv22] I went on quickly. "They picked him up and booked him and slapped him in the Tombs. That was Thursday?" [No23] He nodded. [Nv24] "And Saturday morning they found him hanging in his cell. Case closed."

[No18] triggers Narrated Vocalization beat [Nv19]. [No20] is an initiating Narrated Observation beat that leads to Narrated Thought beat [Nt21]. [Nt21] leads to Narrated Vocalization beat [Nv22]. [No23] is an initiating Narrated Observation beat, which triggers Narrated Vocalization beat [Nv24].

> [No25] "Is that your view? That the case is closed?"

> [Nv26] "From a law enforcement standpoint."

> [No27] "That's not what I meant..."

Finally, [Nv24] leads to an exchange of dialogue in beats [No25] through [No27]. This is all DCE, one beat leading to or triggering the next, notated as Direct NCE.

NORTAV Analysis #12: Lexi Revellian's *Replica*

PROSE SAMPLE

For this analysis we will look at an excerpt from *Replica*, a novel by Lexi Revellian. For more information about Lexi and her work, you can visit her blog at http://lexirevellian.blogspot.com/

... "It's not like you to be difficult, Bethie. She hasn't got anyone but me to ask."

Beth bit her lip, staring unseeing at the computer screen on her desk. Was she being difficult? "What about her boyfriend?"

"He's away."

"Can't she do it herself? With a glass and postcard, she wouldn't have to touch it." Beth remembered the self-help book she was currently reading, Just Say No: every woman's guide to assertive behaviour. Rob could not read her mind; she needed to tell him what she wanted. "I was really looking forward to this evening."

"Spiders freak her out." Down the line, Rob's voice took on a fond, indulgent tone. "A high-flying investment banker, and one tiny insect reduces her to a scared little girl."

Beth started to say, "I don't think spiders are insects..." but Rob spoke through her.

"We can go tomorrow, it'll still be on. You're free Saturday, aren't you?"

"Yes..."

"So no problem. By the time I get back it'll be too much of a rush, better to go tomorrow. We can have a pizza first."

"I suppose…"

"That's settled, then. I'll pick you up at the flat tomorrow at seven thirty. Love you."

"Love you." Beth put the phone back on its receiver and reached into her desk drawer for her emergency Cadbury's Fruit and Nut. She tried to stifle a sense of failure – so much for asserting herself – peeled back the paper and foil and bit off a chunk. It didn't really matter. It was natural Rob should want to help Chloe; they'd lived together for two years, and it was nice they were still friends, even though she'd chucked him and made him miserable for a while. It showed what a kind man he was, willing to drive across London whenever her laptop played up, or her taps needed new washers, or she couldn't put together some flat-packed furniture. Only the month before she'd bought a chandelier for her bedroom, with no idea how to put it up. Rob went straight over, and was gone all day. On his return, he'd taken Beth out to dinner, and spent a big chunk of the evening telling her what a tricky job it had been, and how he'd been about to admit defeat when he finally hit on the idea of accessing the joist from the attic.

He wasn't cheating on her, she was sure, and she wasn't exactly jealous, that would be silly; but it did seem to her that Chloe was taking advantage of him a bit.

She sighed and glanced at the clock. Twenty past six. The building was so quiet she could hear the hum of the air-conditioning; nobody hung about on a Friday, except the

Professor, who viewed his home life as a tiresome interruption to his work. And of course, the security guards that came with a government research institute were still on duty...

NORTAV ANALYSIS

Narrative Mode: *NCE 1*

 Narrator: *Omniscient*

 Narrative Intrusion: *Yes*

 Focal Character(s): *Beth*

 Prose Type(s) and/or Beat Types(s): *NCE and DCE. Style uses mostly DCE with the occasional beat of NCE.*

 Narrative Tense: *Past*

 Additional Constraints: *None*

Narrative Pattern: *NCE 1 throughout.*

Analysis:

[No1] "It's not like you to be difficult, Bethie. She hasn't got anyone but me to ask."

[Nr2] Beth bit her lip, [Na3] staring unseeing at the computer screen on her desk. [Nt4] Was she being difficult? [Nv5] "What about her boyfriend?"

Lexi opens with [No1], a Narrated Observation beat. This triggers [Nr2], a Narrated Reaction beat and leads to [Na3], a Narrated Action beat with some incidental observation tacked on. [No1] also triggers [Nt4], a Narrated Thought beat, and [Nv5], a Narrated Vocalization beat. So far, each beat could stand as DCE.

[No6] "He's away."

[Nv7] "Can't she do it herself? With a glass and postcard, she wouldn't have to touch it." [Nt8] Beth remembered the self-help book she was currently reading, Just Say No: Every Woman's Guide to Assertive Behaviour. Rob could not read her mind; she needed to tell him what she wanted. [Nv9] "I was really looking forward to this evening."

Here [No6] is an initiating Narrated Observation beat. This triggers [Nv7], a Narrated Vocalization beat, which leads to [Nt8], a compound Narrated Thought beat. [Nt8] leads to/triggers [Nv9], a Narrated Vocalization beat. This all could stand as DCE.

[No10] "Spiders freak her out." Down the line, Rob's voice took on a fond, indulgent tone. "A high-flying investment banker, and one tiny insect reduces her to a scared little girl."

[Nv11] Beth started to say, "I don't think spiders are insects..." but Rob spoke through her.

[No10] is an initiating Narrated Observation beat. This triggers [Nv11], a Narrated Vocalization beat. Note that these two beats push the mode from DCE to NCE. "Down the line" feels like a narrative intrusion, and [Nv11] is most definitely the narrator telling the reader about Beth's vocalization. For me, these two beats along with how some of the DCE beats are combined and phrased made me label the narrative mode as NCE-based rather than DCE-based. It's a gut call.

[No12] "We can go tomorrow, it'll still be on. You're free Saturday, aren't you?"

[Nv13] "Yes..."

[No14] "So no problem. By the time I get back it'll be too

much of a rush, better to go tomorrow. We can have a pizza first."

[Nv15] "I suppose…"

[No16] "That's settled, then. I'll pick you up at the flat tomorrow at seven thirty. Love you."

[Nv17] "Love you."

Here [No12] through [Nv17] is dialogue rendered as an exchange of Narrated Observation and Narrated Vocalization beats, all of which could stand as DCE.

[Na18] Beth put the phone back on its receiver and reached into her desk drawer for her emergency Cadbury's Fruit and Nut. {Nr19} [Nt20] She tried to stifle a sense of failure – so much for asserting herself – [Na21] peeled back the paper and foil and bit off a chunk. [Nt22] It didn't really matter. It was natural Rob should want to help Chloe; they'd lived together for two years, and it was nice they were still friends, even though she'd chucked him and made him miserable for a while. It showed what a kind man he was, willing to drive across London whenever her laptop played up, or her taps needed new washers, or she couldn't put together some flat-packed furniture. Only the month before she'd bought a chandelier for her bedroom, with no idea how to put it up. Rob went straight over, and was gone all day. On his return, he'd taken Beth out to dinner, and spent a big chunk of the evening telling her what a tricky job it had been, and how he'd been about to admit defeat when he finally hit on the idea of accessing the joist from the attic.

He wasn't cheating on her, she was sure, and she wasn't

exactly jealous, that would be silly; but it did seem to her that Chloe was taking advantage of him a bit.

[Nv17] leads to Narrated Action beat [Na18]. {Nr19} is an implied initiating Narrated Reaction beat (a sense of failure) brought on by the entire incident of the phone call. This triggers Narrated Thought beat [Nt20]. Narrated Action beat [Na21] continues the action from [Na18].

The lengthy compound Narrated Thought beat [Nt22] continues the thought from [Nt20].

[Nr23] She sighed and [Na24] glanced at the clock. [No25] Twenty past six. The building was so quiet she could hear the hum of the air-conditioning; [Nt26] nobody hung about on a Friday, except the Professor, who viewed his home life as a tiresome interruption to his work. And of course, the security guards that came with a government research institute were still on duty.

Finally, [Nt22] triggers Narrated Reaction beat [Nr23]. [Nt22] also leads to Narrated Action beat [Na24]. [Na24] leads to Narrated Observation beat [No25], which triggers compound Narrated Thought beat [Nt26].

NORTAV Analysis #13: Michael Stackpole's *Tricknomancy*

PROSE SAMPLE

For this analysis we will look at an excerpt from *Tricknomancy*, a novel by Michael Stackpole. For more information about Michael and his work, you can visit http://www.stormwolf.com/.

> ... There were lots of reasons I hated Johnny Dawes. The way he slapped my back as he entered Club Flesh was fast moving up on the list. It hurt. He always caught me on the scar from the bullet that shattered my left shoulder blade.
>
> It was easy for him to hit me there. He'd been the one who pumped that bullet into me. That one, and a couple more.
>
> That shooting thing, that was pretty high up on the list, too.
>
> The same question always came with the backslap. It bugged the hell out of me.
>
> "No one's killed you yet, Molloy?"
>
> "No one's that good."
>
> I always gave him the same answer. It bugged the hell out of him.
>
> He stared at me with cold, dark eyes. I'd heard it said he'd once killed with a glance. I almost let myself believe it. His gaze did send a chill through me, but the club's dark, stuffy heat warmed me again fast.

He broke off the stare and smiled at the bartender. "The Dom, Eddie, please."

"Sure thing, Mr. Dawes. Up in VIP, right?"

"Perfect." Dawes purred the word and Eddie's face brightened. That tone, that smile; Dawes was feeling generous. He expressed it with C-notes, and they came in showers. That made everyone around Club Flesh happy—servers, dancers, even the other bouncers.

Hell, me, too. I was no Boy Scout. I took my cut. I always used it to buy myself the biggest, bloodiest steak I could find.

It reminds me what I'd looked like after he shot me.

Eddie gave me a glance and shook his head. "I don't know why you don't like him, Trick. Guys like that don't have to be generous."

I nodded. Dawes was the sort of sugar-daddy all girls dreamed of. Tall, slender, dark and handsome, a flashy dresser without resorting to cheap jewelry, he could have stepped off a fashion-show runway in Milan or New York. The touch of grey at his temples made him more distinguished. Even the banded collars and slender black chokers he wore, with that big ruby broach at his throat, made him look sinister—and lots of girls squealed over that.

"It ain't that he dresses better than you, is it?"

"Nope, Eddie, it ain't that." I turned away from the bar, hoping Eddie wouldn't continue. He already knew all the reasons I hated Dawes—the shooting, being framed for a crime that got me busted from the force, Chrystale, all that. Just none of them worked for him. He kept trying to find the real reason.

Eddie jammed the bottle of champagne into the ice bucket with a wet crunch. "It's a talent-thing, right?"

"Prolly." Like anyone else who couldn't use magick, for Eddie, the mysteries of life became explained by magick. Since the vast majority of people had no talent, they flat didn't believe it existed or were very afraid of it. Sometimes both—which is why televangelists flourish still...

NORTAV ANALYSIS

Narrative Mode: *NCE 1*

Narrator: *Molloy*

Narrative Intrusion: *Yes*

Focal Character(s): *Molloy*

Prose Type(s) and/or Beat Types(s): *NCE and DCE. Style uses an even mix of NCE and DCE. NCE is mostly created by revealing the narrator through phrasings and beat order.*

Narrative Tense: *Past*

Additional Constraints: *None*

Narrative Pattern: *NCE 1 throughout.*

Analysis:

{No1}[Nt2] There were lots of reasons I hated Johnny Dawes. The way he slapped my back as he entered Club Flesh was fast moving up on the list. It hurt. He always caught me on the scar from the bullet that shattered my left shoulder blade.

It was easy for him to hit me there. He'd been the one

who pumped that bullet into me. That one, and a couple more.

That shooting thing, that was pretty high up on the list, too.

The same question always came with the backslap. It bugged the hell out of me.

Michael opens with {No1}, an implied Narrated Observation beat. This leads to [Nt2], a compound Narrated Thought beat which includes the implied observation using beat substitution. Notice two things here. First, it is only due to the way these beats are phrased that I am labeling this sample NCE-based. Though this comes across as the focal character's thoughts, it definitely feels as if they are being told to the reader by the character narrator at some point after the story. Second, does this style look familiar? It should. It is very close to the same writing style we saw in Michael's previous sample.

[No3] "No one's killed you yet, Molloy?"

[Nv4] "No one's that good."

Here [No3] is an initiating Narrated Observation beat. This triggers [Nv7], a Narrated Vocalization beat.

[Nt5] I always gave him the same answer. It bugged the hell out of him.

Here [Nv4] leads to Narrated Thought beat [Nt5]. Again, this beat feels as if this is the narrator telling us how he felt back at the time of the story.

[No6] He stared at me with cold, dark eyes. {Nr7}[Nt8] I'd heard it said he'd once killed with a glance. I almost let myself believe it. His gaze did send a chill through me, but the club's dark, stuffy heat warmed me again fast.

[No6] is an initiating Narrated Observation beat. [No6] triggers implied Narrated Reaction beat {Nr7}, which leads to Narrated Thought beat [Nt8]. [Nt8] includes the implied reaction using beat substitution.

> [No9] He broke off the stare and smiled at the bartender. "The Dom, Eddie, please."
>
> "Sure thing, Mr. Dawes. Up in VIP, right?"
>
> "Perfect." Dawes purred the word and Eddie's face brightened. [Nt10] That tone, that smile; Dawes was feeling generous. He expressed it with C-notes, and they came in showers. That made everyone around Club Flesh happy—servers, dancers, even the other bouncers.
>
> Hell, me, too. I was no Boy Scout. I took my cut. I always used it to buy myself the biggest, bloodiest steak I could find.
>
> It reminds me what I'd looked like after he shot me.

[No9] is a compound initiating Narrated Observation beat. [No9] triggers [Nt10], a compound Narrated Thought beat.

> [No11] Eddie gave me a glance and shook his head. "I don't know why you don't like him, Trick. Guys like that don't have to be generous."
>
> [Na12] I nodded. {No13}[Nt14] Dawes was the sort of sugar-daddy all girls dreamed of. Tall, slender, dark and handsome, a flashy dresser without resorting to cheap jewelry, he could have stepped off a fashion-show runway in Milan or New York. The touch of grey at his temples made him more distinguished. Even the banded collars and slender black chokers he wore, with that big

ruby broach at his throat, made him look sinister—and lots of girls squealed over that.

[No11] is an initiating Narrated Observation beat. [No11] triggers [Na12], a Narrated Action beat. [No11] also leads to/triggers implied Narrated Observation beat {No13}, where we infer that Molloy studies Dawes's appearance. {No13} leads to compound Narrated Thought beat [Nt14].

[No15] "It ain't that he dresses better than you, is it?"

[Nv16] "Nope, Eddie, it ain't that." [Na16] I turned away from the bar, [Nt17] hoping Eddie wouldn't continue. He already knew all the reasons I hated Dawes—the shooting, being framed for a crime that got me busted from the force, Chrystale, all that. Just none of them worked for him. He kept trying to find the real reason.

[No15] is an initiating Narrated Observation beat. [No15] triggers [Nv16], a Narrated Vocalization beat. Narrated Action beat [Na16] is triggered by compound Narrated Thought beat [Nt17], which is narrated out of its normal order.

[No18] Eddie jammed the bottle of champagne into the ice bucket with a wet crunch. "It's a talent-thing, right?"

[Nv19] "Prolly." [Nt20] Like anyone else who couldn't use magick, for Eddie, the mysteries of life became explained by magick. Since the vast majority of people had no talent, they flat didn't believe it existed or were very afraid of it. Sometimes both—which is why televangelists flourish still.

Finally, [No18] is an initiating Narrated Observation beat. [No18] triggers [Nv19], a Narrated Vocalization beat. [No18] also triggers compound Narrated Thought beat [Nt20].

NORTAV Analysis #14: Terri Reid's *Natural Reaction*

PROSE SAMPLE

For this analysis we will look at an excerpt from *Natural Reaction*, a novel by Terri Reid. For more information about Terri and her work, you can visit her website at http://terrireid.com/.

... The bell pealed its final warning and two dozen high school students quickly rushed in from the grey locker-walled hallway into the Chemistry lab. But even though they were in his classroom, Charlie Thorne, their teacher, knew they were more concerned about the upcoming Spring Fling than anything else. "Okay, ladies and gentlemen," he yelled over the clamor of voices. "I need you to quiet down and pay attention."

"But Mr. Thorne," bubbled Rosie Meriwether, the Homecoming Queen and a shoo-in for Prom Queen, "They just announced the band for the Spring Fling is going to be The Nomadds."

"And yet they still allowed classes to continue," he teased.

"Coach Thorne," Stevo Morris, the shortstop for the high school baseball team Charlie coached, said. "This is a really big deal. The Nomadds are cool."

"Thank you, Stevo," Charlie replied, "And as cool as they are, the only cool we are going to discuss today are endothermic reactions."

A low groan was emitted from the students and Charlie

chuckled. "Cheer up," he said. "Today's experiments are fun and if you get them right, you won't have to write the fifteen page paper on displacements instead of going to the Spring Fling."

The class was immediately alert and quiet. "Yeah, I thought that would work," he laughed.

He moved to the front of his lab table and looked around the room. He was younger than most of the teachers in the school by at least ten years. Because of his good natured personality, he was a favorite among the students. But he would be surprised to know that he was also considered the "dream man" for many of the high school coeds."

"Okay, Stevo, explain single displacement," he said.

Stevo grinned. "You mean the Raquel Welch Displacement Theory, sir?"

Charlie nodded. "Yes, that's the one."

"Okay, so I walk in the classroom with Raquel Welch on my arm," he explained. "And then we walk over and meet you, right? So, she sees you and ditches me for you, because you're a studlier element or a more active element."

Charlie nodded and chuckled. "Exactly, single displacement," he said. "She leaves Stevo for me because; well she has good taste..."

The class laughed at his joke.

"And because I am a more active element than Stevo."

"Except in practice when we run laps, coach," Stevo added. "Then I'm more active."

Charlie nodded. "And that's why I'm the coach and you're the shortstop."

He walked over to the chalkboard and wrote:

$$NH_4OH + HNO_3 = NH_4NO_3 + H_2O$$

"This is an example of the Raquel Welch, Brigitte Bardot Double Displacement Theory," he explained. "It's the same premise, except instead of just one active element replacing a less active element, there are two separate changes going on here. In this case, I am the ammonium ion and I replace the positive hydrogen ion from the nitric acid, HNO_3, and bond it to me. The remaining Hydrogen ion is left with the OH and becomes H_2O or..."

NORTAV ANALYSIS

Narrative Mode: *NCE 1*

   Narrator: *Omniscient*

   Narrative Intrusion: *Yes*

   Focal Character(s): *Charlie Thorne*

   Prose Type(s) and/or Beat Types(s): *NCE, DCE, and Narration. Style uses mostly DCE and Direct NCE, with the occasional Narration added to provide background.*

   Narrative Tense: *Past*

   Additional Constraints: *None*

Narrative Pattern: *NCE 1 throughout.*

Analysis:

   [No1] The bell pealed its final warning and two dozen

high school students quickly rushed in from the grey locker-walled hallway into the Chemistry lab. [Nt2] But even though they were in his classroom, Charlie Thorne, their teacher, knew they were more concerned about the upcoming Spring Fling than anything else. [Nv3] "Okay, ladies and gentlemen," he yelled over the clamor of voices. "I need you to quiet down and pay attention."

Terri opens with [No1], a Narrated Observation beat. [No1] triggers [Nt2], a Narrated Thought beat. Here, the narrative intrusion "their teacher" begins to set the style of the writing, which is essentially DCE with small narrative intrusions inserted in places to provide the reader with necessary background information. As we know, this makes the narrative mode NCE-based.

[Nt2] leads to [Nv3], a Narrated Vocalization beat.

[No4] "But Mr. Thorne," bubbled Rosie Meriwether, the Homecoming Queen and a shoo-in for Prom Queen, "They just announced the band for the Spring Fling is going to be The Nomadds."

[Nv5] "And yet they still allowed classes to continue," he teased.

[No6] "Coach Thorne," Stevo Morris, the shortstop for the high school baseball team Charlie coached, said. "This is a really big deal. The Nomadds are cool."

[Nv7] "Thank you, Stevo," Charlie replied, "And as cool as they are, the only cool we are going to discuss today are endothermic reactions."

Here [Nv3] leads to an exchange of dialogue between Charlie and his class. [No4] through [Nv7] are mostly DCE, but notice we continue to get small bits of incidental narrative information added to the DCE (in [No4] and [No6]), which helps to keep the narrative mode consistent.

[No8] A low groan was emitted from the students and [Nr9] Charlie chuckled. [Nv10] "Cheer up," he said.

"Today's experiments are fun and if you get them right, you won't have to write the fifteen page paper on displacements instead of going to the Spring Fling."

[Nv7] leads to Narrated Observation beat [No8]. [No8] triggers Narrated Reaction beat [Nr9] and Narrated Vocalization beat [Nv10], which follow the natural response sequence.

[No11] The class was immediately alert and quiet. [Nv12] "Yeah, I thought that would work," he laughed.

[Nv10] leads to Narrated Observation beat [No11]. [No11] leads to Narrated Vocalization beat [Nv12].

[Na13] He moved to the front of his lab table and looked around the room. [N14] He was younger than most of the teachers in the school by at least ten years. Because of his good natured personality, he was a favorite among the students. But he would be surprised to know that he was also considered the "dream man" for many of the high school coeds.

Here [Nv12] leads to Narrated Action beat [Na13]. [Na11] leads to Narration beat [N14]. When [N14] begins, the reader perceives it as a Narrated Observation beat, but by the end realizes this is the narrator providing a piece of background information.

[Nv15] "Okay, Stevo, explain single displacement," he said.

[No16] Stevo grinned. "You mean the Raquel Welch Displacement Theory, sir?"

[Na17] Charlie nodded. [Nv18] "Yes, that's the one."

[No19] "Okay, so I walk in the classroom with Raquel Welch on my arm," he explained. "And then we walk over and meet you, right? So, she sees you and ditches me for you, because you're a studlier element or a more active element."

[Na20] Charlie nodded and [Nr21] chuckled. "Exactly, single displacement," he said. "She leaves Stevo for me because; well she has good taste..."

[No22] The class laughed at his joke.

[Nv23] "And because I am a more active element than Stevo."

[No24] "Except in practice when we run laps, coach," Stevo added. "Then I'm more active."

[Na25] Charlie nodded. [Nv26] "And that's why I'm the coach and you're the shortstop."

Here [N14] leads to another exchange of dialogue between Charlie and the class. Again, [Nv15] through [Nv26] are all DCE or very close to DCE. The phrasing of [No22] sounds more like NCE. Also, notice [Na17], [Na20], [Nr21], and [Na25] break up the exchange of Narrated Observation and Narrated Vocalization beats so the dialogue doesn't become monotonous.

[Na27] He walked over to the chalkboard and wrote:

[No28] $NH_4OH + HNO_3 = NH_4NO_3 + H_2O$

[Nv29] "This is an example of the Raquel Welch, Brigitte Bardot Double Displacement Theory," he explained. "It's the same premise, except instead of just one active element replacing a less active element, there are two separate changes going on here. In this case, I am the ammonium ion and I replace the positive hydrogen ion from the nitric acid, HNO3, and bond it to me. The remaining Hydrogen ion is left with the OH and becomes H2O or..."

Finally, [Nv26] leads to Narrated Action beat [Na27], which leads to Narrated Observation beat [No28]. Simply the way the last two beats are phrased and punctuated gives them an NCE feel. [No28] then leads to Narrated Vocalization beat [Nv29].

NORTAV Analysis #15: Victorine Lieske's *The Gathering*

PROSE SAMPLE

For this analysis we will look at an excerpt from *The Gathering*, a short story by Victorine Lieske. For more information about Victorine and her work, visit `http://www.victorinelieske.com/`.

> ... Danielle smoothed her black uniform and strode along the endless, white hallway. How had she gotten turned around again? The outer ring followed the perimeter of the Holodome, just a huge circle. But for some reason she was always going left instead of right. And since the Holodome encompassed a large area, it took quite a while to circle the entire structure. She ended up having to double back a lot.
>
> A yell from ahead made her slow down. The resequencing rooms...unease swept over her and a lump formed in her throat. She never liked walking past them, but usually they were quieter than this. As she approached the door she heard another scream. Several soldiers marched past. A couple of them stared at the door but no one stopped.
>
> It wasn't any of her business—she was supposed to be finding her partner—but the sound unnerved her. What was happening? She pressed her palm against the metal sensor and the door dematerialized.
>
> A dark-haired teenager was strapped to a resequencing table. His muscles bulged against the thick white bands. Purple veins stood out on his neck as he struggled to break free. He was naked from the waist up except for a

silver nose ring. He jerked his head and let out another frustrated scream.

The two Dyken soldiers on either side of him scrambled. "He's not responding," the tall one said.

The guy twisted on the table, his eyes finding hers. His gaze bore into her. "Help me."

Danielle's heart pounded in her chest. She wanted to tell him they were helping him, but he wouldn't have understood. Instead, she turned away, unable to look any longer. What was wrong? Why couldn't they subdue him? He should be out cold until the end of the procedure. She'd never seen anyone awake in the resequencing room.

She took a deep breath and closed her eyes. Someone swore, and she couldn't stop from looking again. The table had risen a foot off the ground. The soldiers grabbed onto it, struggling to push it back to the floor.

"How can he still have his powers?" the younger soldier asked.

"I don't know. Give him another dose of liquid trimeninite."

The young one paled. "We don't know what that will do to him."

"Just do it!"

Metal clinked as the soldier threw his neural inhibitor on the tray and grabbed the injector. Danielle's gut twisted. She fingered the gadgets on her belt. Guilt pressed over her like a thick blanket.

"Danielle."

She turned to see Benit, her partner, walking toward her down the long curved hallway. He waved the small handheld computer at her. "Our next assignment."

Danielle glanced back at the teen before allowing the door to materialize and shut out the scene. She took a breath and tried to clear the images from her head.

"I'm glad you found me," she said. "I get all mixed up in here for some reason."

"You'll get used to it," Benit said...

NORTAV ANALYSIS

Narrative Mode: *NCE 1*

   Narrator: *Omniscient*

   Narrative Intrusion: *Yes*

   Focal Character(s): *Danielle*

   Prose Type(s) and/or Beat Types(s): *NCE. Style uses a lot of Mixed NCE beats.*

   Narrative Tense: *Past*

   Additional Constraints: *None*

Narrative Pattern: *NCE 1 throughout.*

Analysis:

[Na1] Danielle smoothed her black uniform and strode along the endless, white hallway. [Nt2] How had she gotten turned around again? The outer ring followed the perimeter of the Holodome, just a huge circle. But for some reason she was always going left instead of right.

And since the Holodome encompassed a large area, it took quite a while to circle the entire structure. She ended up having to double back a lot.

Victorine opens with [Na1], a Narrated Action beat. [Na1] leads to Narrated Thought beat [Nt2]. In [Nt2], Danielle reflects back on the recent past, bringing the reader up to speed and also providing the reader with some observations (using beat substitution) of the setting.

[Nm3] A yell from ahead made her slow down. [Nt4] The resequencing rooms... [Nr5] unease swept over her and a lump formed in her throat. [Nt6] She never liked walking past them, but usually they were quieter than this. [Nm7] As she approached the door she heard another scream. [No8] Several soldiers marched past. A couple of them stared at the door but no one stopped.

[Nm3] is an initiating beat of Mixed NCE. It includes an observation and an action or reaction, depending on if she slows down voluntarily or involuntarily. [Nm3] leads to Narrated Thought beat [Nt4], which triggers Narrated Reaction beat [Nr5] and Narrated Thought beat [Nt6] (following the natural response sequence). [Nt6] leads to [Nm7], a beat of Mixed NCE that includes an action and observation. [Nm7] leads to Narrated Observation beat [No8].

[Nm9] It wasn't any of her business—she was supposed to be finding her partner—but the sound unnerved her. [Nt10] What was happening? [Na11] She pressed her palm against the metal sensor and [No12] the door dematerialized.

[No8] triggers [Nm9], a beat of Mixed NCE that includes thought and reaction. [Nm9] triggers Narrated Thought beat [Nt10]. [Nt10] leads to Narrated Action beat [Na11], which leads to Narrated Observation beat [No12].

[No13] A dark-haired teenager was strapped to a resequencing table. His muscles bulged against the thick white bands. Purple veins stood out on his neck as he struggled to break free. He was naked from the waist up except for a silver nose ring. He jerked his head and let out another frustrated scream.

The two Dyken soldiers on either side of him scrambled. "He's not responding," the tall one said.

[No12] leads to compound Narrated Observation beat [No13].

[No14] The guy twisted on the table, his eyes finding hers. His gaze bore into her. "Help me."

[Nr15] Danielle's heart pounded in her chest. [Nt16] She wanted to tell him they were helping him, but he wouldn't have understood. [Nm17] Instead, she turned away, unable to look any longer. [Nt18] What was wrong? Why couldn't they subdue him? He should be out cold until the end of the procedure. She'd never seen anyone awake in the resequencing room.

[No13] leads to Narrated Observation beat [No14]. [No14] is not part of the previous compound beat because it triggers Narrated Reaction beat [Nr15] and Narrated Thought beat [Nt16]. [Nt16] leads to [Nm17], a beat of Mixed NCE that includes action and thought and a slight sensation of reaction. [Nm17] leads to Narrated Thought beat [Nt18].

[Na19] She took a deep breath and closed her eyes. [Nm20] Someone swore, and she couldn't stop from looking again. {No21}[Nt22] The table had risen a foot off the ground. [No23] The soldiers grabbed onto it, struggling to push it back to the floor.

"How can he still have his powers?" the younger soldier asked.

"I don't know. Give him another dose of liquid trimeninite."

The young one paled. "We don't know what that will do to him."

"Just do it!"

Here [Nt18] leads to Narrated Action beat [Na19]. [Na19] is an initiating beat of Mixed NCE that includes an observation and a reaction. {No21} is an implied Narrated Observation beat where Danielle sees the table. {No21} leads to Narrated Thought beat [Nt22], which includes the implied observation (through beat substitution). [Nt22] leads to compound Narrated Observation beat [No23].

[No24] Metal clinked as the soldier threw his neural inhibitor on the tray and grabbed the injector.

[Nr25] Danielle's gut twisted. [Na26] She fingered the gadgets on her belt. [Nt27] Guilt pressed over her like a thick blanket.

[No23] leads to Narrated Observation beat [No24], which triggers Narrated Reaction beat [Nr25], Narrated Action beat [Na26], and Narrated Thought beat [Nt27]. These triggered beats almost, but not quite, follow the natural response sequence.

[No28] "Danielle."

[Nm29] She turned to see Benit, her partner, walking toward her down the long curved hallway. [No30] He waved the small handheld computer at her. "Our next assignment."

[No28] is an initiating Narrated Observation beat. It triggers [Nm29], a beat of Mixed NCE that includes action and observation. [No30] is another initiating Narrated Observation beat.

[Nm31] Danielle glanced back at the teen before allowing the door to materialize and shut out the scene.

[Na32] She took a breath and [Nt33] tried to clear the images from her head.

[Nv34] "I'm glad you found me," she said. "I get all mixed up in here for some reason."

[No35] "You'll get used to it," Benit said.

Finally, [No30] leads to [Nm31], a beat of Mixed NCE that includes action, thought, and observation. [Nm31] leads to Narrated Action beat [Na32], which leads to Narrated Thought beat [Nt33]. [Nt33] leads to Narrated Vocalization beat [Nv34]. [Nv34] leads to Narrated Observation beat [No35].

Index of Definitions

About A. J. Abbiati

A. J. "Jim" Abbiati lives and works in historic Mystic, Connecticut. He holds an MFA in Creative Writing, a BA in English, and a BS in Computer Science. When not writing, Jim works for a major software engineering firm. He is currently at work on his second novel and is considering doctoral programs in either creative writing or narratology.

Jim loves to hear from fellow writers. Contact him at:

`http://thenortavmethod.com/`

`http://ajabbiati.com/`

Made in the USA
Charleston, SC
14 July 2012